'THE HIDDEN LIFE AT ITS SOURCE':
A STUDY OF FLAUBERT'S
L'ÉDUCATION SENTIMENTALE

D. A. WILLIAMS
Senior Lecturer in French
University of Hull

HULL UNIVERSITY PRESS
1987

British Library Cataloguing in Publication Data

Williams, D.A. (David Anthony)
    The hidden life at its source : a study of Flaubert's l'éducation
sentimentale.
    1. Flaubert, Gustave. Education sentimentale
    I. Title
    843'.8   PQ2246.E5

    ISBN 0-85958-464-X

Phototypeset in 10 on 12pt Times by Computape (Pickering) Ltd,
Pickering, North Yorkshire and printed by the University of Hull.

It is the function of the novelist to reveal the hidden life at its source
(E.M. Forster, *Aspects of the Novel*)

Ils sont, ne l'oublions pas, des personnages
(Nathalie Sarraute, *Portrait d'un inconnu*)

Contents

Acknowledgements

I am grateful to Dr A. W. Raitt who has been unstinting in the support and encouragement he has provided throughout the long period during which this study has evolved. Without his timely intervention at a critical stage in its development, this book would undoubtedly have been a good deal more partial and one-sided in its approach. If any imbalance remains, it is, needless to say, entirely the result of the author's obduracy and not of any deficiency in the advice he received. I am indebted to Dr P. M. Wetherill who made available to me his microfilms of the manuscripts of *L'Éducation sentimentale* and gave me the benefit of his own growing understanding of their richness and complexity. The British Academy provided the necessary financial support which allowed me to examine the manuscripts in the Bibliothèque Nationale and my hard-pressed colleagues in the Department of French at the University of Hull undertook the additional teaching which made it possible for me to take study leave in the Autumn Term of 1981. I also wish to thank Hull University Press for their help and advice: Alan Best for overseeing the publication, Barbara Nield and Joyce Bellamy for their painstaking editorial work on the typescript and Jean Smith for her efficient supervision of the production of this work.

University of Hull   D. A. Williams
May 1987

Introduction

It has long been recognised that Flaubert occupies a key position in the evolution of the novel. His literary output has a Janus-like quality; in certain respects his works look back to traditional practice, in other respects they look forward to future developments, in particular the 'nouveau roman'.[1] Still writing under the vast shadow of Balzac, yet also attracted to the idea of 'un livre sur rien', Flaubert is torn between supporting and subverting the novel as a form. So, according to one powerful line of argument, the hidden vocation of this painstaking literary craftsman is to bring about 'le détraquement de la machine à écrire',[2] to make the elaborate signifying machinery of the novel go splendidly haywire. Flaubert is not so much the novelist's novelist – Henry James's view – as the reluctant novelist. In Genette's seminal formulation, 'De *Madame Bovary* à *Bouvard et Pécuchet*, Flaubert n'a cessé d'écrire des romans tout en *refusant* – sans le savoir – , mais de tout son être – les exigences du discours romanesque.'[3] In numerous ways the Flaubertian text, Culler argues, thwarts the reader's expectations, since it seems to be 'written against the novel as an institution'.[4] The fact remains, however, that Flaubert did, whatever his misgivings, comply with some of the traditional requirements of the novel. It would be misleading, as a result, to present him as a thorough-going 'nouveau romancier', bent upon the destruction of 'plot' and 'character' a hundred years too early. In spite of the radical undermining of traditional narrative practice, the Flaubertian text continues to operate within the parameters of nineteenth-century readability, as Roland Barthes has pointed out.[5] Likewise, however innovative Flaubert's presentation of character, he continues to provide some semblance of psychological reality. Thus, if Flaubert is a profoundly problematic novelist, it is not simply because in certain ways he anticipates the 'nouveau roman' but rather because he combines old and new, mixes conflicting modes, simultaneously undermines and perpetuates traditional narrative prac-

1

tice, in such a way as to leave the reader in that exhilarating state of radical uncertainty over how to 'respond' which constitutes, according to Barthes, the highest form of literary 'jouissance'.[6]

While acknowledging the dual, even contradictory, nature of Flaubert's literary practice, recent criticism, alerted by the accolade of essential precursor bestowed upon him by the *nouveaux romanciers*, has tended to stress the innovative, subversive tendencies in his work, gravitating to the later novels in which they become increasingly apparent. As far as *L'Éducation sentimentale* is concerned, much emphasis has been placed on Flaubert's radically new approach to the presentation of character. In an introduction to a recent edition of the novel, Alan Raitt has emphasised the 'instabilité des personnages', compared to *Madame Bovary*: 'Alors que les personnages de *Madame Bovary* apparaissent comme des blocs homogènes, ceux du roman de 1869 font plutôt l'effet de faisceaux d'impulsions et de sentiments à peine reliés entre eux.'[7] It is no longer possible, claims J. Gleize, to find coherence 'hors du texte, dans la psychologie des personnages'[8] and in J. Bem's view 'les personnages ne sont plus que des fragments de texte'.[9] The characters of *L'Éducation sentimentale* appear to many critics to be undergoing a process of decomposition or deconstruction.[10] The difference between Frédéric Moreau and the more clearly delineated Balzacian character is powerfully evoked by Christopher Prendergast: 'Unlike the dynamic, integrated personality of the Balzacian hero, Flaubert's hero is a nullity, a void; lacking any stable centre of consciousness, Frédéric's interiority is an empty space traversed throughout the narrative by a plurality of fragmented, dissociated impressions and sensations that never cohere to form a fully constituted subject', so much so that we see the 'beginning of the deconstruction of the full "Cartesian" subject.'[11] It is not just a question, Prendergast argues, of Flaubert's wishing to de-dramatise the Balzacian novel by portraying a colourless hero, but rather of his seeking to subvert one of the most elementary formal categories and conventions of the Novel: the convention of 'character'.

So radical is Flaubert's approach to the presentation of character that the very legitimacy of viewing the novel as a psychological study of a certain kind of romantic temperament has been thrown into doubt: 'Y a-t-il même ... une étude psychologique à proprement parler, ou bien, ce qui serait à démontrer, une évacuation de la psychologie?'[12] Likewise, it becomes debatable whether it is possible for the critic to arrive at the kind of psychological assessment of the characters that earlier novels permit: 'Psychologiquement – si tant est qu'on puisse faire le portrait psychologique des personnages de *L'Éducation sentimentale* – Madame Arnoux n'est pas de caractère despotique.'[13] The psychological element appears to many recent critics so problematic that it no longer constitutes what is essential. The assumption that the function of the narrative is to elucidate the psychological evolution of Frédéric is itself called into question. What strikes the modern critic most about *L'Éducation sentimentale* is the number of obstacles which appear to have been deliberately put in the way of a clear and unequivocal understanding of the behaviour of the characters. Just as the coverage of the historical events is spasmodic, so only intermittent light is thrown upon the development of Frédéric Moreau.

The fitful illumination of the psychological sphere is to a large extent bound up with a number of fundamental innovations which make *L'Éducation sentimentale* a disconcertingly original work. One of the most fully documented of these innovations is the technique of impersonality – the virtual elimination of opinions, value judgments and commentary of a generalised nature which would have helped to endow the narrator with a recognisable personality. The demise of the opinionated 'Balzacian' narrator, confidently glossing the main developments recorded, expansively reflecting on the general significance of character and conduct, imparting to the reader an accumulated wisdom relating to the variety and meaning of human types, is perhaps the single most far-reaching of all the changes effected by Flaubert and one which has profound repercussions in the psychological sphere. No longer guided by a voluble narrator, the reader is left to elucidate himself the significance of the events described, and for many readers this proves an impossible task. Combined with the choice of mediocre protagonist, impersonality leaves the reader in a quandary over the point of the novel. What precisely are we expected to 'learn' from the painstaking record of failure and disappointment? What is the significance to be attached to Frédéric's lingering attachment to Madame Arnoux? The difficulty experienced by the reader in reaching any clear or straightforward interpretation of the novel as a whole has led one critic to describe *L'Éducation sentimentale* as 'the most striking, most challenging example of thematic indeterminacy'.[14] It is wrong, Christopher Prendergast argues, to try to elucidate the hidden meaning of Flaubert's novel, since 'what is most radical in

L'Éducation is, precisely, the absence of any "sens profond" '.[15] The foreclosing of thematic conclusions has the effect of suspending the characters in a kind of thematic vacuum, and making their presence in the novel seem gratuitous.

Flaubert's originality does not lie solely in the removal of clear guidelines to thematic significance. The narrator in *L'Éducation sentimentale* is made to eschew a good deal more than statements of a generalised or reflective cast. The second most striking feature of the Flaubertian narrator's activity is the close attention he accords to the inner life of the protagonist. Characteristically, the narrator adopts the point of view of Frédéric, conveying his subjective impressions of people and places rather than a potentially more reliable narratorial view. The extensive insight we are granted into Frédéric's perceptions inevitably stands in the way of a more traditional presentation which would have involved looking *at* rather than *with* him and his being an object of investigation rather than a subject with whose consciousness we coincide.[16] More critically, everything that falls within the perceptual field of the protagonist tends to dissolve or to be tinged with uncertainty. External reality loses much of its consistency as M. Raimond has noted: 'le monde flaubertien est frappé d'inconsistance parce qu'il n'est jamais que la succession des apparences qui surgissent.'[17] While in some cases the reader may be in a position to add to or modify Frédéric's understanding, this is not always the case.

More recent novels have accustomed readers of fiction to the subjective presentation of the real. It is, however, not possible to attribute consistently or unerringly the view of events adopted to Frédéric or one of the other characters. One of the most perplexing features of the Flaubertian text is the frequent uncertainty generated not so much over who is speaking – this is, we are usually certain, a depersonalised narrator – but rather who is seeing.[18] Culler has discussed the ways in which Flaubert's account resists recuperation as a sustained presentation of a subjective view of events.[19] A degree of precision, a characteristic abundance of details, an insistence upon a kind of comical heterogeneity make certain descriptive passages appear independent of the perceiving consciousness elsewhere used. As Levaillant has suggested 'à la conscience vivante et globale du sujet percevant se substitue une conscience analytique, séparatrice, celle de l'auteur.'[20] The point about such passages is that the reader has the sense of the novel turning away not just from the tiresome business of telling a story but also from the conscious-ness of the protagonist which it had previously appeared to be faithfully presenting. Unaccounted shifts of this nature raise doubts about how much of the account can be legitimately interpreted as representing the point of view of one of the characters.

This is not the most bewildering feature of the novel, however. Partly, but by no means wholly, on account of the use of point of view technique, the account offered of the development of the generation of 1840 has struck many critics as containing an extraordinary number of gaps, lacunae and omissions. The information relating to many characters and their actions is defective: 'les personnages, au lieu d'être construits tout d'une pièce, sont présentés de façon lacunaire, de sorte que le lecteur ignore presque tout de l'aspect physique de Frédéric, de la jeunesse de Madame Arnoux, des origines sociales d'Arnoux.'[21] It is through its 'absences, ruptures, vides' that Flaubert's narrative 's'écarte d'une pratique narrative antérieure'.[22] On a number of occasions there is a kind of slippage, as it proves impossible to pin the text down: 'Mais on peut aussi trouver que le texte dérape et que le sens se met à errer d'un fragment à l'autre.'[23]

The lacunary nature of the Flaubertian text is particularly evident in the failure to present a clear or explicit account of causal relationships. Many events happen without an apparent cause; there is often a sudden leap from one scene to another; characters appear and disappear with bewildering suddenness. This 'de-emphasis on plot causality'[24] has a significant impact upon the reader's general understanding of psycho-logical matters; our grasp of character is dependent in part upon our ability to perceive a logical connection between the main events recorded. More directly detrimental, however, is the failure to give a clear account of motives, which produces a feeling of unpredictability in the psychological sphere.[25] Frequently event or reaction and motivation are separated.[26] The uncertainty over the motives of characters at key junctures leads to an impression of mystery and opacity.[27]

The uncertainty over psychological matters is compounded by a more general pattern of discontinuity. Victor Brombert has suggested that 'despite the sense of flow symbolically suggested by the river-image, much of *L'Éducation sentimentale* is an exercise in discontinuity'.[28] Flaubert, concludes J. Gleize, has embarked upon a problematic 'recherche d'une cohérence dans et par la discontinuité'.[29] The plot of the novel bifurcates, following the fortunes now of Frédéric, now of Deslauriers, documenting the private life of a romantically-inclined young man on the one hand and the historical development of France on the other, thereby creating the impression of a 'défaut de ligne droite', similar to the one that characterises Frédéric's life. Several critics have commented upon the disconnected nature of the plot of *L'Éducation sentimentale*. Denommé notes the 'replacement of the well-focussed single story line by a multiplicity of seemingly disconnected scenes and fragments'[30] and Raitt asserts that 'la succession des scènes, comme celle des chapitres, produit un effet de décousu'.[31] *L'Éducation sentimentale* lacks the clear pyramid structure of *Madame Bovary*; although structural patterns are numerous and the novel is the result of 'un prodigieux travail d'assemblage',[32] the order tends to be at the level of micro-structure rather than macro-structure.[33] The double ending, while corresponding to the double opening, creates an effect of dispersal. The reader does not gain any sense of direction from the novel as a whole and this has the effect of rendering the psychological element more inconsequential and uncertain.

A further threat to the psychological element is posed by what has been described as the citational energy of Flaubert's discourse, the ambiguous relationship which exists between the text and 'bêtise'.[34] It is possible to read the opening description of Frédéric not as an objective account of a person we are expected to 'believe in' but as a network of citations: the sentence, 'Un jeune homme de dix-huit ans, à long cheveux et qui tenait un album sous son bras, restait auprès du gouvernail, immobile', can be read as 'a kind of generalized quotation that at once refers back to, recapitulates and ironizes, under the sign of "bêtise" an inherited corpus of narrative texts'.[35] The irony at work is not, however, easily contained; the relation between Flaubert's own narrative discourse and the citational mode is problematic. The ubiquity of 'bêtise', the impossibility of ever breaking out of its trammels or of allowing the narrator to occupy a position of transcendence, mean that the citational play of the text swallows up narrator and character alike, immersing both in the *doxa*. What *L'Éducation sentimentale* displays, according to this line of argument, is not so much the desultory life and uncertain times of Frédéric Moreau as the fundamental inability of the novel to rise out of the quagmire of 'bêtise'. As soon as it begins to address itself to a particular area of experience the novel immediately gets bogged down in a welter of clichéd assumptions enshrined in the collective wisdom of the age, caught up in a ritual, the ritual of fiction itself which has become irremediably tainted. Whether this inability to escape 'bêtise' is foregrounded in the text as powerfully as Prendergast claims may be debatable, but as long as it is suggested it has the effect of tingeing the psychological element with uncertainty.

It would be difficult to overstate the difficulties encountered by the reader when seeking to formulate a clear view of the characters of *L'Éducation sentimentale.* Flaubert seems to have subverted or undermined so many of the assumptions and procedures relating to character that had prevailed in the novel that the reader may well be inclined to abandon all attempts at reaching a coherent interpretation of the behaviour of the main characters and relish the way traditional psychological presentation is done away with. The reader who approaches the novel with traditional expectations concerning character is liable to be baffled by the development of a whole battery of new techniques and the most common initial impression may well be that character in the novel is in the process of disintegrating and the traditional psychological thrust of the novel being abandoned. It would, however, be a real impoverishment of the novel if the notion of character were rejected entirely or if it were to be assumed that no effort to throw light upon Frédéric's development is being made. If the extreme hypothesis of a complete evacuation of psychology is accepted, the reader is likely to miss a number of important and valuable features of the novel.

In the first place there is a danger of overlooking what at the time constituted a radically new view of human nature; much of the strangeness and fragmentary quality of the action can be predicated upon a new type of personality-structure, one which is diametrically opposed to that of the go-getting Balzacian careerist and not just a pale copy of the mournful romantic hero. Flaubert's view of Frédéric's personality constitutes a challenge to earlier attitudes to love and ambition as well as to the idea of character as such. Secondly, Flaubert is operating with an extremely complex view of what makes people act as they do, and, in particular, breaking new ground in the presentation of unconscious forces. Much that is puzzling or perplexing about Frédéric's behaviour can be partly explained if the reader is prepared to adduce the existence of forces and complexes which operate at an unconscious level. In spite of the fact that the concept of the unconscious is not clearly developed until late in the nineteenth century, and in spite of the fact that the major findings of psychoanalysis come even later, it is tempting to invoke the operation of unconscious forces in order to explain Frédéric's persistent and in many ways perverse fixation on a figure of saintly purity. That this is a legitimate critical gambit rests upon the indisputable truth proclaimed by Freud that 'the poets and the philosophers discovered the unconscious long before me'.[36] Of course the last thing one wants to do is stretch a fictional character out upon an imaginary couch, forgetting that as a paper being,[37] he lacks a real 'unconscious' as much as real entrails. On the other hand, there is something limiting about the traditional reluctance to accept the invocation of unconscious motives into the panoply of exegetical procedures. Admittedly, as Barthes puts it, 'on développe des connotations, on ne poursuit pas des investigations',[38] but the suggestive force of the text, its problematic depiction of behaviour which in many respects is self-defeating and contradictory, may well connote, for those attuned to the idea of unconscious motivation – and who in this day and age is not? – the operation of unconscious forces.[39] Lastly, although the behaviour of characters is no longer presented in the clear, authoritative manner associated with the traditional novel, it is not because of a sudden loss of interest in the feelings and reactions of characters but rather the result of an intensification of interest. Flaubert devotes more attention to the inner life of Frédéric than had previously been customary, presenting the ebb and flow of his consciousness and showing the world through his eyes. In spite of the problems associated with its presentation, the psychological element is central to the novel and forms the basis upon which it rests.

The main aim of this study will be to show that, beneath its problematic surface, and, to some extent obscured by the various techniques of disconcertation which have been referred to above, *L'Éducation sentimentale* offers a coherent account of the development of Frédéric Moreau. Although far from straightforward, the psychological element is of considerable interest and to reject it on principle is to impoverish the text; it is not immediately apparent, after all, why the destruction of character and evacuation of psychology should be hailed as great literary achievements. Although, as Victor Brombert remarks, 'the very word "psychology" now almost sounds insulting in literary criticism',[40] it is precisely this aspect of the novel which will be reclaimed as a legitimate focus of critical inquiry. As an essential preliminary to the reclaiming of psychology, some indication of the view of character which will be adopted is required, since if character is not firmly established as a coherent category, it is doubtful whether it is possible to speak meaningfully of psychology.

Contrary to what novelists themselves have often maintained – but this was often part of their game – characters are clearly not real people and do not have an existence independent of the work in which they figure. To treat a fictional character as if it were a real person is to fall into the 'superstition littéraire' castigated by Valéry:

> J'appelle ainsi toutes croyances qui ont en commun l'oubli de la condition verbale de la littérature. Ainsi existence des personnages, ces vivants sans entrailles.[41]

In an age of literary agnosticism we must pronounce the death sentence on character as an autonomous entity endowed with an individual essence and recognise that what generations of trusting readers have half taken to be flesh and blood creatures are nothing but paper beings. This is not to say, however, that the notion of character becomes totally redundant. Provided one acknowledges the true nature of the literary character as the end result of a complex series of combinatorial operations performed by the reader on the information contained in the text,[42] there is every reason to discuss the characters of a novel, since for most readers and writers character continues to be the main 'totalizing force' of fiction.[43]

The recognition that characters, far from being real people, are first and foremost textual products might appear to be a dangerous concession opening the door to a certain kind of semiotic criticism which threatens to undermine character as a distinct feature of a work of fiction:

> Under the aegis of semiotic criticism, characters lose their privilege, their central status, and their definition. This does not mean that they are metamorphosed into animate things (à la Robbe-Grillet) or reduced to actants (à la Todorov) but that they are textualized. As segments of a closed text, characters at most are patterns of recurrence, motifs which are continually recontextualized in other motifs. In semiotic criticism, characters dissolve.[44]

In spite of the progress made in recent years in the understanding of the way narratives work, the view of character which has been prevalent tends to be reductive, deadening and contrary to the reader's experience, although some attempts have been made to refurbish the notion of character within a 'semiotic' perspective. Both Seymour Chatman[45] and S. Rimmon-Kenan[46] seek to rescue character from the near oblivion to which it risks being condemned. For Chatman it is wrong to equate character with mere words:

> A viable theory of character should preserve openness and treat characters as autonomous beings, not as mere plot-functions. It should argue that character is reconstructed by the audience from evidence announced or implicit in an original construction and communicated by the discourse, through whatever medium.[47]

Rimmon-Kenan, likewise, brings together two different approaches to character:

> In the text characters are nodes in the verbal design; in the story they are – by definition – non (or pre-) verbal abstractions, constructs. Although these constructs are by no means human beings in the literal sense of the word, they are partly modelled on the reader's conception of people and in this they are people-like.[48]

It is precisely such a view of character, which attempts to do justice both to the way character is rooted in the text but at the same time, as a postulate or construct, able, as it were, to float free of the text, that this work will espouse, always mindful of the fact that the study of character within a semiotic perspective is still very much in its infancy. In this way it is hoped to avoid both the 'vieux psychologisme d'autrefois'[49] which mars much earlier work on character and at the same time the blanket rejection of character as a central, organising element in the text which vitiates certain forms of semiotic criticism.

One of the factors which explains the comparative neglect of character is the primacy accorded to 'story' in current narratological theory, which leads to character being viewed as no more than a support for the action.[50] This primacy is difficult to justify, however, as James's famous insistence on their mutual dependency suggests:

> ' What is character but the determination of incident? What is incident but the illustration of character?[51]

'Story', as much as character, is a construct, arrived at by the reader on the basis of information provided by the narrative text itself. However, partly as a result of the way the term 'histoire' has been adopted as a key concept, it has become axiomatic that the story is more central than character. Originally 'histoire' was opposed to 'discours' by Benveniste in order to distinguish between two types of utterance, one which did not bear any grammatical traces of the speaker, the other which did.[52] Subsequently, however, the two terms were used to refer to fundamentally opposed aspects of narrative: what is evoked, on the one hand, the text, on the other.[53] The terminology used carries with it certain concealed assumptions, in particular the assumption that the story constitutes the bulk of the narrative *content*, which can be set against narrative *form*. This is, however, by no means self-evident and it is in some ways unfortunate that the word 'histoire' was so widely accepted to designate the content-plane of narrative, when another term, 'diégèse', first proposed by Souriau, was available. The difference between these two terms has been discussed by Genette:

> La diégèse, au sens où Souriau a proposé ce terme en 1948, opposant l'univers diégétique comme lieu du signifié à l'univers écranique comme lieu du signifiant filmique, est bien un *univers* plutôt qu'un enchaînement d'actions (histoire): la diégèse n'est donc pas l'histoire, mais l'univers où elle advient . . . [54]

Although the adjective 'diégétique' is now widely used, Souriau's original term, 'diégèse' is not generally opposed to 'discours'. Such a term has the advantage, however, of allowing the parity between character and action to be restored; close to what would be termed in English the fictional world, 'diégèse' encompasses both the story that unfolds in the fictional world and the characters who move in it, with neither one necessarily being more important than the other.

As an aspect of the fictional world, character can be defined as a collection of traits. These traits are not free-floating but organised into a relatively stable pattern. It has been suggested by Hrushovski that character is 'a tree-like, hierarchical structure in which elements are arranged in categories of increasing integrative power'.[55] At the top of the tree-like structure one might place a given personality or character type; on the next level would be a certain number of traits, a trait being any relatively stable or abiding personal quality; each trait in turn could be linked with appropriate attitudes, habits and thought-processes at the next level and each of these features of any particular trait would be linked with specific pieces of behaviour. At this lowest level, 'character' can be thought of as 'meshing' with 'story', or alternatively 'story' can be thought of as a temporal projection of 'character'. Individual readers will not necessarily all 'realise' or 'actualise' such a structure in its entirety but it seems highly likely that what material relating to character they do acquire will be organised along hierarchical lines similar to those proposed by Hrushovski. Such a model might well account for different types of character. The greater the number of traits, the more 'complex' the character; the greater the ease with which pieces of behaviour can be subsumed under categories at a higher level, the more recognisable the character; the greater the similarity between the various traits, the more consistent the character and so forth.

The model of character proposed above corresponds to the static construct which the reader arrives at at the end of his reading(s). How, though, does the reader actually acquire the material which is finally organised into this kind of structure or, putting it slightly differently, how is the information relating to character organised in the narrative account? Rimmon-Kenan suggests that the reader constructs 'character' by 'assembling various character-indicators distributed along the text-continuum and, when necessary, inferring traits from them'.[56] Thus the information relating to character is dispersed throughout the text and needs to be put together by the reader. Different types of information are fed into different levels of 'character'. Direct definition, for instance, obviously relates to the upper levels of maximum integrative power while indirect presentation or 'illustration' relates to the lower levels and depends upon the reader's ability to make the appropriate inferences. Direct definition, which relies upon an 'authoritative' narrator tends to create a 'closed' effect; if the character is 'known' from the outset the function of the story becomes that of confirming or demonstrating the correctness of an initial definition rather than gradually revealing character. Indirect presentation, the mode which has become dominant with the demise of the traditional omniscient narrator, seals the mutual dependency of 'character' and 'story' and tends to create an 'open' effect.[57]

The reader's processing of the various types of information relating to character dispersed throughout the text is subject to various controls. Basic to the whole process of character-construction is nomination; as Barthes points out, the proper name acts as an assembly-point for the gathering together of 'semes' or pieces of information.[58] Once a cluster of traits has become associated with the proper name, it acts as a convenient form of shorthand which 'permet de substituer une unité nominale à une collection de traits en posant un rapport d'équivalence entre le signe et la somme'.[59] The use of proper names has the effect of making characters *appear* to be more than simple collections of traits, fostering the illusion that there is an entity, independent of the words on the page and difficult to define, which the text is seeking to flesh out:

> Ce qui donne l'illusion que la somme est supplémentée d'un reste précieux (quelque chose comme l'individualité, en ce que qualitative, ineffable, elle échapperait à la vulgaire comptabilité des caractères composants), c'est le Nom Propre, la différence remplie de son propre. Le Nom Propre permet à la personne d'exister en dehors des sèmes dont cependant la somme la constitue entièrement. Dès lors qu'il existe un Nom vers quoi affluer et sur quoi se fixer, les sèmes deviennent des prédicats, inducteurs de vérité, et le Nom devient sujet.[60]

The proper name functions in different ways allowing an elementary organisation of semic material but also creating more complex 'character' effects, in particular, the impression that character exists independently of the text.

The material used to construct character comes from many different quarters; virtually any aspect of the fictional universe can have relevance to character. It is, however, the sequence of actions making up the 'story', which can be thought of as forming the horizontal axis of the work, which usually makes the richest source of information. Along this horizontal axis there is a premium on repetition: 'Lorsque des sèmes identiques traversent à plusieurs reprises le même Nom Propre et semblent s'y fixer, il naît un personnage.'[61] Stendhal's famous definition of character ('J'appelle caractère la manière habituelle d'un homme de chercher son bonheur') is a reminder that in real life as in fiction the recurrent or habitual response plays a vital role in shaping our notion of character. But while in real life the perception of personality involves 'the process of abstracting an invariant from the multitude of bodily and behavioural transformations during the whole life of the individual',[62] fiction presents the reader with a ready-made selection of 'discriminated occasions' in which the recurrent element is frequently foregrounded. Against the habitual response must be set the revelatory act or gesture which comes as a surprise and forces the reader to revise his notion of what constitutes a character's character. Julien Sorel's shooting of Madame de Rênal, for instance, stands opposed to his habitual behaviour, pointing to a new dimension in his character and refuting the notion of 'what he is like' that has been built up so far.

The actions which make up the story vary considerably in psychological import; the bearing of what might be called an 'historical event' like 'la marquise sortit à cinq heures' is very different from that of a mental occurrence such as 'X se demanda longtemps si . . . '. Historical events will often take on a specific meaning in context, just as physical happenings will often have psychological implications. Thus, 'x bites his finger-nails and glances around the room' implies that 'x is nervous'.[63] So, even where there is little direct information relating to the inner experience of a character, it is frequently possible for the reader to form an idea of how the character is responding at any given moment in the narrative. Narratives vary considerably in the demands that they make upon the reader in this respect. Although a narrative may withhold direct information about what a given character is experiencing, it may stimulate the reader to bring into play various codes – logical, cultural, generic – in order to guess or infer the hidden state from the surface behaviour.

The process of character-construction involves more than making the appropriate inferences from material arranged along the horizontal axis of the work; it is possible to visualise another axis, vertical rather than horizontal, along which material of a different kind is projected.[64] Most narratives contain a good deal of information which does not contribute to the forward movement of the story; information relating to setting, appearance, the permanent or fixed aspect of things cannot be thought of as advancing the narrative in the way that descriptions of actions and events can. Such information may well have a bearing upon character, however. The physical appearance of a character is often endowed with a rich significance, as may be a certain posture or presence in a certain environment. The motionless posture of Frédéric Moreau as he is borne along by the river steamer at the beginning of the novel carries strong overtones of a deep-seated psychic passivity. Details of this kind often have an extremely powerful effect and may threaten to short-circuit the narrative, conveying to the reader in a flash what is going to be established more laboriously by the long account of the character's actions that follows. It is not just symbolic details, however, which suggest a 'vertical' dimension to any narrative, opposed to a horizontal story-line. In building up a notion of character, the reader also relies upon a process of systematic comparison with other characters. Like the elements which make up a linguistic system, the elements composing a fictional system assume their meaning by virtue of the relations of similarity and difference which exist between them and other elements of the same kind. Character is in part constituted through differential relations: 'La "signification" du personnage ne se constitue pas tant par répétition ou par accumulation, que par différence vis-à-vis des signes du même niveau du système, que par son insertion dans le système global de l'œuvre.'[65] For the differential relations between characters to be perceived, the reader needs to arrange material vertically, superimposing the reactions of other characters in similar situations, which have been described at a different point in the narrative, on that of a given character at a specific juncture. The full significance of Frédéric's aim-inhibited attitude to the opposite sex, which constitutes an important part of his character, emerges most forcibly when the very different attitudes of Arnoux or Deslauriers are recollected. Lastly, it is possible to envisage the provisional notion of character as arrived at at any particular juncture of the narrative by the reader as a 'paradigm of traits' which form a 'vertical assemblage intersecting the syntagmatic chain of events'.[66] At any given moment of reading 'the whole set of a character's traits established up to that moment'[67] hovers, as it were, over the horizontal story-line, presenting itself for confirmation, modification or expansion, as the case may be. In other words, there is a constant interaction between the vertical and horizontal dimensions of narrative, between the static and the dynamic. The process of character-construction involves a constant movement from one to the other. A preliminary segmentation of information belonging to the horizontal axis is followed by the vertical projection of symbolic details or differential relations but once this supplementary operation has been carried out the meaning it yields in the form of an enriched view of character is, as it were, ploughed back into the interpretation of 'what is taking place' at a particular juncture of the narrative, as character and action are brought into yet another temporary vertical alignment.

The case for continuing to view 'character' as a central feature of narrative fiction has been stated at some length because it is essential to refurbish the notion of character if the 'psychological' dimension of the novel is to be taken seriously. Although it is theoretically possible, as Nathalie Sarraute has argued, to do away with character, at least as it is traditionally conceived, and yet purvey 'une substance psychologique nouvelle',[68] in practice it is difficult to dissociate the notion of psychology from a certain view of character as a kind of space in which psychology unfolds. 'Character' and 'psychology' stand or fall together in so far as the dissolution or disintegration of character – which some critics see taking place in Flaubert – would leave the 'état psychologique' Flaubert claimed to be seeking to represent[69] floating perilously free. Without some notion of character – albeit one which takes stock of the fact that character originates in a 'réseau impersonnel de symboles' – [70] it would be difficult to defend the idea that in *L'Éducation sentimentale* Flaubert is successfully conducting an investigation into a complex psychological state. It may be true that at times the character of Frédéric Moreau seems to dissolve in a succession of 'états d'âme' and fails consequently to minister to traditional expectations; ultimately, however, these 'états d'âme' are predicated upon a radically new view of character as a system of tendencies corresponding to a certain temperament and activated by certain cultural pressures. In Flaubert a growing awareness of the complexity of the psychology of modern man ('je ne vois de simplicité nulle part dans le monde moderne')[71] leads to a rejection of clearly defined characters and the simple psychology associated with the traditional novel but also makes possible the creation of totally new characters – shadowy, uncertain, vacillating – and the exploration of a new kind of psychological state – intractable, contradictory, self-defeating.[72]

This study is based on the premise that Flaubert was not totally misguided when he spoke of the importance of the psychological aspect in his work or undertook in *L'Éducation sentimentale* to represent a complex psychological state. It will attempt to recuperate the psychological element in a number of ways. First, Flaubert's conflicting ideals as far as psychology is concerned will be examined with a view to showing that he was torn between two opposing approaches which were finally reconciled in the concealment of psychology in the text rather than its complete elimination. Secondly, the long and painstaking preparation of the novel will be investigated. Since the Bibliothèque Nationale acquired the plans and rough drafts for the novel, it has been possible to study the development of *L'Éducation sentimentale* through the various stages of its composition. In particular, the growth of the psychological aspect can now be examined in the same detail as for other novels. The *scénarios* for *L'Éducation sentimentale* throw considerable and at times surprising light upon the psychological element, often making explicit what is left uncertain in the final version, and revealing how concerned Flaubert was to give the novel solid psychological foundations. Fascinating though much of this preparatory material is, it cannot be used directly in support of the argument that *L'Éducation sentimentale*, in the final version, which is all most readers are familiar with, offers a coherent account of a complex psychological state in spite of its many departures from traditional narrative practice. Accordingly, the main part of this study is concerned with the final version of the novel, which will be examined first from the point of view of form, then from a thematic perspective. One of the most disconcerting features of the novel is its curiously unmemorable, disconnected and extended plot. The chronology, the handling of time and causality, as well as the overall significance of the events themselves, will all be discussed with a view to ascertaining whether the novel's plot produces an overwhelming impression of fragmentation, which would militate against the notion of an ongoing psychological development, or whether, on the contrary, beneath its fractured surface some kind of continuity can be detected. Equally problematic is the narrative practice of the novel, which will be examined in the next chapter in an attempt to determine the effects produced in the psychological sphere both by Flaubert's innovations in technique and by the remnants of traditional practice.

The originality of *L'Éducation sentimentale* does not lie solely in the unusual plot and narrative techniques employed. As startlingly original, in many respects, is the content of the novel. In the first place, the novel develops a new emphasis on inner determination in the presentation of the motive forces underlying the behaviour of the characters, although other factors are not ruled out. Frédéric and Deslauriers may not reach any significant conclusion when reviewing the disappointing course of their lives in the last chapter but they do succeed in isolating some of the most important factors which, in varying degrees, underlie the various kinds of failure presented. It is perhaps most markedly in the presentation of relations between the sexes that *L'Éducation sentimentale* breaks new ground. Frédéric's complex relationships with various women will be examined in detail, as will the attitudes of the women themselves, in an attempt to show how perceptive Flaubert's treatment of the theme of love is. Although the psychology of love is Flaubert's central concern, *L'Éducation sentimentale* also explores the psychology of friendship and once again, as will be seen in the next chapter, the account offered is both novel and penetrating. Where Flaubert is at his most original is in the alignment of psychology and history which permits the use of historical material to extend and illuminate in at times quite radical ways what is taking place in the psychological sphere, particularly at an unconscious level, which are discussed in the following chapter. Finally, in the conclusion, the originality of the novel as far as the presentation of psychology is concerned will be examined and the nature of the characters that emerge discussed.

I

Analysis, Synthesis and Hidden Psychology

Although the strength and importance of the psychological element in Flaubert's work is now the subject of intense critical debate, Flaubert's own expectations regarding this aspect of the novel were consistent. There can be little doubt that he attached considerable importance to 'psychology', both in the sense of the thoughts, feelings and motives of the protagonists, and in the sense of a coherent presentation of these thoughts, feelings and motives. The stress laid by Flaubert on the psychological aspect in *Madame Bovary* is well known.[1] Although the subject of *Salammbô* did not lend itself to the same treatment as far as psychology was concerned, Flaubert continued for a long time to think of the psychological element as vitally important.[2] Like the two novels which preceded it, *L'Éducation sentimentale* was first and foremost a psychological study, a representation of a complex psychological state.[3] Only with *Bouvard et Pécuchet* do serious doubts about the importance of psychology surface in Flaubert's *Correspondance*, although even there the preoccupation with psychology does not disappear completely.[4] In the light of this constant emphasis upon psychology as the basis upon which the novel rests, the view that Flaubert is evacuating psychology from the novel needs to be treated with caution.

It was not simply a question of claiming that 'psychology' is important rather as one might claim that human relations are important. Flaubert's observations on his own novels and on those sent to him for comment reveal that he had a set of very precise expectations relating to psychology. To ensure the coherence of the psychological aspect it was essential that character and action should be bound together in a pattern of mutual implication,[5] that characters should possess a certain consistency,[6] that the development of the main character should possess an inner logic,[7] that clear motives should be provided for the major actions,[8] and that descriptions should always have a bearing upon the behaviour of the character.[9] Many of these requirements are enunciated by Flaubert as if they were incontrovertible principles; the *Correspondance* lays down with remarkable firmness and clarity the fundamental tenets of what was once called psychological realism.

However definite Flaubert might have been in arguing that the various elements of the novel should be bound together in a pattern of mutual implication in order to elucidate the psychological progression of the protagonist, which constituted the basis upon which the novel rested, when it came to actually working out the psychological development of the protagonist in the plans he frequently experienced considerable difficulty.[10] More importantly, when it came to actually accounting for this development in the novel, he frequently found himself confronted with problems which were difficult to resolve. Although Flaubert was strong in his conviction that the psychological element was of fundamental importance, he was less certain over the question of how this element, once elaborated, should be conveyed. 'J'ai des *idéaux* contradictoires', Flaubert admitted;[11] the truth was that he found himself pulled in different directions when it came to actually presenting psychology in his works, torn between the conflicting ideals of analysis and synthesis and able to reconcile them only with a certain amount of difficulty in a practice akin to what Maupassant called 'psychologie cachée'.

Flaubert consistently thought of himself as undertaking in his works an analytic account of human behaviour. He is most at home, he claims, with 'les sujets d'analyse'[12] and not the least important of the two 'bonshommes' who are at loggerheads within him is 'celui qui fouille et creuse le vrai tant qu'il peut, qui aime à accuser le petit fait aussi puissamment que le grand, qui voudrait vous faire sentir presque matériellement les choses qu'il reproduit'.[13] The son of an eminent surgeon whom, as a child, he had observed dissecting corpses in the Hôtel Dieu in Rouen, Flaubert retained a strong interest in medicine in general and dissection in particular.[14] It was all too easy, therefore, for him to think of his pen as a kind of scalpel and writing as a dissective art. Debarred from actually operating on other people, Flaubert is driven to self-dissection.[15] This activity provides him with invaluable material for his novels:

> Que de fois j'ai senti à mes meilleurs moments le froid du scalpel qui m'entrait dans la chair! *Bovary* . . . sera sous ce rapport, la somme de ma science psychologique et n'aura une valeur originale que par ce côté.[16]

Flaubert's adoption of the family emblem, the scalpel, is not a simple act of filial homage, however. Sartre has argued that Flaubert's attitude towards his father was a complex mixture of dread and devotion, respect and resentment and that he was led, by virtue of his constitutional passivity and subordination to his father's will, to adopt against his own deepest inclinations the 'scientific', analytic approach to life with which his father was associated.[17] More specifically Flaubert attempts to constitute himself as a person by interiorizing his father's analytic gaze in the form of what he called the 'coup d'œil médical'.[18] Analysis, according to this interpretation, becomes a kind of superego,[19] and represents the most significant manifestation of the father's domination: 'le père ennemi, installé en lui, comme une force étrangère, le domine et le dirige à son gré'.[20] But, by the same token, it does not correspond to Flaubert's true needs:

> Voici donc l'analyse, comme schème opératoire, introduite sournoisement en Gustave et se substituant chez lui à l'expérience acquise, devenant, de par l'autorité paternelle, un impératif méthodologique et se prétendant équivalente à l'expérience existentielle.[21]

Analysis is then a curse, something foisted upon a defenceless infant by an all-powerful father.[22] It is, however, completely ineffective: 'Gustave, à l'inverse de son père, qui pratique la vertu sans y croire, croit à l'analyse, sans jamais la pratiquer'.[23] Thus, according to Sartre, Flaubert is able to grasp himself only as an object of analytic penetration[24] and fails abysmally in his attempts to 'faire un plan' or analyse Emma's feelings.[25]

Although Sartre's estimation of Flaubert's capacity for analysis is questionable, the skill with which he identifies the implications and associations of analysis for Flaubert cannot be doubted. The sight of the father dissecting corpses in the Hôtel Dieu is a key experience, predisposing Flaubert to associate analysis with death, putrefaction and everything that is loathsome. When dissecting the human heart, Flaubert expects to be dealing with something that has reached an advanced stage of decomposition: 'la psychologie, pour Gustave, est une mortisection qui nous découvre l'état cadavérique de l'âme'.[26] This helps to explain why Flaubert was compelled to divide his life into two distinct 'existences';[27] Flaubert creates the myth of the 'death' of his first self not simply in order to account for his profound inability to 'live', but in order to be able to perform figuratively his own autopsy. Unlike Renan, for whom analysis yielded a higher beauty,[28] Flaubert was conditioned into expecting it to expose nothing but the unpleasant: 'La plus belle femme n'est guère belle sur la table d'un amphithéâtre avec les boyaux sur le nez ... O non! c'est une triste chose d'analyser le cœur humain pour y trouver égoïsme.'[29] As Sartre graphically puts it, 'Ce sera pour Flaubert une règle générale: l'objet du savoir pue.'[30]

Flaubert's predisposition towards analysis cannot be accounted for solely in terms of his family situation. There is clearly an important literary precedent set by Balzac which Flaubert was in no position to ignore. The image of the scalpel is already found in one of Balzac's novels, in connection with the subject-matter that Flaubert himself takes up,[31] and the analytic posture is one which the earlier novelist often, though by no means invariably,[32] adopts. Secondly, respect for the scientific method and achievement was not confined to the Flaubert household but rather constitutes what has been called the 'leurre idéologique' of the age.[33] Along with the emphasis on 'généralités', and the prescription of impartiality, the recommendation of a rigorously analytic approach can be directly related to Flaubert's frequently expressed admiration for science and scientific method.[34] It has been argued that 'l'esprit scientifique que Flaubert insuffle au roman n'a rien de très original ni même de très vivifiant',[35] but what has been termed his 'scientificité' constitutes an essential element in his literary project and acts as a necessary corrective to a profoundly sceptical and defeatist tendency in him. Temperamentally Flaubert was averse to 'reality', philosophically, he had doubts about its objective existence,[36] and artistically he was agonisingly aware of the impossibility of grasping it. The point about Flaubert's 'scientificité' is that it forces someone who might otherwise have turned his back on 'reality' to address himself to it and to overcome his scepticism on account of the attraction of 'l'utopie féconde d'une série de lois qui doivent pouvoir se découvrir, mais non s'inventer'.[37] Science represented for Flaubert one acceptable way of accommodating a hated reality.

The analytic method associated with science allows Flaubert to deal with reality without betraying his profound antipathy for it: 'Disséquer est une vengeance'.[38] Secondly, the notion of analysis gives Flaubert the impression that he is in possession of insights into the general pattern of human experience which provide the necessary basis for the psychological dimension of his fiction. Lastly, unlike the 'affres du style', analysis was a finite process; when he wore his analyst's hat, Flaubert experienced the reassuring sense of making definite progress. Although the extent and effectiveness of the analytic dimension in Flaubert's novels are open to question, the belief that he was engaged in analytic activity gave Flaubert a much needed sense of security and helped to offset the profound doubts and uncertainties about the value of his work by which he was constantly assailed.

Although there were many reasons for Flaubert's enthusiasm for analysis, there is considerable evidence to suggest that it was not his most characteristic mode of apprehending the real; as he confesses, at an early stage, in *Souvenirs, notes et pensées intimes*, 'Je saisis et je sens en bloc, en synthèse, sans m'apercevoir du détail'.[39] In spite of the powerful influences to which he was exposed, Flaubert senses that his true vocation lies in the global perception of the real, in the synthesizing approach. Certainly, his attraction to the analytic method did not blind him to the merits of synthesis. In an important passage in the first *Tentation* the need to go beyond a purely analytic approach is clearly apparent in the ambition attributed to the allegorial figure, La Science:

> Si je pouvais pénétrer la matière ..., comprendre l'être dans tous ses modes, et de l'un à l'autre remontant les causes, comme les marches d'un escalier, réunir à moi ces phénomènes épars et les remettre en mouvement dans la synthèse d'où les détachés mon scalpel ... peut-être alors je ferais des mondes.[40]

While the scientific method entails the fragmentation of a given totality into its component parts, these parts need to be reassembled or reconstituted into the original totality in a higher process of artistic creation. As Sartre suggests, it is not a question of replacing scientific analysis with artistic synthesis[41] but rather of going one stage further than analysis, as the following account of the creative process makes clear:

> L'artiste non seulement porte en soi l'humanité, mais il reproduit les phases dans la création de son œuvre: d'abord du trouble, une vue générale, des aspirations, l'éblouissement, tout est mêlé (époque barbare); puis l'analyse, le doute, la méthode, la disposition des parties (l'ère scientifique); enfin, il revient à la synthèse première, plus élargie dans l'execution.[42]

Analysis and synthesis are, therefore, complementary rather than mutually exclusive operations within the creative process as a whole.

It would be misleading, however, to suggest that analysis and synthesis coexist in a state of perfect unison, or that there is no discrepancy between the two types of outlook associated with them. If the analytic approach is associated with the discovery and exposure of all that is disagreeable, the synthesizing approach is linked with the discovery and reconstitution of harmonious totalities. Flaubert can swing from extreme loathing to pantheist exultation in the face of the real, according to whether he apprehends the part or the whole. The first *Éducation sentimentale* charts the oscillation between the two ways of apprehending the real in a particularly revealing way. Initially morose and disillusioned, full of disgust when confronted with his memories of various and apparently unrelated experiences in his past life, the artist-figure, Jules, on adopting a synthesizing approach, suddenly intuits an order in what had first appeared chaotic: 'en le synthétisant et en le ramenant à des principes absolus, il aperçut une symétrie miraculeuse rien que dans le retour périodique des mêmes idées devant les mêmes choses, des mêmes sensations devant les mêmes faits'.[43] Not only his past but also all Creation, viewed from the same synthesizing standpoint, take on a new harmony: 'Alors la suprême poésie, l'intelligence sans limites, la nature sur toutes ses faces, la passion dans tous ses cris, le cœur humain avec tous ses abîmes, s'allièrent en une synthèse immense, dont il respectait chaque partie par amour de l'ensemble'.[44] The validity of the synthesizing solution proposed here has been questioned.[45] Even within the novel there is a suggestion that Jules's synthesizing tendency is too strong: 'en faisant de l'analyse il se préoccupait trop de la synthèse, de sorte que le détail lui échappait . . .'.[46] More powerfully, the famous dog episode, which comes immediately after his perception of the 'symétrie miraculeuse' and the 'synthèse immense', can be read as a questioning of his synthesizing euphoria. Jules has theoretically arrived at a position where he can accept all aspects of existence as integral parts of a total harmony but when confronted by a mangy dog he is unable in practice to come to terms with it. Whether it symbolizes the isolated detail which cannot be transformed by its integration into the 'synthèse immense', or the 'synthèse immense' itself, now registered under the sign of ugliness, the dog seems to undermine Jules's recently acquired belief in harmonious totalities.[47]

Whatever the validity of the belief adopted by Jules, there is no doubt that it has profound repercussions on his whole view of the process of artistic creation. In order that art should reflect the underlying 'symétrie miraculeuse', the artist transforms himself into a vehicle for the absorption and expression of the world, viewed as a harmonious totality: 'tout vient vers lui, tout en ressort, flux du monde, reflux de lui-même; . . . et lui-même tout entier il se concrétise dans sa vocation, dans sa mission, dans la fatalité de son génie et de son labeur – panthéisme immense, qui passe par lui et réapparaît dans l'Art.'[48] In organising and structuring his work he need do no more than adopt the same basic 'procédés' which render the world itself harmonious like a work of art: 'habituons-nous à considérer le monde comme une œuvre d'art dont il faut reproduire les procédés dans nos œuvres.'[49]

Perhaps the most important of these 'procédés' relates to the mode of the Creator's presence in his Creation. In moments of pantheist euphoria, when he perceives the world as a harmonious unity, Flaubert recognises a Spinozist God immanent in and consubstantial with Creation.[50] The first *Tentation* contains the fullest exposition of this view of God forming an indissoluble unity with Creation, embracing matter and spirit, good and evil, perceived reality and perceiver, in a single totality: 'Dieu vit donc dans la vie, se pense dans la pensée; du moment que tu es, il est en toi; de l'instant que tu le comprends, tu es en lui; il est toi, tu es lui, et il n'y a qu'Un.'[51] It is inappropriate to look for the source or higher purpose of the universe in such a God, so deeply interfused is He with its fabric: 'Mais le séparer de la création pour l'expliquer davantage, ce n'est pas lui-même l'expliquer davantage, et il reste maintenant aussi incompréhensible hors d'elle que la création, tout à l'heure, l'était sans lui.'[52] It is this type of identity or consubstantiality of Creator and Creation, leading to the disappearance of the one into the other, that Flaubert wishes the novelist to emulate:

> L'art étant une seconde nature, le créateur de cette nature-là doit agir par des procédés analogues. Que l'on sente dans tous les atomes, à tous les aspects, une impassibilité divine et cachée.[53]

The novelist, whom he repeatedly compared to God in creation, should be nowhere seen, everywhere felt.[54]

To what extent can this ideal of a divinely impassible creator accommodate Flaubert's analytic leanings? In his numerous pronouncements Flaubert asserts that the novelist should refrain from philosophising, judging, confiding, all of which would risk endowing him with a recognisable personality and detract from the impression of impassibility he wished to create. He does not, however, proscribe statements of an analytic cast, as the following advice to an aspiring novelist makes clear: 'Pourquoi faites-vous des réflexions qui coupent le récit? Une réflexion ne vaut pas une analyse'.[55] But who, it might be asked, is responsible, according to Flaubert, for the 'analyse' which he prefers to evaluation? When discussing the ideal of impersonality, Flaubert refers to 'le romancier', 'l'auteur' and 'le créateur' but not to 'le narrateur', failing to make a distinction between the narrator, the fictional construct to whom the task of telling the story falls, and the author, the real-life person who actually produced the work. As a result of this conflation of author and narrator, he does not in practice simply suppress statements which could be interpreted as evidence of the author's presence in the work but also, in spite of his theoretical justification of analysis, seeks to attenuate the narrator's presence, by restricting his omniscience. He does this most typically by using the technique commonly known as point of view, which involves looking *with* rather than *at* character: 'le principe même de ce mode narratif implique en toute rigueur que le personnage focal ne soit jamais décrit, ni même désigné de l'extérieur, et que ses pensées ou ses perceptions ne soient jamais analysées objectivement par le narrateur.'[56] Logically, the technique of point of view or 'focalisation interne' may imply a modicum of omniscience (as much as is required to see into the mind of another person) but the effect it produces is that the narrator has disappeared or 'merged' with the character,[57] which in turn enhances the impression of the fictional world simply existing. The extent to which Flaubert uses this technique means that in practice his analytic tendency is severely checked by his attempt at achieving the same identity with his fictional world as is postulated for a Spinozist God with Creation.[58]

The full extent of the dilemma facing Flaubert is highlighted by Maupassant's well-known distinction, made in the controversial essay 'Le Roman', which was first published as a preface to *Pierre et Jean* in 1885, between two types of novel, the 'roman d'analyse' and the 'roman objectif', each with its own supporters:

> Les partisans de l'analyse demandent que l'écrivain s'attache à indiquer les moindres évolutions de l'esprit et tous les mobiles les plus secrets qui déterminent nos actions, en n'accordant au fait lui-même qu'une importance secondaire ... Les partisans de l'objectivité ... prétendent, au contraire, nous donner la représentation exacte de ce qui a lieu dans la vie, évitent avec soin toute explication compliquée, toute dissertation sur les

motifs et se bornent à faire passer sous nos yeux les personnages et les événements.[59]

Maupassant appears to associate the 'objective' novel with Flaubert,[60] but his practice does not in fact conform to either of the over-simplified categories proposed. Had Flaubert been committed unequivocally to either analysis or synthesis he would have been able to align himself with one or other of the two camps and sought either total transparency of mind and motive or adopted the restricted, quasi-behaviourist perspective described by Maupassant. It is precisely because he is attracted to both analysis and synthesis that he is pulled in opposite directions and led to combine different narrative modes, presented as diametrically opposed by Maupassant.[61]

The conflict between analysis and synthesis is directly connected with the status of psychology in the novel. While analysis entails the direct exposure of psychology, the narrative modes associated with synthesis lead to its concealment. This radically new status of psychology for 'objective' novelists is underlined by Maupassant; 'Pour eux, la psychologie doit être cachée dans le livre comme elle est cachée en réalité sous les faits de l'existence.'[62] This is not to say, however, that psychology is totally abolished. The suppression of explicit analysis of psychological states and motives leads to a displacement of psychology from the surface to the interior of the work: 'Ils cachent ... la psychologie au lieu de l'étaler, ils en font la carcasse de l'œuvre comme l'ossature invisible est la carcasse du corps humain.'[63] The image of the skeleton underlines the vital supportive role of psychology when treated in this way. Paradoxically, the less prominent the psychological element is in the narrative account itself, the greater its importance in holding the novel together is likely to be. Following a long tradition, an equation can be made between what is hidden and what is essential, between secrecy and centrality.[64] To the extent that he is drawn to the practice of the 'objective' novelist, therefore, Flaubert will tend to place psychology in this new unseen supportive role. To the extent that he retains a residual commitment to the analytic mode, on the other hand, he will continue to locate the psychology of the novel more conventionally in the explicit account provided.

Flaubert's actual practice, it will be seen, does not conform to the simple model proposed by Maupassant but the idea of hidden psychology does open up an interesting perspective both upon the way he set about writing and upon the way the reader might be thought to react to his works. Flaubert's production of a novel falls into two quite distinct phases which can be clearly related to the notion of 'psychologie cachée'. In the first phase, that of the planning of the novel, a record of which is to be found in the *scénarios*, he gives free rein to his analytic tendency, carefully establishing motives for various actions and attempting to ensure a rigorous 'enchaînement des sentiments'[65] which is designed to constitute the 'ossature invisible' of the work. In the next phase, that of the actual writing of the novel, much of the explanatory and connecting material elaborated in the *scénarios* is removed, leaving the carefully erected psychological patterns standing without the support of the original scaffolding. Thus it is that Flaubert can engage in a considerable amount of psychological analysis without this being apparent to the reader confronted with the final version. When working on *Madame Bovary*, Flaubert wrote:

> Je tourne beaucoup à la critique. Le roman que j'écris m'aiguise cette faculté, car c'est une œuvre de critique, ou plutôt d'anatomie. Le lecteur ne s'apercevra pas, je l'espère, de tout le travail psychologique caché sous la forme, mais il en ressentira l'effet.[66]

Flaubert's painstaking dissection of feelings and motives prior to the actual composition of *Madame Bovary* reflects his analytic bent, while the urge to present a fictional world in which the hand of the creator is nowhere apparent is accommodated by the concealment of the fruits of his analytic labours beneath the surface of the work.

The effect of this concealment is not necessarily to suspend the reader's interest in psychology, but rather to stimulate him to complete the incomplete.[67] The best recipe, it would appear, for whetting the reader's interest in psychology, is to cover it with a veil of silence, the removal of which constitutes the best part of the reader's pleasure. In other words, the psychological element need not be permanently hidden; it should be possible for the reader to reconstruct the missing moods and motives. 'Tu devineras la psychologie sous les faits', concludes Flaubert, at the end of a long account of his day's activities, soon after Gautier's death, in which his personal feelings are not referred to directly.[68] In real life it is possible to infer from the cues and context of a factual account of a person's behaviour the emotional state which subtends that behaviour.

The same applies, Maupassant argues, to the account offered by the 'objective' novelist:

> Au lieu d'expliquer longuement l'état d'esprit d'un personnage, les écrivains objectifs cherchent l'action ou le geste que cet état d'âme doit faire accomplir fatalement à cet homme dans une situation déterminée. Et ils le font se conduire de telle manière, d'un bout à l'autre du volume, que tous ses actes, tout ses mouvements, soient le reflet de sa nature intime, de toutes ses pensées, de toutes ses volontés ou de toutes ses hésitations.[69]

The objective novelist, Maupassant suggests, provides the reader with innumerable inference tickets which give access to that inner realm of which the novel does not overtly speak. This assumes, of course, a close nexus, ultimately deterministic in nature, between inner state and outer behaviour in real life and in fiction. Only if there is a necessary connection between physical behaviour and psychological state can the former signify the latter. Where this sense of necessary connection is absent, the signifying mechanisms break down. Maupassant, and perhaps Flaubert too, at times seem unduly sanguine about the ease with which it is possible to deduce inner state from outer action and appearance.

The central issue, in fact, raised by the notion of hidden psychology is the one which Henry James was not slow to perceive: 'If psychology be hidden in life, as, according to M. de Maupassant, it should be in a book, the question immediately comes up, "From whom is it hidden?"'[70] Concealment should not be thought of as something absolute and what is hidden from one person may be apparent to another. James is more concerned with the question of motives, reasons, relations and explanations in real life rather than the novel, but it is equally pertinent to ask from whom psychology is hidden in a work of fiction. It is often the case, of course, that all that can be subsumed under the term 'psychology' may be hidden from the participants in the action. The main character in a novel, has, as a rule, only limited insight and understanding of both his own behaviour and that of other characters. Generally speaking, however, the person apparently responsible for the telling of the story, the narrator, can be expected to have a greater degree of insight into psychology. In the case of the type of novel recommended by Maupassant, however, the narrator will refrain from being specific about psychology. But although psychology may appear to be hidden, in that case, from the narrator, it is not necessarily hidden from the reader. According to Maupassant's argument the reader is in a position to deduce or infer what is happening 'inside' characters. Similarly, Flaubert claims that the reader will feel the effect of the psychological planning that has gone into the making of the novel. What, then, is the agency within the novel which allows psychological inferences to be made and the psychological planning to produce some kind of effect? Maupassant is silent on this point but Flaubert's concept of a creator consubstantial with his created world, nowhere seen but everywhere felt, goes some way to providing an answer to the question. Over and above the narrator entrusted with the actual telling of the story, whose knowledge of psychological matters may be restricted, can be set an organising intelligence notionally responsible for the articulation of the narrative as a whole in such a way as to allow psychology to be divined, if not perceived, by the reader. How this notion can be related to the narratological category of the 'implied author' will be discussed in a later chapter. At this point it is sufficient to suggest that Flaubert's notion of the novelist as a hidden presence in the work may go some way to accounting for the way in which psychology can be simultaneously hidden and felt.

While the narrator, activated by the demon of analysis, is made to keep a relatively low profile in the Flaubertian text, with the result that a good deal of the 'psychology' is passed over in silence by him, the *deux absconditus* or organising intelligence behind the work, who cannot be silenced since he has no voice to speak with, does much to compensate for the gaps in the narrator's account and the distortions of the protagonist's consciousness, by mobilising a whole range of expressive detail which so enriches, complicates or contradicts the narrator's explicit version of events as to make it seem that the psychological element is emerging, warts, unconscious forces and all, like the shape of the skeleton in an X-ray, from a narrative which is all darkness. Analysis and synthesis, narrator and hidden creator complement rather than contradict each other, ensuring that the reader will, in the hermeneutically controlled game of hide-and-seek the text entices him to play, have some measure of success in lighting upon his illusory and elusive quarry, what Forster aptly described as 'the hidden life at its source'.[71]

II

The Planning of *L'Éducation Sentimentale*

Carnet 19

After completing *Madame Bovary*, Flaubert had escaped from the modern world, which he made a habit of saying he despised, by undertaking to explore in *Salammbô* the vast resplendent passion of Mâtho, the leader of an army of mercenaries, for a Carthaginian princess, the daughter of Hamilcar Barca.[1] In exchanging nineteenth-century France for sixth-century Carthage Flaubert was also moving away from complex psychology, the exploration of which had at times during the composition of *Madame Bovary* given him considerable problems. The main characters in *Salammbô* are relatively simple; apparently swayed by and at times almost indistinguishable from the elemental forces of the sun and the moon, their behaviour is much more straightforward and single-minded as Flaubert himself pointed out: 'Mme Bovary est agitée par des passions multiples; Salammbô, au contraire, demeure clouée par l'idée fixe. C'est une maniaque, une espèce de sainte Thérèse.'[2] But however much he relished his immersion in a more colourful and, in certain respects, less demanding subject-matter, Flaubert did not seek permanent release from the difficulties associated with the depiction of the present. In 1859 he reports that 'le besoin de faire du moderne me reprend'[3] and finally opts for a project in which psychological complexity is of the essence, as he subsequently somewhat despairingly recognised: 'On n'arrive à de grands effets qu'avec des choses simples, des passions tranchées. Mais je ne vois de simplicité nulle part dans le monde moderne.'[4]

The gestation of *L'Éducation sentimentale* was, partly on account of the inherent complexity of the modern age, a protracted one. Before embarking upon the composition of the novel in September 1864 Flaubert spent a considerable period of time thinking about various other possibilities for a modern novel and trying to work out his main ideas. As

31

early as March 1862 Flaubert told the Goncourt brothers that he wished to 'faire deux ou trois petits romans, non incidentés, . . . qui seraient le mari, la femme, l'amant'[5] but it was not until May 1864 that he could claim that 'l'idée principale s'est dégagée et maintenant c'est clair'.[6] The plans in the *Carnet 19*, first published in Madame Durry's *Flaubert et ses projets inédits*, were in all probability drafted in the earliest phase of the preparation of *L'Éducation sentimentale*, which began in 1862.[7] Although they represent a minute fraction of the preparatory work that Flaubert undertook,[8] they provide a fascinating record of the initial decision-making process that helped to determine the final shape the novel was to assume.

When he first set about trying to find a suitable subject for a modern novel Flaubert's interest centred on the triangular relationship between husband, wife and lover. The germ of *L'Éducation sentimentale* is to be found in a series of projected novels all of which would explore the complications of modern marriage. 'Un ménage moderne' concerns the attempts of an apparently respectable married woman to extract from a young man who is in love with her a sum of money which she intends to give to a former lover who is in financial difficulties.[9] 'Le Roman de Me Dumesnil', though not alluding to a lover, shows the married woman finding an alternative outlet for her energy in the attractions represented by fine materials and fine clothes.[10] Finally, 'Me Moreau (roman)' depicts a kind of amatory stalemate: 'Le mari, la femme, l'amant tous s'aimant, tous lâches'.[11] In all these projects, although Flaubert is concerned with several participants and their complex inter-relationship, the main emphasis falls on the woman. For a wide variety of reasons, not the least of which is the constitutional passivity diagnosed by Sartre, Flaubert tends to project himself most easily into the existential situation of the unhappily-married woman. In the course of the first stage of planning represented by the plans in the *Carnet 19*, however, he gradually came round to the view that the young man rather than the married woman should be the central character and thereby ensured that he would not simply produce another *Madame Bovary*, a danger Bouilhet had warned him against.[12]

In what is generally taken to be the earliest plan Flaubert envisaged that the married woman would commit adultery[13] but rapidly made the famous revision:

Il serait plus fort de ne pas faire baiser Me Moreau qui chaste d'action se

rongerait d'amour. – Elle aurait eu son moment de faiblesse que l'amant
n'aurait pas vu dont il n'aurait pas profité. (f.35 verso)

This decision has far-reaching consequences; the opposition between
two different types of woman, which was perhaps present in Flaubert's
mind from the outset,[14] is strengthened, which in turn throws the
emphasis onto the young man:

> Mais s'il y a parallèlisme entre les Deux femmes l'honnête et l'impure
> l'interet sera porté sur le jeune homme – (ce serait alors une espèce
> d'Education sentimentale?). (f.36)

From the beginning Flaubert had wished the sexual element in the
relationship between Madame Moreau and the young man to be problematic;[15] the decision to leave their love unconsummated, however,
opens up a whole new area of experience and allows Flaubert to express a
series of analytic insights into the nature of modern love which, he
believed, tended to be strongly idealistic. *L'Éducation sentimentale* may
have originated in Flaubert's shocked reaction to the news of Madame
Schlesinger's nervous illness[16] but the autobiographical element in the
first of the plans[17] is almost immediately expunged and the project
modified in order to accommodate the highly critical approach to love
which Flaubert believed was typical of his age.[18]

In his early works Flaubert takes a sympathetic view of the deep-
seated tendency in human nature to reach out to a mystical ideal[19] but
already by the time he is writing *Madame Bovary* he is formulating the
view that mystical longing leads women to demand more than is humanly
possible with fatal consequences: 'Ce que je leur reproche surtout, c'est
leur besoin de póetisation ... Elles ne voient pas le vrai quand il se
rencontre, ni la bcauté là où elle se trouve.'[20] The idealising urge is,
however, by no means confined to the opposite sex, as Flaubert insists in
the following extract from a letter written in 1859, which is directly
relevant to *L'Éducation sentimentale*:

> Quant à l'amour, je n'ai jamais trouvé dans ce suprême bonheur que
> troubles, orages et désespoir. La femme me semble une chose impossible
> ... Je m'en suis toujours écarté le plus que j'ai pu. C'est un abîme qui attire
> et qui me fait peur! Je crois du reste, qu'une des causes de la faiblesse du
> 19ème siècle vient de sa *poétisation* exagérée. Aussi le dogme de l'Im-
> maculée-Conception me semble un coup de génie de la part de l'église. Elle

a formulé et annulé à son profit toutes les aspirations féminines du temps. Il n'est pas un écrivain qui n'ait exalté la mère, l'épouse ou l'amante. – La génération, endolorie, larmoie sur les genoux des femmes, comme un enfant malade. On n'a pas l'idée de la *lâcheté* des hommes envers elles![21]

The romantic idealisation of woman is seen by Flaubert as doubly detrimental; on the one hand it channels feminine energy into a limiting quest for the 'purity' and 'perfection' with which the Virgin Mary is associated and leads women to think of themselves solely in the capacity of self-sacrificing mothers; on the other hand, it encourages in men a deplorable passivity which stems from a regression to a state of infantile dependence upon a woman who is seen first and foremost as a mother-figure.[22]

Flaubert was hostile to the idealising tendency present in modern love on account of its hypocritical attitude to sexuality. All human affection, Flaubert believed, was rooted in sexuality,[23] including what he once referred to as 'l'adoration religieuse de la femme':[24] 'La femme, pour nous tous, est l'ogive de l'infini. Cela n'est pas noble, mais tel est le vrai fond du mâle'.[25] Such, however, is the blindness induced by the excessive 'spirituality' of modern love that the sexual origins and nature of the male's reverence of the opposite sex are obscured. Flaubert was also opposed to the religious adoration of woman on the grounds that it was excessively inward looking. Challenging G. Sand's belief in disinterested love, Flaubert wrote:

> Nous faisons toujours Dieu à notre image. Au fond de tous nos amours et de toutes nos admirations, nous trouvons *nous*, ou quelque chose d'approch-ant.[26]

Adoration of woman involves concentrating on oneself. Not only is it infantile, it is also profoundly narcissistic. Flaubert was keenly aware of how easy it was for the lover to engage in a kind of 'masturbation morale', revelling in the inner turbulence produced by the obsession with idealised figures who exist only in the mind.[27] Nothing, then, is what it appears to be; 'l'adoration religieuse de la femme' may be experienced as a spiritual impulse but in fact is fuelled by sexual desire and it may seem to reach out to another human being but in reality involves focussing attention inwards. Not without cause did Flaubert say 'je ne vois de simplicité nulle part dans le monde moderne'.

The decision to leave the young man's love for 'Me Moreau' uncon-summated may have brought the novel into line with Flaubert's convictions about the essential nature of modern love, but it still required extensive validation. Motives needed to be established to justify the change of plan. Mme Moreau's new-found 'virtue' rests upon Frédéric's timidity ('N'osant declarer son amour . . .', f.35 verso), upon the alternative outlet he finds for his sexual energy ('l'idée ne lui vient pas qu'il peut la baiser tranquille de sens du reste, car ils ont, par les filles publiques un derivé naturel et frequent', f.36 verso), and upon the affection of her husband ('Bien que courant les filles, il aime sa femme', f.35). But in spite of the fact that he has accepted the postulate that the novel will be 'une espèce d'Education sentimentale', Flaubert is mainly preoccupied with the motivation of the married woman. The plans in *Carnet 19* bear witness to his desire to throw the full weight of his sense of complex causality behind the vacillating, self-denying reactions of 'Me Moreau'. The most important factors adduced are internal; Flaubert speculates that she 'a ‹doucement› basé son refus sur la Vertu, les devoirs' (f.35 verso), that she wishes to feel superior to her husband ('Les vilenies de la Debauche de son mari l'ecartent de l'adultère elle veut pouvoir le mepriser, dans sa conscience', f.38) and that she worries about the effect of her lost reputation upon her children (f.38 suite). But the question of timing is crucial ('Elle aurait eu son moment de faiblesse que l'amant n'aurait pas vu', f.35 verso) and the element of chance plays a crucial part ('le hazard aussi s'en mêle, les faits exterieurs, bref, l'occasion est à jamais manquée', f.37). Finally Flaubert brings inner and outer factors together in a complex interaction: 'quant à l'empêchement de baiser quand tout est mûr pr cela il n'y a pas que sa vertu qui l'empêche mais une circonstance fortuite – le moment precis est passé psychologi-quement –' (f.38 suite). Chance, which in *Madame Bovary* is excluded as much as possible, is from the outset given an important role in *L'Éducation sentimentale*, counterbalancing a powerful inner determinism and masking the ultimately arbitrary nature of the narrative line for which Flaubert has opted. The sexual embargo pronounced by Flaubert constitutes, therefore, an important watershed from which a good deal of psychological speculation flows. Flaubert devotes most of his analytic energy in this early stage to convincing himself that he is right to change his mind.

The early plans also show Flaubert attempting to envisage a coherent development both for Frédéric and the other major characters. The basic situation from which the novel grows is essentially static, the main protagonists all being frozen in their set reactions to each other, and even much later Flaubert's aim is to 'représenter un état psychologique', conceived in terms of a set of unvarying tendencies and constant urges.[28] The decision that Madame Arnoux should retain her virtue compounds the problem; how can the amatory stalemate which lies at the heart of Flaubert's projected novel be made to yield the change and progression which narrative by its very nature requires. The 'action' which Flaubert seeks to extract from the initial narrative configuration is inevitably psychological in nature and consists of variations in intensity rather than of fundamental shifts in attitude; around the pivotal rue Tronchet episode, in particular, passions wax and wane (f.37). One plan deals at length with the various phases through which Frédéric's passion moves (f.36 verso) and Flaubert establishes from this very early stage its intermittent quality in the famous note: 'La passion de Fr, foudroyante d'abord, puis timide et constante, puis repoussée ... a des intermittences' (f.38). Likewise, an appropriate evaluation for the husband and wife is also laid down; the former 'va ... en progressant dans une voie sentimentale et presqu' idyllique' (f.37 verso suite), while the latter 'finit folle, hysterique' (f.36). The underlying 'principe' which governs the projected development of the main three characters is that 'jamais deux êtres ne s'aiment en même temps';[29] locked in mutual dependence, the main characters are not able to synchronise their desires. At this early stage, however, Flaubert has only begun to envisage the detailed illustration of his deeply pessimistic view of human relations.

Scénarios d'ensemble

The plans in the *Carnet 19* are extremely fragmentary and in many ways at variance with the novel as we now know it. For a long time, however, they represented all the documentary evidence relating to the planning of the novel. In 1975 the position changed dramatically with the acquisition by the Bibliothèque Nationale of six dossiers of plans and rough drafts for the novel which had previously been in the hands of a private collector.[30] In a preliminary classification the rough drafts and the plans were separated; as a result the bulk of the plans can be found in a single volume.[31] The plans for the novel are found in two distinct batches; folios 65 to 104, slightly smaller in size, were the first to have been drafted, while folios 1 to 64, much more detailed, were written at a later date.[32] It is highly likely that the first set (folios 65–104), which cover the whole of the novel in numbered sequences and can be classified as *scénarios d'ensemble*, were written in the first half of 1864, when Flaubert was working intensively on the planning of the novel, often with the help of Louis Bouilhet.[33] The second set of plans which cover either a whole part or a chapter of the novel and can be classified as *scénarios partiels*, were probably written, for the most part, as and when required, that is to say immediately prior to the composition of the relevant section of the novel.[34] Flaubert's *Correspondance* reveals that he was still engaged in the drafting of plans for parts and chapters of the novel long after the actual composition had begun.[35] In addition to these two sets of plans there are also a number of résumés, notes on characters and fragments of various kinds, bound in the same volume, most of which appear to have been written at the same time as the *scénarios d'ensemble*. Finally, interspersed among the rough drafts are a large number of sketches (*esquisses*), much more detailed than the *scénarios partiels*, covering as a rule a scene or part of a chapter, which were almost certainly drafted just before the first rough drafts (*brouillons*) for the corresponding section was written. These various documents provide a fascinating insight into the various stages of the long drawn out, immensely painstaking planning which preceded the actual composition of *L'Éducation sentimentale*.

The stage which is perhaps of greatest interest for this study is the first. Over a period of several months in 1864, before the composition began in September, Flaubert worked intensively on the plans in a concerted attempt to clarify the main outline of the novel, declaring finally in May 1864: 'L'idée principale s'est dégagée et maintenant c'est clair.'[36] At this early stage Flaubert is concerned with the overall shape of the novel, which rests essentially upon the development of the protagonist, Frédéric Moreau. His main aim is to establish a plausible 'enchaînement des sentiments', a sequence of appropriate reactions and responses to the various situations in which Frédéric finds himself.[37] While at a later stage there is a deliberate blurring of the account which is given, when first working seriously on the projected novel it is clarity of outline which is being sought, as Flaubert seeks to determine the exact nature of

Frédéric's development. Similarly, he also seeks to define the various characters who surround Frédéric as sharply as possible, although subsequently they too are destined to become indistinct. The *scénarios d'ensemble* stand, therefore, at an important juncture in the evolution of the novel. Considerably more detailed and closer to the final version than the decidedly inchoate plans in the *Carnet 19*, they reveal the psychological backbone of the novel in its embryonic state, as Flaubert gradually establishes a logical development which will provide adequate support for the rest of the novel. Although, in the *scénarios partiels* the psychological evolution of Frédéric will be analysed in more detail and, in some cases, modified, its broad outline and underlying postulates do not change. The *scénarios d'ensemble* mark an important stage in the planning of the novel, determining the broad shape it will assume.

In spite of their considerable importance, no systematic study of these plans has yet been made. In the work that has been done so far, the pattern has been to take one episode or chapter and follow its development through the various stages of planning and composition.[38] The relationship between the various *scénarios d'ensemble* themselves and between these plans and subsequent plans has not been discussed in any detail.[39] The following account is, as a result, necessarily exploratory and may have to be modified in the light of subsequent findings. As far as can be ascertained, there were originally three distinct sets of plans written at this stage, each covering the whole of the novel and numbered from 1 to 22 by Flaubert.[40] There are some sizeable gaps in each of these runs, which could be the result of some of the plans having been lost or, possibly, of Flaubert feeling that certain sections of the novel had been sufficiently well planned for the corresponding *scénario* to be carried forward into the next run[41] and certain sections of the novel are covered much more fully than others. The beginning and end of each part of the novel are relatively under-represented at this stage, while the central section, in which the major psychological developments take place, are more fully covered, possibly reflecting the greater attention that they were accorded. It may well be that all the material relating to this crucial stage in the planning of the novel has not survived, however, and the way in which Flaubert's ideas developed at this stage cannot be fully established as a result. None the less, the material which is available is more than adequate for the purpose of determining the main postulates underlying Frédéric's development and the way in which the characters were envisaged by Flaubert.

The general course of events mapped out in the plans produced at this stage bears a strong similarity to the final version. Although a number of differences do exist, as will be seen, Flaubert seems to have arrived at a clear view of the overall shape of the novel at a relatively early stage. The essential details of plot and character remain, for the most part, fixed, although this did not reduce the amount of time and energy Flaubert was to spend on the planning of the novel. The early plans, therefore, reveal that Flaubert had from the outset a clear sense of direction, an exact idea of how the novel was to end. He did not, however, immediately divide the long narrative sequence of the novel into the segments which correspond to the existing chapters; both the number of chapters and the placing of the divisions between them change considerably.

In Part I most of the events are the same but the order is sometimes different; in the first chapter Frédéric was originally to see Madame Arnoux before her husband,[42] the dinner at which he meets her again was to have taken place before he gets to know Arnoux's circle of friends,[43] the visit to Saint-Cloud precedes Madame Arnoux's absence in Chartres.[44] There is also a 'partie de campagne' which is envisaged in some detail before being suppressed.[45] Part I originally contained five chapters of which the third contained material which was to develop finally into the fourth chapter and the fourth contained what was to become the fifth chapter.[46] In Part II Frédéric's 'installation' and house-warming originally preceded the ball scene,[47] and the order of events after he gets to know Rosanette is different in several respects: the visit to the races takes place before the quarrel between Madame Arnoux and her husband while the trip to the factory comes earlier, before the quarrel.[48] Originally there were nine chapters in Part II, the last covering events which are finally included in the first chapter of Part III.[49] In Part III Madame Dambreuse was originally to become Frédéric's mistress before the reconciliation with Madame Arnoux.[50] The death of Monsieur Dambreuse does not at first coincide with the birth of Frédéric's child and the pattern of events surrounding the departure of the Arnoux was originally different in several respects.[51] Once again the number of chapters envisaged at first was higher, ten in this case, and these are gradually reduced in the *scénarios d'ensemble*.[52] The overall shape and outcome of Frédéric's relationships are not seriously affected by these various modifications; there is no change as drastic as the original decision in the *Carnet 19* that the relationship between Frédéric and Madame Arnoux should not be consummated. On the other hand, the constant shifting of chapter boundaries is an indication that the actual presentation of events in a narrative discourse, as opposed to the main events themselves, is going to undergo a prolonged development.

Flaubert's main preoccupation in these plans is with the development of Frédéric. The early *scénarios* painstakingly plot his reactions at various junctures in his life, from the first appearance of Madame Arnoux onwards. Although the development of his serious relationships is already beginning to be worked out in detail and a succession of scenes over a long period of time is already being envisaged, Flaubert also seeks to define the overall shape of Frédéric's life. In a résumé[53] the three parts of the novel are entitled 'Les Rêves', 'La lutte' and 'l'Experience', a Balzacian scheme which does not seem to fit the material. More persuasive is the division of Frédéric's life into three main phases:

1ere epoque – rêve et poesie
2e = nerveuse – angoisseuse
3e pratique, jouissante, degoutée. (f.120)

What is strongly emphasised at this stage is the way in which Frédéric, who is at the outset essentially a naive dreamer,[54] gradually deteriorates once his love for Madame Arnoux begins to fade and he is exposed to the deleterious influence of various milieux:

L'enervement causé par le Demi-monde l'a preparé aux lâchetés du Vrai-Monde. Il n'a plus d'energie, de mouvement spontané. il se laisse aller; (f.101)
l'ambition politique ‹resultat du monde qu'il voit›, sous sa forme la plus vulgaire, le prend – il veut se pousser et se remet à la remorque de Mr D., pr. s'en servir, et l'exploiter; (f.100)
Mariage de Mlle Arn. Fr, que le monde a pourri, n'y va pas par negligence. (f.101)

It is in this way that Flaubert fulfils his express wish to 'le faire un peu vil' (f.138).

Frédéric's character is defined to a large extent through the opposition with Deslauriers, who did not figure in the plans in the *Carnet 19*. Although Frédéric's romantic temperament and propensity to dream may be implied in certain details of the opening scene, it is in the next chapter that his character and preoccupations emerge most clearly:

Deslaur a l'amour latent du pouvoir et de la richesse.chacun aime le luxe mais differemment l'un comme vanité et moyen l'autre comme but et sensualité. Fr pense plus aux femmes, au monde des sensations poétiques (influence de Byron et du type de d juan.) – ils sont au fond naifs, aucun d'eux n'est vierge. Fr est le dern des romantiques Desl le dernier des penseurs. (f.67)

The opposition between the two is sustained in the rest of Part I:

D donne des repetitions de droit, travaille beaucoup. contraste de son activité avec la nonchalance rêveuse de Fr; (f.73)
Par economie il a pris pr maîtresse une petite couturière qu'il eblouit par son esprit. il l'a <u>faite</u> lestement en contraste avec les langueurs de Fred; (f.74)
Fr et D. s'ecrivent Fr exh sa tristesse en long. lettres lyriques D. en vain tache de le reconforter la corresp devient plus rare et plus courte, l'un rentrant dans son passé, l'autre allant vers l'avenir. (f.75)

Although the character of Deslauriers may have first come into being as a result of Frédéric, once established, he serves to sharpen and strengthen the latter's failings.

The bulk of the analysis of Frédéric's development relates to his preoccupation with the opposite sex, in particular with Madame Arnoux, who provides the focus for the kind of idealising love Flaubert believed to be characteristic of the modern age:

La jeunesse a l'esprit tragique et n'admet pas les nuances. – en fait de femmes deux [classes] ‹manières d'etre› seulement. – ou putains comme Messalinc – ou immaculées comme le Ste Vierge (<u>Cela doit dominer la Iere partie</u>). (f.67 verso)

Gradations within this set pattern of blinkered adoration are carefully established, ranging from the 'eblouissement' of the first encounter (f.65), to the 'enchantement' of the next meeting when Frédéric 'rentre dans son atmosphere' (f.70) and the more intense 'exaltation' (f.70) of a subsequent meeting when he is seated next to her. It is, however, the fixed nature of the idealising urge which is stressed:

Me Arn devient une habitude de sa pensée – l'ideal Elle resume toutes les autres femmes. toutes sont en elle et elles la font. car les excitations qu'elles lui envoient retournent à celle-là seule ‹et s'y fondent›, actrices, ecuyères, bayadères des cafés, filles publiques. il lui trouve partout des ressemblances

et des affinités – et tout ce qui est beau dans la nature et dans l'art la lui
rappelle par des transitions brusques et insensibles. (f.73)

And, at the same time, there is a recurrent suspension of sexual desire:

Il ne pense pas qu'elle puisse avoir un sexe. c'est comme un parfum qui
l'ennivre et l'abrutit; (f.69)
ce qu'il sent pr. elle ce n'est pas tant le desir de son corps que la curiosité
infinie, inassouvissable de sa personnalité c'est pr cela qu'il est si inactif et
que la vue ‹de Me Ar.› le fait tomber en reverie. (f.74)

And a tendency to latch onto anyone and anything in any way connected
with Madame Arnoux, apparent both in the 'absorption infinie' (f.66) in
all that surrounds her on the steamer and his attachment to her
household: 'Il aime son mari, ses enfants, les domestiques, la rue etc.
tout ce qui de près ou de loin la touche' (f.72). It is for this reason that he
is not jealous of Arnoux: 'il n'est pas jaloux d'Arn il fait partie d'elle.
c'est un des ses attributs comme sa robe. Il lui suffit qu'elle soit heureuse'
(f.70). Lastly, Frédéric typically in Part I makes excessive demands of
himself, feeling that all his energies should be directed towards Madame
Arnoux:

Desl canotte le Dimanche. (partie de campagne – gigot, enguelade de
Senecal et de Desl du logis de Me xx) Fr une fois s'y laisse entrainer. – puis a
des remords de s'etre amusé, il trouve qu'il se manque et à elle aussi. (f.74)

The overall effect of his wanton idealisation is to make Frédéric
problematically inactive; there are, however, sudden bouts of febrile
enthusiasm as well as the more characteristic indolence:

tour à tour motif à activité cerebrale à projets, à elans de travail et de genie –
et cause de nonchaloir et de faineantise. (f.74)

In Part II Frédéric's attitude to Madame Arnoux is complicated by the
appearance of Rosanette; Madame Arnoux's qualities and his reactions
to them are defined in opposition to those of Rosanette in the major
'parallèle' of this part of the novel:

Me Arn le charme par sa bonté, tous ses gestes avaient l'air d'aumone.
"Comment il n'est pas heureux de l'avoir", il s'excite les sens chez la Mle, le
cœur chez Mme Arn et selon qu'il vient de les voir l'une ou l'autre il a des
dispositions morales differentes. il rêve [une] ‹un genre de› vie approprié à
l'amour de chacune. et à l'excitation particulière qu'elle lui procure. (f.76)

In spite of his attempts to differentiate between the two women, the two loves become confused:

> ‹s'excite les sens chez l'une le cœur chez l'autre qqfois il a comme un seul desir, fait de ses 2 desirs reunis. une confusion s'eleve dans son âme. près de l'une il rêve à l'autre et elles s'echauffent reciproquement, cepend predominance de Me Arn›. (f.77)

A good deal of Flaubert's analytic energy is directed towards explaining why Frédéric does not seek to make Madame Arnoux his mistress. One factor is the vacillation in the face of two women which allows him to conceal from himself his own timidity:

> ‹L'impression parallelique est arrivée trop vite pr. qu'il penche nettement d'un côté ou de l'autre – il delibère laquelle des deux sera sa maîtresse. choississons se dit-il pr se cacher à lui-même sa timidité›. (f.78)

But other reasons are not hard to find:

> S'il n'essaie pas de baiser Me Arn c'est que la chose lui semble impossible Il n'a pas l'idée qu'elle puisse faillir. D'ailleurs comment s'y prendre embarassé qu'elle est par son menage, au milieu de ses enfans etc; (f.79)
> c'est un sphinx dressé devant lui. cet œil profond et noir le regarde impassiblement. il voudrait la connaitre à fond. il a une curiosité infinie. ‹une des causes de son inaction d'a present c'est l'inaction d'autrefois. puisque ça n'a pas été prquoi serait-ce!›. (f.79)

A sexual response does, however, develop in the course of Part II, initially surfacing in the second encounter, only to be immediately postponed till after the quarrel between Madame Arnoux and her husband:

> Elle le reçoit dans sa chambre à coucher, c'est pr. la Iere fois et la vue du lit [lui fait l'effet d'un voile qui tombe. ‹Pas ce jour-là› Mais c'est tout.]; (f.76)
> Il arrive au milieu d'une dispute violente. à propos de la facture du cachemire ((...)) Il fait semblant de la plaindre. Mais il se rejouit, il se delecte et se retient pr. bondir de joie, car ça pourra avancer ses affaires. La voilà donc humaine, enfin – belle dans les larmes d'ailleurs – et comme il a de l'espoir, il l'aime davantage, desir violent. (f.79)

As the friction between Arnoux and his wife develops Frédéric's determination increases, leading to the 'tentative vaine' (f.83) in the factory. As there is no *scénario d'ensemble* covering the last chapter of Part II, it is unfortunately not possible to establish how Flaubert envisaged the culmination of this aspect of Frédéric's relationship with Madame Arnoux at this stage in the planning.

In Part III Frédéric has considerably less contact with Madame Arnoux:

> Il semble à Fr qu'il a trahi Me Arn, il n'ose y retourner Arn qui s'ennuie de ne pas le voir le ramene. Me Arn est ironique Fr lui repond par des forfanteries, ils se blessent mutuellement. (f.95)

His lasting obsession with her is none the less apparent in a number of reactions; he has the feeling that she is somehow present when he makes love to Rosanette, as his embarrassment with Arnoux shows:

> [Mais Fr est gené devant lui. il a peur qu'il ne devine son secret quand il dit elle il pense à Me Arn. ne la possede-t-il pas tous les jours dans les bras de la Mle?]. (f.91)

Secondly, when he meets her in the flesh, he responds strongly on occasion; at the Dambreuse dinner, he 'sent son cœur s'elancer vers elle' (f.155) and consummation seems close in the scene of reconciliation:

> L'attendrissement arrive il vient de lui jurer que depuis longtemps il a rompu avec la Mle et ils vont peut-etre se baiser. – silence, extase. (f.96)

Even at the end, when he goes again to the rescue of Arnoux, he still hopes to be paid in kind:

> il lui offre les 30 mille fr, indispensables – elle hésite – intervention d'Arn en pleurs. – enfin ils acceptent. Fr malgré son beau mouvement pense ‹vaguement› qu'il sera payé en nature. (f.103)

When, however, at the very end Madame Arnoux visits him in what he suspects is a receptive state, Frédéric's final response is a rejection of the possibility of fulfilment which has come too late:

> reapparition de Me Arn qui rapporte l'argent – vient-elle s'offrir?veut-elle le payer ... mais degradée physiquement vieille. Il a peur d'en avoir [horreur] ‹degout› – Il fait semblant de ne pas comprendre. (f.104)

Frédéric's reactions to Rosanette both contrast with and echo his responses to Madame Arnoux, to whom, in his mind at least, she is diametrically opposed. In the first instance it is a whole lifestyle which fascinates him and strengthens the powerfully sexual nature of her appeal: 'le fard, le maquillage, la prostitution, les empressements des hommes, tout cela l'embellit etend son sexe, en fait une femme plus femme que les autres' (f.77). Given her blatant sexuality and given the way in which he seeks to direct a specifically physical response to her, Frédéric's failure to make Rosanette his mistress, which duplicates a similar failure with Madame Arnoux, requires a good deal of motivation:

> Ce qui fait qu'il ne baise pas la Mle c'est que: elle est toujours occupée elle a du monde, elle le reçoit entre deux portes. ‹elle a ses affaires 'c'est comme l'autre.'› puis ils se connaissent deja depuis trop longtemps, ils sont trop familiers. ils ont l'habitude d'etre amis. Leur ton ‹perpetuel› de blague [repousse] ‹empêche› tout dialogue serieux; (f.78)
> ‹puis elle a certains› cotés agaçants, genre enfant, faux. 'ce sera quand je voudrai'se dit-il – c'est ainsi qu'il se donne à lui-même de fausses raisons pr excuser sa timidité. – et puis il croirait manquer à son amour. (f.79)

As with Madame Arnoux, however, hesitation and timidity are gradually overcome as Frédéric comes to believe that his desires are about to be fulfilled, only to meet with parallel rebuffs:

> enfin elle lâche son entreteneur. et vit seule. Fr qui attendait ce moment-là en a une gde joie. mais c'est pr.prendre en liberté le christ dramatique. Fr s'en aperçoit et comme il se considerait comme futur amant il eprouve une deception comique; (f.78)
> Diner au Café anglais. Hussonnet comme rendant compte des courses s'y trouve Fr n'a pas assez d'argent. – humiliation de frequenter les gens riches. – La Mle s'en va avec Mr de Cisy en lui disant un mot amer et dur.Fr se sent enragé contre elle. (f.84)

Once again it is not possible to establish how the reversal of this trend in the last chapter of Part II is explained at this stage since the relevant *scénarios* are missing.

Frédéric's reactions to having Rosanette as his mistress are predictable:

> ‹Frédéric est heureux il a tout le charme de la passion, sans le delire. fierté de la conquête et de la possession sentiment de virilité satisfaite›. (f.95)

The limits of his relationship become apparent, however, in the Fontainebleau episode:

il epuise la lune de miel. impossibilité de se faire comprendre.(f.92)

Subsequently the balance between attraction and repulsion alters. On the one hand, there is a strong physical satisfaction: 'c'est un collage physique ardent. elle le fait jouir de plus en plus' (f.94); on the other hand, feelings of irritation and degradation:

> cependant il en veut à la Mle des cadeaux qu'elle reçoit naïvement, et dont il profite, de ses anciens amants, etc de ses connaissances, de son passé, du present, de ce qu'elle a été, et de ce qu'elle est. tout ce qui l'excitait autrefois le degoute – il ne tient plus à elle que par l'habitude et l'irritation; (f.100) il se degrade et le sent et pr.tant elle le fait jouir de plus en plus. (f.93)

These feelings intensify as Rosanette's physical charm diminishes and she begins to make what he considers inappropriate demands:

> La Mle qui commence à vieillir (elle s'est fait mettre un ratelier) rêve le mariage, le pot au feu ‹Elle prêche à Fr. le renoncement aux vanités, la poesie du foyer› – c'est une bourgeoise declassée comme Me D est une lorette manquée. son charme diminue comme son train de maison ((. . . .)); [Il en est excedé. misères du concubinage]. (f.97)

Ironically, the very strength of Rosanette's feeling for Frédéric is counter-productive:

> ‹par vertu elle ne reçoit plus d'argent de ses amants – et n'ayant plus d'elegance n'a plus de charme›. (f.102)

Rosanette's compliance makes it more difficult for him to leave her, however: 'D'ailleurs comment rompre? sous quel pretexte, car elle est douce, excellente' (f.93). As a result there is no immediate break, only increasing neglect ('il neglige la Mle de plus en plus' (f.98)) as Frédéric embarks upon his 'vie double' (f.98).

Madame Dambreuse's appeal is closely connected with his dissatisfaction with Rosanette. Initially she had not made much impact upon him: 'il va [un soir] ‹au bal› chez Me D. mais comme il est ce soir-là dans un jour d'espoir Me lui cause peu d'impression' (f.82). Once his life with Rosanette degenerates, however, Madame Dambreuse's attraction increases:

> Par suite de sa vie un peu ignoble avec la Mle il en rêve une autre toute elegante et decente avoir pr.maitresse une femme du monde! aussi est-il très assidu chez les Dambr. attiré par le confortable doré. (f.94)

There is something contrived about this third relationship and the ease with which it is consummated is an indication of its lack of depth: 'tous deux posent et se mentent bref Fr arrive à la baiser facilement ‹et sans presque s'en apercevoir› (parce qu'il l'a peu profondement desiré) (f.101). The satisfaction Frédéric derives from his conquest is, however, limited:

> mais le cœur n'est pas content
> ni le corps non plus Me D est un mauvais coup. Cependant il eprouve un certain plaisir d'orgueil quand il la voit dans le monde, recevant chez elle, froide, convenable, honorée et il s'en estime davantage. (f.101)

It is not long, consequently, before the demands Madame Dambreuse makes begin to prove irksome and any superiority over Rosanette evaporates:

> Cependant lui fait des reproches de ne pas venir plus souvent exigences de la femme du monde. correspondances regulières. blagues forcées. La verité est tout aussi impossible à [savoir] ‹connaitre› avec celle-là qu'avec l'autre, son âme aussi fermée, son passé encore plus et elle a plus d'hypocrisie en outre. (f.97)

Although Madame Dambreuse represents material prosperity, this contrasts with the emotional poverty of Frédéric's responses:

> Frederic va devenir riche. il s'enfonce de plus en plus dans la canaillerie. mais il sent fermement qu'il n'aime pas Me Dambreuse. gde amertume au cœur. (f.103)

It is not surprising, therefore, that when she stubbornly insists on buying the casket at the auction her behaviour provokes in Frédéric a 'haine subite' (f.103).

Of his four relationships with women, it is the one with Louise which is least fully covered in this set of plans. When she is mentioned, Frédéric's reactions are not analysed in any depth until the Dambreuse dinner in Part III:

> souffrance de Mlle Desroches qui le devore des yeux. Elle est provinciale et assez ridicule Fr. en a honte. (f.92)

When confronted directly by Louise, Frédéric is casually evasive:

> Le soir il est obligé de prendre le bras de Mlle Desroches – et elle lui demande nettement ses intentions. mais on vient de lui faire des avances. il

vient de revoir Me Arn. il est engagé avec la Mle. 'il n'y faut plus penser'
dit-il à Mlle Desroches. 'plus tard' etc – bref il la refuse. [vaguement –
plaisante] et va coucher le soir chez la Mle. commodité du sans-façon. (f.92)

Any feeling of abandonment he experiences on discovering Louise's
marriage is, therefore, unlikely to elicit much sympathy: 'il arrive à
Nogent comme ils sortent de la Mairie–seul–tous l'ont abandonné' (f.104).

Although the main emphasis in the *scénarios d'ensemble* is upon
Frédéric's relations with various women, the pattern of his relations with
other men is also outlined. Frédéric's early attitude to Deslauriers is one
of unqualified admiration: 'Fr.l'admire beaucoup C'est son père intellectuel' (f.66). In spite of their different enthusiasms, they have certain
things in common and share the same desire to go to Paris: 'tout deux
execrent L Philippe-rêve commun d'avenir aller à Paris l'année prochaine, dans le monde!' (f.67). The differences that exist between them
are destined, however, to become a source of dissatisfaction. When
Deslauriers finally joins Frédéric in Paris, it is not long before the
'premiers dissentiments' (f.69) begin to emerge. Frédéric finds Deslauriers unsympathetic to his 'expansions sentimentales' (f.146), while
Deslauriers finds Frédéric's inactivity annoying ('et comme c'est un
homme actif et qui a le gout du pouvoir l'inactivité de Fr l'agace lui
semble une espèce de desobeissance envers lui', f.74) and envies him his
social success ('Envie sourde de Desl en voyant Fr. s'habiller pr aller chez
elle', f.69). In Part II, when Frédéric spends most of his time with the
Arnoux, Deslauriers feels let down ('Desl est blessé de cet abandon',
f.83). From this point, the contact between them is less close; when
called upon for help, each either fails or betrays the other. It is only after
learning that Deslauriers's final act of treachery in marrying Louise has
not brought him much joy that Frédéric becomes reconciled with him at
the end (f.104). Interestingly, although the weaker of the two in many
respects, Frédéric has a strong influence upon his friend:

Par l'effet de la frequentation continue de Fr. Desl a pris plus de besoins;
(f.141)
Deslauriers imite constamment Fr. [lequel] ‹qui› il a [pr lui] une faiblesse
nerveuse invincible. Ainsi il a voulu baiser Me Ar, – il baise la Mle, et
epouse la petite Roque; (f.111 verso)
prêche Deslaur et l'enregimente dans la reaction où Deslauriers le depass-
era. (f.95)

Already Flaubert senses that friendship both depends on and dissolves differences in temperament and outlook.

Frédéric's friendship with Arnoux is also described in some detail. Frédéric is instinctively drawn to him: 'Fr se sent pr lui de la sympathie' (f.66). His attitude towards him is inextricably bound up with his attitude to his wife.

> Fr retourne au Bureau, loin d'etre indigné des manigances d'Arn comme il le devrait, il en est ebloui, c'est le reflet de Mme. – et puis l'effet d'une concordance de temperament entre Arn et Fr. (f.69)
> il n'est pas jaloux d'Arn. il fait partie d'elle (f.74)

In Part II his early admiration gives way to feelings of incomprehension and exasperation:

> ‹la conduite d'Arn envers sa femme lui semble incomprehensible: comment 'il n'est pas heureux de l'avoir'›; (f.82)
> il fait à Fr. sur le seuil de sa porte des confidences conjugales intimes. Fr est decidé à n'y plus remettre les pieds separation muette et enragée sous un reverbère. (f.89)

Arnoux, in contrast, becomes increasingly fond of Frédéric ('il veut rompre avec lui mais Arn l'adore et ne peut plus se passer de sa compagnie', f.89). At this stage of the planning, the guardroom scene is already envisaged in considerable detail, dominating the first chapter in Part III:

> Arn l'agace horriblement. – une fois en maniant un fusil devant lui, au corps de garde, l'idée fantasque et subite le prend de le tuer comme par megarde. La vue d'un foulard ‹sur son cou› à elle, l'arrête. Le soir ils se soulottent ensemble – concordance de gouts et de temperament. Arn en titubant lui fait encore l'eloge de sa femme. (f.91)

In what constitutes, in effect, a kind of dénouement of their relationship, an underlying similarity in their make-up finally proves stronger than the feelings of oedipal rivalry that come to a head at this point.

In comparison, relatively little is said about Frédéric's relations with various other men. Frédéric's attitude to Monsieur Dambreuse is defined in part in contrast to his attitude to Arnoux: 'et il sert Mr Dambr. – sans en être dupe cette fois ce n'est plus de la fascination comme avec Arnoux' (f.94). The precise nature of his reactions to a wide range of other friends is not discussed in any detail; Frédéric's attitude is determined to a large extent by his need to enlist their aid in his various relations with women. For instance, Sénécal is used in an elaborate erotic strategem ('Pour avoir qq'un à lui près d'elle, pr.la posseder d'une façon détournée, il place Senecal, ‹alors sans emploi› dans l'usine de son mari', f.80) but when it comes to nothing need no longer be treated differently: 'changement de manière de Fr. vis-à-vis de Senecal des que celui-ci lui est inutile' (f.78). Of all his acquaintances, it is perhaps Dussardier who treats him best and Cisy whom he most closely resembles: 'Parmi ses etudes à bâtons rompus Fr. etudie le gothique. c'est là le joint avec Mr de Cisy (sans compter l'elegance des façons, une certaine parité d'education)' (f.67 verso).

Although the main character of the novel is quite clearly by this stage Frédéric, other characters are not viewed consistently from his viewpoint as they tend to be at a later stage. Flaubert felt the need to draw a series of thumb-nail sketches of nearly all the characters, giving details of their physical appearance, way of life, political convictions and main characteristics. Grouped together, these sketches are not to be found in the *scénarios* themselves but on separate sheets, written at the same time.[55] In this initial roll-call, Flaubert runs through his cast, pinning each one down in a firm and authoritative manner which is destined to be superceded by a more uncertain and fragmentary presentation. Elsewhere he plots an appropriate development or career for each of the characters, determining how they will change with changing circumstances and how each is destined to end up. In addition, Flaubert establishes suggestive pairings of characters, based upon contrasts and similarities between their outlook, behaviour or situation:

> ((Dussardier)) fait la paire avec Senécal. comme de leur coté Fr et Deslauriers; (f.109 verso)
> Le père Desr et la mere de Fr font pendant. Considérée pieuse, Ste Monique, finit par faire des canailleries par amour pr. son fils (comme le père Desr pr. sa fille); (f.139)
> Frederic a des affinités nerveuses avec Arn et des idées communes avec Deslauriers. (f.120)

The irony of Frédéric being in the same position as Arnoux in Part II is not lost on Flaubert: 'Arnoux est dans la même situation morale. il aime ‹à la fois› sa femme et sa maîtresse "ma pauvre femme" (f.77). At times

the perception of unsuspected similarity begins the process of undermining stereotypes: '((Rosanette)) est une bourgeoise declassée comme
Me D est une lorette manquée' (f.97). But although Flaubert may have a
clear view of the characters as they float in a kind of timeless limbo, they
still need to be integrated into a narrative account whose main concern is
the development of Frédéric, and this process of integration and development necessarily involves a blurring of the clear outline with which
they initially are endowed.

At the stage of the *scénarios d'ensemble* two characters have already
achieved a certain complexity. Deslauriers is fully and clearly described
in a detailed portrait which begins with his physical appearance, relationship with Frédéric and political convictions, before going on to define his
main characteristics:

> [très laborieux], apre, beaucoup d'àplomb et cependant jovial, d'une gaité
> sèche et bavarde. nature de charlatan et de despote. (f.66)

The account is not, however, totally unsympathetic for Deslauriers's
harshness is grounded in hardship: 'beaucoup de mauvaises choses de
son caractère [dissimulation et durete] derivent des contraintes de son
enfance et de sa jeunesse' (f.66). Deslauriers's subsequent experience
does nothing to alleviate his characteristic surliness: 'Desl a echoué pr.
une place d'agregation à l'Ecole de droit – il est devenu ‹plus› sombre et
apre – enragé de politique, amer, ultra-radical' (f.77). Although, at one
stage, his 'amour latent du pouvoir' (f.67) is satisfied ('Desl. red. d'un
petit journal où il fait de la politique, il est ‹enfin› arrivé à qquechose',
f.86), his success is short-lived and his resolutely self-seeking nature
manifests itself in a series of actions directly detrimental to his best
friend's interests.

The other character who is also well developed at this stage is Arnoux,
who, like Deslauriers, owes this privilege to the fact that he acts as a foil
to Frédéric. Arnoux is typical of a certain category of man which Frédéric
defines at length in an early fragment: 'Il y a aussi des hommes courtisans
qui ont une faculté d'aimer, à pouvoir cherir tout un harem, naifs, de
cœur et de sens.ils mettent la tendresse dans la débauche, ont [le] lyrisme
de la chair' (f.126 verso). Although his professional, moral and physical
decline is already outlined, it is Arnoux's attitude to women which
receives most attention. Unlike Frédéric, Arnoux does not seek to make
a rigid distinction between his wife and his mistress: 'il aime ‹à la fois› sa

femme et sa maitresse' (f.77). Arnoux's attachment to Rosanette differs from Frédéric's in its liberality ('Arn entretient maintenant à lui seul la Mle.Elle lui mange beaucoup d'argent', f.83) and the desire to have a child by her ('Arn. souhaite une re-famille avoir un enfant de la Marechale', f.118). This affection for Rosanette does not, however, detach him from his wife in the way Frédéric hopes: 'Bien que depensant beaucoup pr la Mle il aime sa femme "ma pauvre femme"' (f.89). His subsequent erotic itinerary is also mapped out: 'Arn a pris le gout des grisettes, (amour des jeunes filles où il se mêle qque chose de l'amour paternel). elles le trompent indignement' (f.94); 'Il entretient une petite ouvrière, c'est moins cher et plus jeune' (f.93). As his health declines, however, he returns to the conjugal fold: 'Arnoux a deux attaques d'apoplexie coup sur coup. affaibli un peu – retourne à sa femme, ne peut plus se passer d'elle' (f.99). Although Arnoux's attitude to women differs considerably from Frédéric's, they are the main cause of his downfall too.

Dussardier is from the outset envisaged as the only character with a heart of gold:

> enfant naturel, constitution athletique, douceur d'agneau grosse chevelure blonde sanguin, ‹n'a pas fait d'etudes.› excellent, soigne Fr. dans une maladie – intelligence mediocre, cœur hardi. – affamé de justice, un peu gobe mouche. (f.109 verso)

Originally he was to devote himself to a woman: '[se marie à une petite ouvrière, pr laquelle il s'extenue et qui le plante là]' (f.109 verso) and his kind heart, generous nature and outstanding bravery are apparent in numerous good deeds:

> emeute à l'Ecole de droit. ((. . .)) Dussardier, tres brave, ‹prend la defense de . . . et terrasse un agent de police›; (f.69)
> Dussardier, par bonté, pr. Pellerin vient lui dire que Pellerin se plaignait amerement de ce que lui Fr ne lui achetait pas de tableaux; (f.82)
> Duss achète des oiseaux pr leur donner la liberté. les regarde partir de sa fenêtre va va!". (f.118 verso)

Even in straitened circumstances he retains a certain nobility: 'il faut à la fin de V (3e) que Duss fut dans la misère – [noble] resiste à une infamie venant naïvement de Fr' (f.120). The striking composure of the most impoverished character in the novel is also underlined: 'Placide au milieu de sa vie dure, tandis que les autres, plus heureux materiellement sont plus agités' (f.140). Flaubert's vision of humanity is not totally negative, as the brief comment 'Dussardier seul vertueux' (f.103) suggests. In contrast to Dussardier, Sénécal appears lacking in generosity and behaves in a way which is detrimental to those around him. The early portrait suggests an unappealing rigidity of outlook: 'Cheveux en brosse, rigide, s'inquiete des systèmes sociaux, fort appétit, a horreur des parfums, extremement honnete comme argent, admire Louis Blanc et Proudhon, n'aime pas à etre dupe, dur pr sa femme de menage' (f.109 verso). A boorish killjoy in the 'partie de campagne' (f.72) and the house-warming (f.77), he is consistently resentful of Frédéric's prosperity and equally hostile towards Arnoux.

The presentation of the remaining minor characters is frequently trenchant and incisive. Pellerin possesses 'beaucoup d'idées, aucun talent plastique' (f.109 verso), Martinon is 'naturellement bas devant le pouvoir' (f.109 verso), Monsieur Dambreuse is 'par tempérament ami de tous les pouvoirs' (f.109). One character originally seems to be of particular interest to Flaubert, although his role in the final version is not particularly significant. Originally called Halbout, then Ambert, Regimbart has developed a love of a very special kind whose origins are traced and whose complexity is stressed:

> Halbout (le petit Richer) – prend l'amour du café par la lecture des journaux – puis ‹le billard – puis› l'amour du café n'a plus besoin de pretextes.
> Varie successivement ses boissons – Ie la demi-tasse. – puis le petit verre – puis le grog etc – et arrive en allant du composé au simple au Bol! (f.71 verso)
> L'amour du café est comme l'amour du Monde. qqchose de complexe. ce n'est le billard, ni les boissons qu'on aime. Mais le café. – pr lui-même. (f.111)

According to Flaubert 'tous les piliers ont de jolies femmes' (f.111) and Regimbart's neglect of his wife is also dwelt upon. It is, perhaps, the obsessive quality of Regimbart's behaviour which attracted Flaubert, who may have seen in it a parodic distortion of Frédéric's equally compulsive behaviour.

As far as the female characters are concerned, they are frequently viewed from Frédéric's point of view. The adoption of Frédéric's often puzzled perspective has the effect of rendering Madame Arnoux a particularly enigmatic figure whose real attitudes remain uncertain:

> irritante, impenetrable comme un sphinx. elle parait insensible aux fre-
> daines de son epoux. est-ce froideur native. ‹ou sottise› cependant elle
> embrasse ses enfans d'une façon emportée, fievreuse. mais elle est trop
> occupée de son menage. (f.78)

As long as Frédéric admires her from afar, it is possible for her true nature to be left undefined, but as soon as his advances become more direct the question of her attitude to him needs to be resolved. While there is little doubt about the state of her relationship with her husband and whilst she does reject Frédéric's request that she leave him, Flaubert does not seem to be completely sure how she should react at this critical stage:

> querelle. intimité Mais comment l'intimité, peut-elle finir ‹elle a peur et
> s'en va?› car il n'est pas naturel que F s'arrête; (f.125)
> Me Ar. ne comprend pas Fr. ou fait semblant de ne pas le comprendre.
> s'arrange de manière à ce qu'il ne fasse pas de declaration. (f.137)

In Part III when Frédéric's contact with her is reduced, on the other hand, the account of Madame Arnoux's inner feelings is a good deal less tentative:

> comme elle aime Fr plus que jamais et qu'elle a peur de faillir, elle ne le
> reçoit pas seul; (f.95)
> Me Arn a emmené son mari dans une province eloignée pr faire des
> economies et se soustraire à Frederic. (f.103)

As the disintegration of her family makes her increasingly unhappy, the stereotype of the 'femme vertueuse' (f.83) becomes increasingly inappropriate: 'Me Arn s'est acquitté de son vœu per probité. Mais perd peu à peu toute religion à mesure que ses malheurs augmentent' (f.100). Even so there is no unequivocal answer given here (as opposed to in the earlier plans of the *Carnet 19*) to the question Frédéric asks himself – 'vient-elle s'offrir?' – on the occasion of the last visit (f.104).

Many of the comments relating to Rosanette suggest that like Madame Arnoux she is not quite as Frédéric imagines her to be:

> La Mle n'a pas l'esprit d'intrigue nécessaire pour exploiter les hommes et
> faire fortune. tout au premier mouvement et à la fantaisie de son cœur ou de
> ses sens. Bonne fille dans la force du mot et legère. (f.122)

Her attitude to Arnoux reveals her to be only as mercenary as necessary:

> Elle voudrait se debarrasser du raffineur et qu'Arn seul l'entretint et elle est
> amoureuse du christ dram.; (f.76)
> Pour pouvoir coucher toutes les nuits tranquillement avec son cabot, elle
> voudrait se debarrasser de son raffineur et qu'Arn l'entretint à lui seul. (f.78)

Although Frédéric is initially subordinated to both Arnoux and Delmar, in Part III she does not keep up her old way of life out of choice:

> [La Mle] ‹elle› commence à l'aimer serieusement. Si elle couche avec
> d'autres pr. de l'argent. c'est ‹d'abord par habitude puis› afin de subvenir
> plus abondamment aux frais du menage; (f.94)
> Cependant ‹elle voudrait devenir vertueuse et si› elle continue à coucher pr.
> de l'argent. c'est d'abord par habitude puis pr. subvenir plus abondamment
> aux frais de la communaute. (f.93)

Fundamental to Flaubert's conception of Rosanette is a mismatch between aspirations and opportunity.

The early comments on Madame Dambreuse mark her out as a 'vraie femme du monde' (f.109), superior in certain respects ('la plus intelligente des 4 la seule lettrée', f.120) and yet, in spite of her privileged position in society 'envieuse des lorettes' (f.109) and even a 'lorette manquée' (f.97). There is something highly contrived about the way, while waiting her turn for confession, she 'repasse un rôle pr. jouer la comedie en societé' (f.120), about her bogus interest in good works ('fait partie de toutes les societés religieuses, par chic', f.109) and her hypocritical strictness ('sévère sur les mœurs pr. ses domestiques et sur les lectures que peut faire sa nièce', f.109). In contrast, Louise is presented as someone who harbours genuine feelings. The effect Frédéric has upon her is described in the same terms as the one produced upon him by Madame Arnoux: 'eblouissement qu'il lui cause par ses affaires de toilette elegances' (f.75). Louise, however, is unproblematically demonstrative: 'Elle a un mouvement passionné quand il part. Elle lui saute au cou' (f.75). Wearing her heart upon her sleeve does not make her any happier. The emphasis in Part III falls on her suffering:

> Souffrance de Mlle Desroches qui le devore des yeux; (f.92)
> ‹Mlle D. est dans un etat horrible et sur le point de faire un eclat›; (f.92)

If she finally betrays Frédéric, he has only himself to blame, as the brief overview of her development suggests:

I. Fr a fait lire des poetes à Mlle Desr.
II. sceptique.raille tout
III. elle profite de ses leçons. (f.120)

The plans produced at this early stage in the development of the novel do not reveal any awareness on Flaubert's part of the potentially problematic aspect of the whole undertaking. There are no signs of any resistance to working within the constraints of 'psychological realism'. Indeed, one set of reminders of future work to be done issued by Flaubert to himself show that for him the essential function of the *scénarios* is to establish a clear and coherent pattern of events, consistent with the characters presented.[56] But although Flaubert claimed, in all probability on completing these plans, that 'l'idée principale s'est dégagée et maintenant c'est clair', the multiplicity of characters and events, the long time-span, the almost unbroken pattern of decline and degradation all mean that he will – perhaps without fully realising it – be working at the very limits of what is normally associated with psychological realism. It would seem from the plans produced at this stage that there is a contradiction between the aims and methods adopted, which broadly speaking are the traditional ones of the novelist who sees himself as investigating the complex reality of the human heart, and the material with which Flaubert is working, which is potentially intractable, lacking in dramatic appeal and generally problematic as he himself recognised once he had begun to write the novel:

> C'est un livre d'amour, de passion; mais de passion telle qu'elle peut exister maintenant, c'est-à-dire inactive, Le sujet, tel que je l'ai conçu, est, je crois, profondément vrai, mais, à cause de cela même, peu amusant probablement. Les faits, le drame manquent un peu; et puis l'action est étendue dans un laps de temps trop considérable. Enfin j'ai beaucoup de mal et je suis plein d'inquiétudes.[57]

From relatively modest and inauspicious beginnings ('une série d'analyses et de potins médiocres'),[58] the work has already begun its steady advance towards the impossible novel that constitutes Flaubert's true but hidden vocation.

Scénarios partiels

The next stage of planning is represented by the second set of plans, folios 1 to 64, which are far more detailed and either cover in sequence a whole part of the novel or are devoted to single chapters. For each of the three parts of the novel there are at least two, and in some cases three, sets of plans as well as chapter plans for most of the chapters.[59] Although these plans were all drafted after the first batch, it is not possible to say with absolute certainty whether they were all written immediately before the composition of the corresponding part or chapter. The use of the name Laroque for Roque in one set of plans for each of the parts of the novel suggests that in 1864 Flaubert was already working on part plans for all three parts of the novel and not just the first part.[60] It seems likely, on the other hand, that all the other plans were written immediately prior to the section of the novel which they cover. Thus, before embarking upon Part III Flaubert wrote: 'Je tâche d'arranger le plan de ma dernière partie'[61] and, before composing the last two chapters, he wrote 'Depuis mon retour, j'ai travaillé le plan de mes deux derniers chapitres'.[62] Thus, while in all probability there was no gap in the case of part plans for Part I between the *scénarios d'ensemble* and the *scénarios partiels*, in the case of part plans for Parts II and III the time lapse is likely to have been considerable. What this means, therefore, is that folios 1 to 64 contain plans which correspond to a distinct stage in the planning of the novel, one which is virtually coextensive with the composition of the work. It is to be expected that they will reflect the considerations operative throughout the composition of the work as modified by the actual experience of writing.

The main function of these plans is to amplify and, in some cases, correct the material contained in the previous set of plans. Taking the earlier set of plans as his starting point, Flaubert goes over the ground again, expanding the account of events, extending the analysis of reactions and motives and defining character in greater detail. Adding to, rather than modifying, the original outline of plot and character, Flaubert painstakingly moves towards a fuller and clearer view of the fictional situation he is about to evoke. These plans reveal a strong determination on Flaubert's part to achieve a kind of total control over the material for his novel, one which would leave nothing to chance or the inspiration of the moment, which would leave no reaction unexplained, no event unmotivated. In the light of the obscurity of the final version Flaubert's quest for complete clarity at this stage is perhaps surprising. Why bother to work out in such detail the precise nature of the motives of characters when these motives are destined in many cases to be left undefined or obscure? Does Flaubert need to have a Balzacian basis upon which to start his writing even if that writing takes the form of undermining such a basis?[63] Or is it, perhaps, a question of his believing that the psychological material elaborated, though partially obscured in the process of writing, should still be worked out clearly in order to be apprehended through hints and suggestions by the reader? Before he could begin the process of concealment, Flaubert seems to have needed to know exactly what he was going to hide.

The process of ordering and segmentation of the material for the novel, begun in the first set of plans, continues in folios 1 to 64. Changes made to Part I, as might be expected, are fewer than for other parts. The two separate dinners originally planned to take place at Arnoux's house are reduced to a single evening which coincides with Deslauriers's arrival.[64] The 'partie de campagne', which had figured in several of the scénarios d'ensemble, is retained in the part plans but suppressed in the chapter plans,[65] while the projected visit to the 'chaumière ou à un café chantant' finally becomes the trip to L'Alhambra.[66] As in the scénarios d'ensemble, there are still five chapters in Part I in the part plans, Chapter iv covering the ground of Chapters iv and v in the final version.[67] By the time he was drafting chapter plans, however, Flaubert had increased the number of chapters to six with Chapters v and vi beginning at their present point.[68] By the part plan stage the visit to the factory in Part II has been deferred and the quarrel over the shawl has been brought forward.[69] Frédéric's house-warming party now occurs after visits to Rosanette and Madame Arnoux[70] and a visit to Madame Dambreuse is added to the visits to Rosanette and Madame Arnoux.[71] The trip to the races, which occurred earlier in the scénarios d'ensemble, now takes place after the abortive visit to the factory.[72] Deslauriers's attempted seduction of Madame Arnoux, which takes place at the same time as Frédéric's outing with Louise Roque, is still described after it.[73] Part II, which originally had as many as nine chapters, now has six chapters.[74] At first, the second chapter was to end with the Dambreuse ball and the quarrel over the shawl was to come at the beginning of the next chapter but Flaubert decided to make it end with the quarrel over the shawl.[75]

Other divisions coincide with the present ones. In Part III, the scene of reconciliation with Madame Arnoux is brought forward to its present position and the death of Monsieur Dambreuse is now made to coincide with the birth of Rosanette's child.[76] Although the pattern of events surrounding the departure of the Arnoux is closer to the final version, it is still envisaged that Frédéric should give money to them.[77] At first there are nine chapters for Part III, which are gradually reduced to the present seven.[78] What is now III i at the part plan stage formed two chapters, the second beginning with the Fontainebleau episode.[79] What became Chapter iii was originally divided into two chapters, the second beginning with the contacts with the Dambreuse, leading to the seduction of Madame Dambreuse.[80]

The *scénarios partiels*, like the *scénarios d'ensemble*, are primarily concerned with Frédéric and his development. In Part I his deficiencies are outlined in greater detail. In the opening scene he ineffectually 'essaie de dessiner sur son album' (f.2); living in Paris fails to produce the expected effect upon him: 'Il s'ennuie mortellement. ‹son genie a baissé. Paris loin de l'echauffer le refroidit›' (f.4); his interest in painting flags: 'Fr travaille peu à la peinture, n'etant pas né artiste. il est de l'ecole de l'inspiration' (f.8); in Deslauriers's eyes, at least, he is despised because he 'garde sa chasteté' (f.9); in Nogent where he might have been expected to show up to advantage, he disappoints on account of his 'defaut d'exactitude, de science et d'intelligence' (f.15) and the way in which he fails to resist the pressure to work in the lawyer's office reflects the 'mollesse de sa nature' (f.14); most significantly, the very fact that he stays in Nogent indicates his lack of drive: 'S'il avait été un homme energique, il eût été à Paris tout de meme' (f.13). In Part II the future at one point looks brighter: '[son avenir s'annonce splendidement tout lui réussit]' (f.24). Frédéric does not, however, fulfil the high hopes both he and others have of him: 'plus d'exaltation intellectuelle. Depuis qu'il frequente La Mle il mène la vie du boulevard, mange un peu trop d'argent – rêve une gde fortune, – en somme mène une vie bête. Sa mère a raison. il sent qu'il faut faire qque chose' (f.25). It is not, however, solely the relationship with Rosanette which saps his resolution: 'tout croule, par suite de son amour pr. Me Arn' (f.30 verso). Frédéric's decline is already well underway in Part II but in Part III it is more marked. Flaubert documents more fully the way he is corrupted. After the February Revolution he is 'gagné par la contagion parlante' (f.47) and after the June Days at the Dambreuse dinner, 'Privé de toute passion politique, il domine l'assemblée et brille en contant l'histoire de Dussard.' (f.49) The deleterious influence of the Dambreuse circle, already analysed in the earlier *scénarios*, is restated: 'Le milieu hypocrite où il se trouve chez les D le prend' (f.53) but he is now accorded a kind of charm which he perhaps could have well done without: 'Il avait le charme des putains – par le seul developpement de sa vie analogue à la leur' (f.57). At one stage Flaubert seems to have considered the possibility that he might partially redeem himself: 'il est devenu canaille. se releve à la fin par un Bon Mouvement qui trompé le fait finir par un aimable scepticisme' (f.30 verso); in the event, although he does go to the aid of the Arnoux, nothing mitigates the 'Dessechement et aridité de sa vie' (f.62) and his decline is complete.

The main features of Frédéric's responses to the various women in his life remain unchanged in the *scénarios partiels*, which tend to give a fuller account of his underlying attitudes and to analyse in more detail his inner feelings in scenes which had been only rapidly sketched in the earlier plans. As far as Madame Arnoux is concerned, the main process in Part I to be accounted for is the gradual increase of his passion:

> Par suite de son desœuvrement et de l'inassouvissement de sa passion, la passion augmente. c'est un amour sans nul espoir; (f.9)
> sa passion pr. Me Arnoux augmente à mesure qu'il la voit davantage. (f.12)

More emphasis is laid upon his timidity:

> Fr. ne pense qu'à Me Arn. il n'ose lui faire de visites. qqu' envie qu'il en ait. Battement de cœur au bruit de la sonnette se repercutant dans les appartemens. soulagement quand on lui dit que Me n'est pas là; (f.9)
> motiver la timidité de Fr. Il est sûr, par des mots qu'elle lui a entendu dire que toute tentative serait vaine. – et elle devient une habitude de sa pensée. (f.11)

A number of scenes are expanded. The effect of the 'soirée intime chez Arnoux' upon Frédéric is defined: 'Il s'en revient au clair de lune sur les ponts. Comme elle lui a parlé peinture il veut etre peintre, devenir gd homme. – Paris, la nuit. son cœur deborde. (f.9) Frédéric's failure to understand Madame Arnoux's distress on returning to Paris from the country is fully evoked (f.7 and f.3). Much of the time, however, it is a question of analysing Frédéric's thoughts about an absent idealised figure, as when he gazes at what he takes to be her window ('pensait à Me Arn. regardait les fenêtres du Ier etage, croyait que c'est là qu'elle habitait. la cherchait vaguement', (f.4) or pines for her in Nogent ('Mais s'il n'y va pas (i.e. to Paris), il y pense. – et à Me Arnoux [,et à tout le reste] ‹aussi›. Le souvenir et l'absence donnent à tout cela des proportions colossales, des embellissements, – lui procure des excitations enragées et melancoliques', f.15).

The implications of the 'parallèle' established between Madame Arnoux and Rosanette are worked out in more detail in the *scénarios partiels*:

> Dès lors Frederic les frequente simultanement. ((..)) Me Arnoux [le charme] pas sa vertu, son serieux, sa bonté; (f.25)
> Me Arn est trop serieuse, trop occupée de son menage, – froide, sans doute. cependant elle embrasse ses enfants d'une manière exaltée. (f.25)

The confusion which exists in Frédéric's mind is added to: 'une sorte de confusion de sentiments s'etablissait, provoquée d'ailleurs par les objets exterieurs' (f.25). Many more meetings take place in Part II, requiring amplification and clarification of Frédéric's reaction. Frédéric's disappointment on meeting her again after a long period in which she had been idealised ('[Pendant ses deux ans de sejour à Nogent son amour par la reflexion et la distance avait gdi, s'était poetisé]', f.19) is fully explained:

> Le cadre de sa passion etant changé, la passion diminue; ‹il est derouté, un voile lui tombe des yeux› – Il sort froid et s'en va au café anglais souper seul. (f.19)

The suspect basis upon which intimacy grows is spelt out:

> Comme Fr aime naïvement les Arnoux, il fait part à Me de ce que l'on dit des aff. d'Arn. D'abord elle se recrie bien haut, defend son mari – puis avoue ses inquietudes [sur la prodigalité d'Arnoux]. ce qui fait un commencement d'intimité, etablit entr'eux une espèce de lien. (f.18)

So, too, is the ambiguous way he relishes discord which he has helped to create:

> Afin d'envenimer les choses et de les hater, il vante à Arnoux la fidelité de la Mle ((...)) Il a volé le mouchoir de Me Ar. trempé de larmes – et [(contraste de naïveté)] le soir, dans son lit il s'en couvre le visage. (f.24)

The account of Frédéric's reactions in Chapter vi is of particular interest since *scénarios d'ensemble* are missing. The first meeting at her house is briefly evoked: 'l'aveu mutuel se fait de soi-même. baiser sur les yeux–ivresse. il touche à son rêve. l'enfant entre' (f.42) The subsequent stage of frustrated desire is described as a kind of illness: 'ils sont malades. ils ont l'adultère sans l'adultère. ils trebuchent sur une pente' (f.42). Frédéric's hopes in arranging the rue Tronchet meeting are also made clear:

> Il l'a demandé comme une marque de confiance. esperant qu'il l'entrainera sous la porte cochère d'un hotel. il loue donc d'avance une chambre garnie dans un hotel de la rue tronchet. y apporte des objets de toilette, des parfums, des fleurs se prepare à un coup splendide. (f.40)

Frédéric's state of mind on meeting Madame Arnoux again at the Dambreuse is characteristically hopeful:

> Fr. (un peu fatigué de la Mle, il a eu une querelle avec elle avant de venir) en revoyant <u>Me Ar</u>. sent son cœur s'elancer à sa rencontre. mais elle se montre froide et même ironique. (f.50)

The scene of reconciliation is slightly modified by the significant omission of 'peut-être' from 'ils vont se baiser' (f.54) and the reaction of Frédéric in the final scene becomes more complicated: in place of the bare 'il a peur d'avoir degout plus tard', Flaubert substitutes: 'Elle ne le degoute pas. Par l'effet de son vieil amour, il eprouve qqchose d'inexprimable. mais il a peur d'avoir degout plus tard. et il fait semblant de ne pas comprendre' (f.156).

The *scénarios partiels* give a more detailed account of the impact of Rosanette upon Frédéric: 'Rosanette le charme par sa grace, ses vices, sa legereté, ses fantaisies' (f.25). The motivation of the failure to make Rosanette his mistress is amplified:

> [Mais] la familiarité qui existe entre Fr et la Mle est un obstacle. ils ont debuté sur un ton de blague qui continue. ils sont trop amis pr. devenir amants. il se declare vingt fois mais d'un ton folatre quand ce serait le ton tout opposé qui reussirait. (f.25)

Exasperation and desire now become more closely linked:

> Puis elle l'agace par ses airs factices, tour à tour enfantins et bonne femme, par l'impossibilité de savoir le vrai, par sa fugacité essentielle, et il a envie de la posseder moins pr. en jouir que pr. la dompter. (f.25)

The pattern of high hopes and comic disappointment is finally broken in the rue Tronchet episode (missing in the *scénarios d'ensemble*):

> reaction de Fr. il court chez la Mle, est si eloquent qu'il la baise. – par perversité il l'emmene dans le logis preparé pr. l'autre, et pleure sur l'oreiller. 'qu'as-tu cher amour?' 'c'est excès de bonheur il y avait trop longtemps que je te desirais.' (f.40)

The limitations inherent in all human relationships are made clearer in the Fontainebleau episode: 'mais ni l'un ni l'autre ne disent absolument toute la verité, à cause de l'impossibilité generale et particulière d'un hymen complet' (f.44). Part III is mainly concerned with charting the inevitable deterioration of Frédéric's feelings for Rosanette. Although postponing the final break, the child Frédéric has by Rosanette does nothing to bring them together, either when first announced or when it dies, on account of his lasting infatuation with Madame Arnoux:

> embêtement de la decouverte puis reaction de tendresse paternelle à l'idée que l'enfant pouvait etre ((de)) Me Arn et dans l'espoir que ce sera peut-être une fille, il l'appelera "Marie" – il se radoucit; (f.54)
> Mort de son petit garçon, ce qui l'afflige mediocrement, tout preoccupé qu'il est de Me Arn. (f.62)

Nor does physical satisfaction undermine his hostility: 'Elle le fait jouir malgré l'espèce de haine qu'il lui porte. C'est un goût des sens, âcre, violent, brutal. Il souhaite sa mort' (f.57). It is not that Frédéric is lacking in feeling, rather a question of his capacity for feeling never being developed in a productive context, as the comment on his reaction to his child's death ('insensibilité d'un coté, tendresse de l'autre', f.63) suggests. He is never less than totally unfair to Rosanette, particularly when frustration at having been duped by the Arnoux leads him to break with her:

> Dans le ressentiment de sa duperie et ne sachant sur qui faire passer sa fureur il s'en prend à la Mle et rompt avec elle, brutalement, malgré ses protestations pathetiques. (f.63)

In the expansion of the account of Frédéric's relationship with Madame Dambreuse, more emphasis is laid upon a profanatory response:

> Pour la seduire, il fait tout ce qu'il faut. Il lui raconte comme senti pr. elle ce qu'il a, autrefois, ressenti pr Me Arn. Elle lui resiste. Il voit ‹tristem› qu'il

n'y a pas dans tout ce qu'elle exprime un mot de vrai, n'importe! il y tient!
et puis, Me D. l'excite d'une façon irritante et depravée Elle est du tiers
ordre de St Dominique. Il goute un plaisir pervers à l'idée de souiller les
amulettes; (f.53)
Madame D est un mauvais coup. il est obligé pr jouir de penser à Me
Arnoux ou à la Mle. (f.57)

On the other hand, the rewards of the relationship are also spelt out:

Puisqu'il baise Me D. il se croit, se sent dans son hotel, chez lui; (f.59)
Amour exquis de la femme de quarante ans. Elle lui fait des cadeaux, lui
envoie des fleurs, montait tout à coup dans un fiacre et arrivait chez lui. Fr.
se sent passé à l'état d'idole. (f.58)

These are not sufficient, however, to prevent the 'rupture froide et con-
tenue, mais irrevocable' (f.62) after the auction.

The brief comments relating to Frédéric's attitude to Louise in the
scénarios d'ensemble are amplified in the *scénarios partiels*. In Part I vi,
'Il s 'eprend de cette petite nature ardente qui se developpe – c'est la
seule personne originale de Nogent' (f.16). In Part II she helps to
assuage his wounded pride, as well as representing provincial inno-
cence: 'Revenu dans sa ville natale, Fr. fait le parisien, etale son
elegance, et se venge de ses déboires en s'amusant à chauffer Mlle
Roque. Promenade amoureuse au bord de l'eau. Souvenirs d'enfance,
de la Iere communication etc' (f.41). When Frédéric returns to Paris he
does not wish to see Madame Arnoux 'etant d'ailleurs un peu pris pr. la
petite Louise' (f.42). The reactions of Frédéric in III ii do not change
appreciably; Flaubert simply multiplies Frédéric's reasons for not taking
her seriously at this point in his life:

quand on s'en va, elle laisse son père derrière elle, prend le bras de
Frederic et lui demande, nettement, ses intentions. Mais il a revu Me
Arnoux, il est engagé avec la Mle, on vient de lui faire des avances de
toute nature, il a pris la resolution d'etre positif, de ne plus donner dans le
sentiment. Donc il la refuse ((...)). (f.52)

The clearest expression of all that Louise stands for in his eyes is
perhaps to be found in the chain of associations which make him think
of Louise Roque at the end of the novel:

Dessechement et aridité de sa vie. Vue d'un zouave, caressant un enfant à
la porte d'un café. = une bonne famille tableau de greuze. alors Fr.

regrette son enfant. Il pense à la famille, à la province, à la petite Roque. (f.62)

As well as plotting the collapse of Frédéric's relationships with women in greater detail, Flaubert also works out more fully how friendship too declines. In the case of Deslauriers, it is, in the first place, other friends who are to blame:

> Le contraste entre [les deux amis] ‹Fr et Deslaur› s'accuse. ils ne sont pas de meme sentiment sur les amis. Senecal est desagreable à Fr. Hussonnet à Deslaur etc.; (f.8)
> 1er dissentiment entre Desl et Fr. à propos de Senecal. ‹car› Senecal dès la lere visite a blessé Fr à propos de Me Ar indirectement. quand il est parti Desl et Fr s'echangent à son propos qq mots aigres. (f.9)

But the underlying cause remains Frédéric's doting upon Madame Arnoux: 'Desl ne comprend rien à toutes ses delicatesses ((...)) Fr. lui semble un peu niais et mou. de là besoin de société – il forme un cenacle où viennent les amis communs. – cenacle (indirect) – dissentiments à propos des amis – La symp se denoue' (f.9). Separation at the end of Part I simply allows the rift to widen: 'La correspondance se rarefie et se raccourcit – car ils finissent par ne plus se comprendre. il est choqué de ses jeremiades' (f.15). Details of the promise of financial help and the failure to provide it (f.36, f.39) serve to bring out the commitment to different goals and fall well short of the 'communisme' (f.9), or sharing, both practise in Part I. Although Frédéric and Deslauriers are finally reconciled at the end, they are not totally frank with each other (any more than Frédéric and Rosanette in III i); each of them withholds something, as Flaubert is at pains to establish:

> Deslauriers avoue à Fr. qu'après sa rupture avec Rosanette, il a profité de son emotion pr. la baiser. – Fr. fait là-dessus, bonne figure, mais lui en veut. Il ignore sa tentative près de Me. Arnoux, qu'il eut plus aisément pardonné, puisque Desl ayant été repoussée, c'était une espèce de triomphe pr. lui. Mais cet aveu de Deslauriers touchant Rosan est une delicatesse de sa part, il l'a fait par une sorte de remords de n'avoir fait l' autre aveu ‹qui etait› plus grave – Fr ne dit pas la dernière visite de Me Ar. chez lui. (f.64)

The pattern of Frédéric's responses to Arnoux, already well defined in the *scénarios d'ensemble*, receives further clarification. When Frédéric discovers that Rosanette is betraying Arnoux with Delmar, he feels protective towards him: ('Il est pris pr. lui d'une tendresse subite. veut l'eclairer, court à son domicile. – puis à la porte s'aperçoit qu'il va faire une infamie', f.24). The conflicting claims of love and friendship are neatly illustrated in an incident planned for II iii when Arnoux is trying to allay his wife's suspicions:

> il lui dit ‹devant Fr› que Fr. est l'amant de la Mle. [il prie même] ‹embarras de Fr. qui proteste. – Arn. badine puis supplie› Fr. de lui laisser croire ça à sa femme et de lui dire adroitement qqchose qui le lui persuade – indignation et reproches de Fr. (f.34)

The guardroom scene is retained virtually unaltered but the original 'concordance de gouts et de temperament' which defuses the oedipal rivalry between the two men becomes 'une excessive concordance de gouts et de temperament' (f.45) The attitude of Frédéric to various other friends remains superficial in comparison. Flaubert works out in detail how almost all his friends at some point do something damaging, either to Frédéric's interests or the Arnoux's, but he does not seek to establish fine variations in his responses to them.

Flaubert continues in the *scénarios partiels* to discuss the reactions of various characters independently of Frédéric's perception of them, adding further detail in many cases to the account presented in the *scénarios d'ensemble*. Deslauriers's motives in a key episode missing in the earlier plans throw further light on his assertive, impressionable nature:

> à force d'entendre Fr. parler de Me Arn, il est devenu excité. puis il veut voir sa force – ça le posera à ses propres yeux – il est aussi poussé par l'imitation de Fr. qu'il admire en depit de lui-même. ‹Desl est ebloui par l'am de Fr. pr Me Arn. Les gens comme Desl. croient que les jeunes gens riches ont plus de femmes que les autres. – et les respectent en [ces] ‹cette› matières›. (f.42)

As well as following in Frédéric's footsteps in his relations with women, Deslauriers also seeks to replace him in business matters: 'Desl qui a envie de se substituer à lui dans l'affaire des houilles l'engage aussi à quitter Paris' (f.39). This type of analysis is, however, most marked in the case of the female characters. Madame Arnoux's responses at key junctures are clearly indicated. She experiences a 'jalousie subite qu'elle ne peut contenir' (f.42) on being told by Deslauriers that Frédéric is about to marry and her thoughts about the consummation of their

relationship are formulated: 'ils ne doivent pas s'appartenir. 'il m'es-
timerait moins' pense-t-elle. elle lui déclara que s'il allait plus loin, il ne
la reverrait plus' (f.42). Rosanette's reasons for giving Cisy a hard time
are explained: 'Mais Cisy n'eut pas beaucoup d'agrement. Elle songeait
à l'equipage de Me Dambr. – et Me Arn pleurant d'avoir été insultée
par la mtresse de son mari' (f.39). Flaubert also emphasises her fulfilment in Fontainebleau ('La Mle n'a jamais eprouvé ce qu'elle ressent.
Elle entrevoit un horizon de bonheur serieux', f.44), and explains her
desire to be virtuous: 'Sa maternité prochaine la purifie' (f.155). The
clarification of Madame Dambreuse's various motives and reactions
does not make her any more attractive. She adopts a different attitude
to Frédéric because she is 'depitée contre Martinon' (f.50) and then
artificially whips up her passion for him: 'Me Dambr se fouette à la
jalousie pr. avoir de la passion'; (f.55). The more detailed account of
Louise's reactions, given her 'intelligence primesautière' (f.14), makes
her more appealing. Flaubert describes how Frédéric 'lui produit l'effet
d'un Prince de Conte de Fees' (f.14) and how literature effects her
'caractère violent et fantasque' (f.16): 'Macbeth trad par Letourneur la
ravage. Elle se croit Lady Macbeth et se lave les mains – espèce d'accès
de folie' (f.16).

Flaubert's persistent interest in the motives of a wide range of
characters is consistent with a more general tendency apparent in these
plans, the tendency to try to fit all the events in the novel into a single,
infinitely complex causal scheme, even though aspects of this causal
scheme are destined to be veiled in obscurity in the final version.
Flaubert goes to great pains to establish the precise nature of the various
characters' reactions to each other, the exact reasons why the paths of
characters cross, the pattern of obligations, often financial, which bind
them together and the limits of each one's knowledge of the other.
Flaubert seems reluctant to allow anything to happen by chance; each
event must be connected with some prior event. Of the invitation to
dinner he receives from Arnoux in I iv he asks 'cette invitation doit etre le
resultat de?' (f.8); referring to the presence of Sénécal and Deslauriers in
the Champs Elysées in II iv he writes 'ne pas les faire trouver sur sa route
par hazard', f.39); an explanation of Madame Arnoux's presence at the
races is provided ('Me Ar. est venue là, sur une lettre anonyme de la
Vatnas, afin de surveiller son mari qui devait se trouver avec la Mle',
f.39); sometimes Flaubert is not satisfied with the explanation he has

provided, writing for instance of Sénécal's visit to Frédéric in II iv 'trouver un meilleur motif' (f.39). Flaubert takes a strong interest in money matters, working out in considerable detail the precise details of Arnoux's business activities in Part II and his bankruptcy in Part III ('La faillite d'Arnoux est la consequence de faits dont Fr. n'a pas suivi la filière (marquez-la pr.le lecteur)', f.59) as well as Madame Moreau's indebtedness to Le Père Roque. But although Flaubert displays an almost neurotic aversion for the unmotivated happening and the gratuitous response, he does not seek to establish a sequence of events which is totally predictable. Indeed, on several occasions he expresses a desire to mislead the reader about the outcome of events:

> [Le lecteur doit croire qu'il va baiser Me Arn]; (f.24)
> il faut qu'on croie qu'il va devenir l'amant de la Mle; (f.27)
> faire croire au lecteur que Fr. va epouser la petite Roque; (f.39)
> faire croire au lecteur que sa vie va changer. (f.53)

The significance of such comments should perhaps not be exaggerated but it may well be that they reflect Flaubert's growing realisation that, however foolproof the logic of events the plot of the novel rests upon, there is no reason why it should not fool the reader, since there is a constant discrepancy between what has been painstakingly established in the plans and what is actually declared in the narrative text to which all the planning gives rise.

Esquisses

All the plans examined so far are to be found in a single volume and correspond to distinct stages in the planning of the novel. In addition to these plans there are a large number of more detailed sketches (*esquisses*), which have been bound with the rough drafts (*brouillons*) – since the other side of the folio is a *brouillon* – but can be distinguished from the *brouillons* on account of their different system of pagination.[81] It seems certain that after completing a chapter plan, Flaubert would not immediately begin the first *brouillon*, needing to expand the chapter plan into a sequence of *esquisses* which provide the basis upon which the first *brouillons* were drafted. The *esquisses* constitute a kind of half-way stage between *scénario* and *brouillon*, sharing with the former the use of the present tense, looser style, outspoken tone and clarificatory function but resembling the latter in the fullness and intricacy with which events are noted, their high degree of focalisation and the large proportion of material which is close if not identical to the final version. The sheer quantity of these sketches makes it difficult to give a comprehensive account of them; the comments that follow are based upon a limited selection of sketches, those pertaining to the first part of the novel.

Although the *scénarios* had plotted Frédéric's development with considerable care, his reactions in various episodes still had to be worked out in fine detail. Referring to the impact made upon Frédéric by Madame Arnoux in I i Flaubert writes 'Avait toute la portée d'un dévouement [l'exaltation vague] ‹et la vague exaltation› que produisent [les choses impersonnelles, les gds spectacles de la nature, les œuvres d'Art, sublimes] les gds spectacles' (17599, f.72 verso).[82] In the next chapter Flaubert notes that 'par pudeur ou impuissance de s'exprimer ((Frédéric)) ne parle pas de Me Arnoux' (17599, f.76 verso). The importance attached to the visit to Monsieur Dambreuse in I iii is outlined fully in a marginal addition: 'cette visite avait une importance extreme pr. Fr. elle allait avoir une influence decisive sur sa vie – un evenement. – si Desl avait dit vrai après tout? en tout cas elle ouvrirait l'entrée des Salons.' (17599, f.156 verso). On receiving evidence of Arnoux's dishonesty in I iv, Frédéric is scandalised but at the same time 'il y eprouve un attirement complexe' (17600, f.54 verso). The sequence of 'mouvements psychologiques' when deprived of a bed for the night by Deslauriers's success with a 'grisette' are carefully listed:

1er elancement vers elle
2 de rage en pensant à ses amis qui jouissent maintenant
3e de lassitude, de decouragement.
4e accablement et fatigue physique. (17601, f.75 verso)

The sequence of Frédéric's thoughts on discovering the state of his mother's finances in I vi is worked out in similar detail:

1e ruiné = mouvement
2e consequences = mediocrité = deshonneur – il passera pour avoir blagué. s'être introduit frauduleusement dans des compagnies supérieures
3e et elle – elle! . . . . comment oser la revoir! . . . puis-je la revoir d'ailleurs, ((illegible words)) avec mes deux mille livres de rente, je ne serai pas meme

à la hauteur d'Hussonnet il faut que je la voie pourtant! . . . bien d'autres
que moi sont sans fortune – ((. . .)). (17602, 4 verso)

At times Flaubert comments in more explicit terms than previously
upon character and behaviour. The impact of Frédéric's reading between
the ages of sixteen and eighteen is discussed and leads to a definition of
his mental characteristics: 'cycle sentimental littérature pr. l'exaltation
des sentiments . . . cela developpait en lui les idées. mais qui n'etaient
que l'echo de ce qu'il lisait ((. . .)) esprit malleable et flottant avec un
sentiment d'autant plus concentré qu'il ne se produit par des formes
nettes' (17699, f.76 verso). The nature of his obsession with Madame
Arnoux is also evaluated: 'Et cet amour, deplacé de son but, cet amour
sans espoir et sans épanchement, sans confidence tourne à la maladie et
devient intolerable' (17601, f.163). Arnoux's guided tour of his house in
Saint-Cloud is tartly glossed: 'Puis comme un bon bourgeois qu'il etait
montre sa propriété' (17601, f.200 verso). Flaubert also continues to
issue reminders to himself which throw interesting light on his aims.
Having specified that Frédéric was to take no positive action to make
contact with Madame Arnoux in I iii, Flaubert adds in parenthesis
'justifier la situation en expliquant longuement sa timidité' (17699, f.156
verso). Even at this point, there is no suggestion that Flaubert is not
totally committed to justifying his account of events in psychological
terms.

The *esquisses* provide the final piece of evidence demonstrating
Flaubert's determination to base his novel on firm psychological foundations. The sheer bulk of the material relating to the planning of the
novel is staggering; few novels can have been prepared with quite so
much care, with the same obsessive determination to provide an explanation of every event, a plausible motive for each action. Of course, as
many critics have noted,[83] much that is clear and explicit in the plans not
only for *L'Éducation sentimentale* but also for other works of Flaubert
becomes obscure or implicit in the final version. This makes the effort
expended by Flaubert in planning the novel seem even more phenome-
nal. Given that in the final version motives are often going to be left
undefined, characters blurred and the connection between events
obscure, what purpose is served by all the painstaking preparatory work?
Given that it is going to be dismantled at a later stage, why erect so much
elaborate explanatory material? There can be no simple answer to this

question. It may be that when it came to the actual composition of the novel, Flaubert could make progress only if he suppressed, could enrich his account only by reducing it, could achieve his desired effect only by rendering the behaviour of his characters obscure.[84] But the plans do more than provide the rubble which has to be cleared before the novel can become suitably unclear. It would seem that (for Flaubert) writing was predicated upon knowing, knowing in the abstract, knowing without saying. Both the bewilderment of the reader and the bewilderment of Frédéric become significant only in relation to a full understanding, not immediately apparent in the text but none the less possessed by its creator. The extent to which that understanding can be recuperated by the attentive reader and the basis upon which it rests are questions that can be resolved only by close scrutiny of the text in its final, definitive form.

III

Plot-Structure

L'Éducation sentimentale has a curiously unmemorable plot; there are few scenes which stand out from the rest, there is no dramatic climax and the uneventful action extends in a desultory manner over a considerable period of time. The 'défaut de ligne droite' which is adduced to explain Frédéric's failure to attain his ideal could also be invoked to account for the failure of the plot of *L'Éducation sentimentale* to make an immediate impact upon the reader by moving in a straightforward way towards a clearly defined thematic goal. Likewise, Frédéric's decision to return to Nogent 'par la route la plus longue' has self-reflexive overtones; as well as anticipating a life of indirection and vacillation, the description corresponds to a plot which appears to many readers to take an inordinately long time to come to a conclusion which might have been reached much earlier were it not for a perversely wayward quality in the organising intelligence behind the work. Although Frédéric is clearly the central figure in the novel and although the bulk of the action revolves round him, there are a number of sections where the focus moves to other characters such as Deslauriers, in such a way as to make it seem that the account offered is digressing or hesitating between rival centres of interest. There is also a certain tension between the fictional material and the historical material; the intrinsic interest of events in the historical sphere leads at times to the temporary eclipse of the protagonist, creating the impression that he is unable to command the narrator's unbroken attention. Whether all this constitutes merely a modification of the kind of plot-structure associated with the Balzacian novel or a more thoroughgoing subversion of plot of any kind is, however, debatable. Although in numerous ways traditional narrative practice is disrupted, the novel as a whole none the less possesses a classical readability.[1]

Recent criticism has stressed the incoherence, discontinuity and lack of clear significance of *L'Éducation sentimentale*. Many of these alleged features of the novel are closely connected with what is traditionally called plot, that is to say, the overall pattern into which a series of carefully selected events are organised. In some respects, however, the term 'plot' is loose, blurring the distinction between the actual information the reader is provided with and the final impression formed by the reader after he has pieced together this information. In order to discuss the plot of *L'Éducation sentimentale* more precisely it is worth recalling the important distinction between the narrative account itself – most commonly referred to as *discours* – and the sequence of events which is constructed by the reader on the basis of the narrative account – most commonly referred to as *histoire*.[2] The fundamental distinction between these two very different aspects of the novel is underlined by Culler: 'the theory of narrative requires a distinction between what I call 'story' – a sequence of actions or events, conceived of as independent of their manifestation in discourse – and what I call 'discourse', the narrative presentation or narration of events.'[3] Although the sequence of events is often regarded as independent of or logically prior to the narrative account, it is, inevitably, only arrived at by the reader through the narrative account. As Rimmon-Kenan points out, 'being an abstraction, a construct, the story is not directly available to the reader'.[4] Although the opposition between *discours* and *histoire* is not without its problematic aspect, in particular when it comes to deciding which determines the other,[5] it none the less allows crucial distinctions to be made when it comes to discussing questions such as coherence and continuity in a novel. The main point to be stressed is that the two should not be assumed to be identical; what obtains at one level of the novel does not necessarily obtain at the other.

It is well established that, with regard to time, the relationship between *discours* and *histoire* is subject to constant variation. Strictly speaking, *discours* does not possess any time: 'The narrative text as text has no other temporality than the one it metonymically derives from the process of its reading.'[6] None the less, by means of a pace-constant, which involves equating a given stretch of narrative with a given amount of time, it is possible to endow the narrative text with a notional element of time. Opposed to the time of *discours* is the time of *histoire*, that is to say the time of the events related, a time which is frequently conceived of on the basis of the linear model which constitutes a kind of 'natural' frame into which the events are placed.[7] The wide range of variations between these two different time-schemes which become possible have been systematically analysed by Gérard Genette. First, the order of events in time may differ; the narrative text does not always present the events in the exact order that they are deemed to have taken place. Secondly, the time taken to narrate events may differ from the time the actual events themselves are reputed to take, although the precise duration of events may not always be recorded. The time-ratio between *histoire* and *discours* is frequently manipulated in order to throw certain events into relief; on the one hand a novelist may, in a panoramic passage, cover a long period of fictional time very rapidly, on the other he may, in a scenic passage, allocate a good deal of textual space, and therefore time, to the recording of events that allegedly take place in a short period of time.[8] Lastly, a novelist may vary the relationship between the number of times events take place and the number of times they are recorded. This usually entails a choice between relating once what occurred once and relating once what occurred several times but theoretically, and occasionally in practice, it is possible to narrate several times what occurred once or to narrate several times what occurred several times.[9]

A second ingredient of plot, closely linked with time, is causality. Once again the relationship between *discours* and *histoire* is not necessarily one of identity, and the status of causality varies considerably, as Rimmon-Kenan points out: 'causality can either be implied by chronology or gain an explicit status in its own right.'[10] A narrative account may avoid specifying or indicating causal links but this does not necessarily mean that at the level of *histoire* all causality evaporates. Frequently the reader is made to supply the missing links, as Todorov has observed: 'Si un récit s'organise suivant un ordre causal, mais garde une causalité implicite, il oblige par là même le lecteur à accomplir le travail auquel le narrateur s'est refusé.'[11] The basis on which the reader is able to postulate causal links when they are not specified varies considerably; the selection of material for description by a novelist is often governed by an implicit norm of causal connection; there is a strong tendency to link temporal succession with causality and there is considerable reliance upon a whole set of unspoken assumptions about the way both the world and experience hang together. Causality can be best thought of as a working assumption; the reader expects that there will be causal connections linking the various events and experiences described, even where these are not explicitly indicated or easy to divine. In much the same way the reader posits a notional continuity at the level of *histoire*. Few novels can claim to be exhaustive in their depiction of experience, offering no more than a highly selective, partial account of what purports to be an ongoing, continuous process. There is, therefore, inevitably, almost always a discrepancy between *histoire* and *discours*, one which is rendered more acute in a panoramic novel with a long timespan and a wide range of characters.

When discussing the plot of *L'Éducation sentimentale* it is necessary to bear in mind the possibility that there may be a significant difference between the explicit narrative account, on the one hand, and the psychological development that the reader abstracts or postulates on the basis of his reading of that account on the other. Although in many ways the narrative account is fragmented and disconnected, the reader may still find himself led into postulating an underlying continuity based upon Frédéric's thraldom to the idealised image of womanhood represented by Madame Arnoux.[12] According to whether one focuses upon the surface account or the ongoing development it is possible to reconstruct, *L'Éducation sentimentale* appears either to be anticipating the 'désagré-gation de l'intrigue' exemplifed by the *nouveau roman*,[13] or alter-natively, to be playing a more complicated game by restoring at one level what is thrown into jeopardy at another. What appeals to Flaubert is not so much the complete subversion of all that is associated with literature as the maintenance of an untenable state of affairs in which literature is both preserved and repudiated.[14]

The aspect of the plot which has received most attention and, when examined under the critical microscope, been found to be marred by a number of minor blemishes, is time. Flaubert's skill in conveying the passing of time, celebrated by Proust,[15] has been called into question. S. Buck has asserted that we are not presented with a 'continuous narrative covering the years 1840 to 1851, but rather a story in three episodes', and has spoken of Flaubert's 'cavalier treatment of time'.[16] More radically, J. Bem suggests that in spite of appearances to the contrary, *L'Éducation sentimentale* possesses 'une structure a-chroni-que',[17] which would mean that what had previously been an essential ingredient of plot was being contested. The basis for Bem's assertion is provided by the contradictions which have been discovered in the chronology of the novel, contradictions which, it must be said, are perhaps more perplexing to the critic who meticulously peruses the text than for the average reader who is unlikely to scrutinise so closely the relatively few and at times imprecise temporal indicators the novel provides.

The most glaring inconsistency in the novel's chronology relates to the length of time Frédéric spends in Nogent at the end of Part I. From the fixed starting-point of the fifteenth of September 1840 given in the first sentence of the novel it is possible to calculate, on the basis of various references to Frédéric's activity, that he returns to Nogent in the summer of 1843.[18] Before his return, however, in a conversation with Frédéric and his friends (p.87), Regimbart is made to refer to the Government's loss of vast sums of money in the campaign against the Moroccans which took place in September 1844. Should Frédéric's return be postponed by a year or should this reference be regarded as anachronistic?[19] A similar uncertainty surrounds the end of Frédéric's stay in Nogent. A second unusually precise reference gives the fourteenth of December 1845 as the date of Frédéric's learning of his inheritance. Frédéric's immediate return to Paris is rapidly followed by the inviting of his friends to his new apartment at the beginning of the following year, yet all the references in the conversation which takes place are to events of 1847 not 1846.[20] Furthermore, the subsequent timing of the development of Frédéric, leading up to the abortive rue Tronchet meeting on the eve of the February Revolution, point to 1846 rather than 1845 as the year of Frédéric's return to Paris, leading Buck to claim that 'for the second time Flaubert has eliminated a year from the story by the simple expedient of moving forward as if no such year existed.'[21] J. Bem has argued that the repercussions of this skipping of two whole years are profound: 'Entourer cet épisode de deux hiatus temporels, c'est très délibérément le détemporaliser, c'est le désinscrire de l'axe du temps, c'est trouver l'équivalent romanesque de l'instant, qui est le contraire de la durée.'[22] In other words, the double 'gap', whether the result of inadvertence[23] or a deliberate blurring of the temporal edges of Frédéric's stay in Nogent, has a de-stabilising effect, throwing the chronology of the novel as a whole into question.

It is debatable, however, whether what is perhaps no more than a characteristic miscalculation[24] on Flaubert's part has quite such a drastic effect. Although the chronology is undoubtedly defective and at least one year somehow gets lost, the dominant impression conveyed is of a long period of time spent languishing in the provinces. During this period the fictional life of Frédéric is 'uncoupled' from the historical development of France. In addition to omitting references to contemporary history, Flaubert also fails to match up the two distinct chronological schemes. The reference to the Camarilla is wrongly placed before Frédéric's return to Nogent and the expressly given date of his return to Paris is inconsistent with the numerous references to events of 1847, rather than 1846, which follow. The effect of such discrepancies is, however, to make the reader aware of the problem of integrating fictional and historical material which faced Flaubert, rather than to produce a radical destabilising of the novel's chronology.

There are other instances, though none quite so serious, of contradictions and inconsistencies in the overall chronological scheme. Buck singles out the third chapter of Part III in which the events of sixteen months, from January 1849 to May 1850, are telescoped into a few pages. If the reader attends closely he will be able to work out that Rosanette has a preganancy which lasts 25 months, truly 'a pregnancy of Gargantuan duration',[25] the difficulty Rosanette has in fulfilling the maternal function contrasting with the rapidity with which Madame Arnoux produces her second child. Once again, however, the problem is created by Flaubert's less than perfect dovetailing of the fictional and historical time-schemes; it follows that an unusually detailed knowledge of the historical background is required if the reader is going to be in a position to correct or modify the relatively imprecise indications of passing time relating to the fictional element of the novel. More perplexing than the various inconsistencies in the novel's chronology which have been detected by hawk-eyed critics is the discrepancy between the few extremely precise temporal indicators examined so far and the calculated vagueness and imprecision which characterise Flaubert's presentation of time elsewhere.[26] In some cases the reader is likely to be in a position to supply the missing date (of the trip to Fontainebleau for instance); in other cases, although Flaubert's documentation is extremely thorough and references to historical events are scrupulously accurate, the actual date of events is not specified. In spite of the frequency of temporal indicators[27] the reader is often left unsure of the exact location in time of the events described, although almost invariably the temporal relationship between the events is clear; 'Le lendemain' occurs on 58 occasions, allowing the reader to situate fictional events in relation to each other but not to 'historical' time.

The inconsistencies in the chronology and the vagueness of many of the references to time point to a relative lack of interest on Flaubert's part in what might be called 'objective' time, which has as its corollary the privileging of 'subjective' time, that is to say of time as experienced by the protagonist.[28] Time does not flow at a steady pace in the novel but rather is subject to constant changes of speed. In a dazzling display of technical virtuousity, Flaubert constantly varies the relation between text-time and story-time in order to create a wide variety of effects, of acceleration and deceleration, of time dragging on endlessly and of a moment of time swelling uncontrollably. Thus in Part I after two chapters which together cover in a total of eighteen pages a single day, the day of the first meeting with Madame Arnoux and the reunion with Deslauriers, the next chapter, only seven pages long, covers a whole year, from November 1840 to November 1841. Flaubert comes dangerously close to breaking a kind of novelistic speed-limit, when he makes time accelerate alarmingly by compressing the events of almost a whole year into two short paragraphs:

> L'hiver se termina. Il fut moins triste au printemps, se mit à préparer son examen, et, l'ayant subi d'une façon médiocre, partit ensuite pour Nogent.
>
> Il n'alla point à Troyes voir son ami, afin d'éviter les observations de sa mère. Puis, à la rentrée, il abandonna son logement et prit, sur le quai Napoléon, deux pièces, qu'il meubla. (p.26)

The effect of this daring variation of the time-ratio, however, while not devoid of subversive force, is to convey the impression of uneventfulness. Similarly, after the full scenic treatment given to the second meeting with Madame Arnoux, which takes up as many pages as the previous year, and the extended account of Frédéric's more eventful life culminating in the Fête de Saint-Cloud, another long scene taking up six pages, time is once again compressed:

> Ces images fulguraient, comme des phares, à l'horizon de sa vie. Son esprit, excité, devint plus leste et plus fort. Jusqu'au mois d'août, il s'enferma, et fut reçu à son dernier examen. (p.86)

The allocation of a few pages to the long period of time Frédéric spends in Nogent comes as yet another striking passage in which time is made to accelerate, completing the picture of a life of little moment.

Part II, though considerably longer than Part I, covers a significantly shorter period of time, just over one year, as opposed to over five years. Throughout Part II time flows more steadily; the opening chapter, covering the first few days of Frédéric's return to Paris, is followed by three chapters, each covering approximately three months. Chapter Five concentrates mainly on the events of a single day (Deslauriers's visit to Madame Arnoux, Frédéric's simultaneous outing with Louise) and is followed by a final chapter which covers a period of six months up to the eve of the February Revolution. Within individual chapters there is an alternation between scenic passages, often lasting a few pages, describing Frédéric's various encounters, and panoramic passages describing his responses to the various people he knows, over a period of time. Part II, as far as the handling of time is concerned, establishes a kind of norm which allows the infractions of Parts I and III to stand out more clearly.

Part III, like Part I, displays considerable variation in the coverage of time. Leaving out the last two chapters, a period of almost four years is covered in 130 pages, giving an overall ratio similar to Part I. If the last two chapters are included, a period of over twenty years is dealt with in 139 pages. As well as depicting important historical developments, the first chapter covers a substantial period of time (four months) but not in a steady fashion. The events of a single day (24 February) take up the first eight pages while the time between the two revolutions is compressed into the next eight pages. The visit to the *Club de l'Intelligence* is given extensive coverage (seven pages) and, most remarkably, twelve pages are devoted to the Fontainebleau idyll, creating the impression that it lasts much longer than three days. The brief second chapter, describing the events of a single day, is followed by a medium-length chapter, covering a period of almost two years, from July/August 1848 to May 1850. The following chapter likewise covers a considerable period of time, from May 1850 to the middle of Autumn 1851. What remains of *L'Éducation* exhibits extreme daring in the handling of time as Flaubert again moves close to the limits of acceptability. Chapter Five records the rapid liquidation of Frédéric's four main relationships and the final destruction of political aspirations, all in the space of a few days. This is then followed by the famous passage in which sixteen years of Frédéric's existence are dismissed in not many more words:

Il voyagea.
Il connut la mélancolie des paquebots, les froids réveils sous la tente,

l'étourdissement des paysages et des ruines, l'amertume des sympathies
interrompues.
Il revint. (p.420)

In addition to using the time-ratio to convey the emptiness of Frédéric's
life, this passage also helps to highlight the importance of the following
scene in which Frédéric and Madame Arnoux are reunited; this scene,
though lasting only a few hours, occupies roughly twenty times as much
textual space as the previous sixteen years of his existence which take up
less than half a page. The same discrepancy throws into greater prominence the final scene in which Frédéric and Deslauriers mull over the
past; ironically, the visit to the brothel originally lasted considerably less
time than it takes – many years later – to recount the episode (p.427).
The impact of these constant variations of the time-ratio is, however,
softened by the underlying steadiness with which the plot follows the
course of time.[29]

While Flaubert contrives constant changes of the time-ratio, he is less
conspicuously innovative when it comes to the order of events. On the
whole, the order of presentation closely follows the order of occurrence,
creating a strong impression of the remorseless forward movement of
time, the element in which the hopes and aspirations of a whole
generation come to grief. Set against the various 'subjective' experiences
of time suggested by variations in the time-ratio, is the 'objective'
framework of linear progression. It is noticeable that Flaubert avoids the
long exposition that in the traditional novel often suspends the forward
movement of time, preferring to present indispensable expositional
material relating to the past lives of the characters in brief passages, often
long after the character has first been introduced. The presentation of
Madame Moreau's past (p.11), of the origins of the friendship between
Frédéric and Deslauriers (p.13), of the upbringing of Louise Roque
(p.94), of the constrasting backgrounds of Sénécal and Dussardier
(pp.233–4) are all sufficiently short and succinct for the impression of
forward movement not to be disrupted, although in each case the
narrator is referring back to events which took place before the main
action of the novel begins. The one occasion where the reader is perhaps
made aware of the plot going, as it were, into reverse, is the account of
Deslauriers's childhood, which coincides with the beginning of a chapter
and shows the influence of Balzac lingering on.[30] But even here Flaubert
deals with his material expeditiously, counteracting any impression that

the novel is in danger of getting becalmed in some temporal doldrums. Elsewhere, essential information is relayed not through the narrator's discourse but through the characters' own accounts of their past, given either in direct or indirect speech. The past of both Rosanette and Madame Arnoux is conveyed through their own subsequent suitably partial or tailored presentation at an appropriate juncture in their relationship with Frédéric (pp.171, 271, 331–2). Technically, such passages do not constitute a 'retour en arrière', since the information about the fictional past is integrated into the conversation taking place in the fictional 'present'.

There is one incident in the past, however, which is presented half through conversation, half through narratorial summary, for which the novel has become renowned. The visit to the brothel, which is the last incident to be recounted in the novel, is the first of any moment to have actually occurred in the chronological sequence which the reader establishes. It might seem somewhat perverse to defer to the very end of the novel the full account of an episode which in Frédéric's disabused estimation constitutes the best thing to have happened to him. So, in addition to the problematic nature of the episode itself is the problematic nature of its placement, which raises questions about the judiciousness of the narrative account offered to the reader. Why, the reader wonders, was I not told about this before? A damaging process of disqualification comes into operation as a result of Flaubert's reversal of chronological and textual order; the narrative account which has dwelt upon Frédéric's lingering infatuation with Madame Arnoux now seems to have somehow missed the point by overlooking or underplaying an episode which is allotted pride of place by the protagonist himself. Having itself been eclipsed by the main narrative account, the brothel episode in turn threatens to eclipse all that subsequently happens to Frédéric.

Although, on the whole, events are presented in their chronological order, at certain points, where the actions to be described are simultaneous rather than consecutive, this is not possible. Incidents, one critic has declared, are more strikingly simultaneous than sequential.[31] Extensive use is made of coincidence and, as will be seen, the element of chance is heavily underlined. In some cases coincidental timing does not pose any problem because the narrative is following only one of the occurrences – usually relating to Frédéric – which are brought together at a given moment of time. There are, however, occasions where the narrative is following two distinct threads and forced therefore to present successively events which are deemed to have occurred simultaneously. The best example of this is II v which describes Deslauriers's visit to Madame Arnoux and Frédéric's outing with Louise Roque. It would, of course, have been more plausible for these two incidents to have occurred at different times but we are told that they take place 'la même après-midi, le même moment' (p.249). In this way the inability of a strictly linear narrative medium to present simultaneously events which take place simultaneously is foregrounded.

It would be difficult to encompass the long time-span of eleven years if a further variation between text-time and story-time – frequency – were not possible. It is true that Flaubert tends to isolate a large number of occasions, some brief, some protracted, recounting once what occurred once, but he also makes use of another option open to the novelist, namely to recount once what occurred on several occasions. Panoramic passages covering a long period of time are often marked by the use of the 'iterative' mode,[32] which represents an economical way of conveying habitual or repeated experiences. A wide range of effects are generated by the use of the iterative mode, ranging from a sense of dreary sameness to subdued ecstasy. At times, it seems to mark an oppressive experience of time flowing monotonously on:

> Il passait des heures à regarder, du haut de son balcon, la rivière qui coulait entre les quais grisâtres, noircis de place en place, par la bavure des égoûts . . . Ses yeux, délaissant à gauche le pont de pierre de Notre-Dame et trois ponts suspendus se dirigeaient toujours vers le quai des Ormes, sur un massif de vieux arbres, pareils aux tilleuls du port de Montereau. (p.64)

Here the iterative imperfect points to a mechanical quality, both pointless and compulsive, in Frédéric's behaviour, but at the same time a characteristically problematic note is introduced; are we really meant to believe that Frédéric behaves the same way time and time again or is the imperfect drained of its normal habitual meaning? By applying the iterative mode to experiences not intrinsically or plausibly repeated or habitual Flaubert creates an impression of seepage, which stems from our feeling that the very capacity of the narrative account to grasp experience is being called into question. A very different use can be seen in the following passage:

Il reconnaissait de loin sa maison, à un chèvrefeuille énorme couvrant, d'un seul côté, les planches du toit; c'était une manière de chalet suisse peint en rouge, avec un balcon extérieur. (p.271)

The euphoric overtones of 'reconnaissait' here stem from the incongruity of the imperfect with a verb which normally records a single happening, which suggests that for Frédéric each visit to Madame Arnoux at Auteuil possesses an ineradicable freshness. The perception indicator which introduces and presents descriptive material dynamically suggests a kind of spell-bound immersion in the contemplated object or surroundings and ultimately a kind of liberation from time.

The initial impression created by the plot of *L'Éducation sentimentale* is of a series of disconnected events, a bewildering multiplicity of loosely related scenes and fragments. What Du Bos referred to as the novel's 'manque de lié'[33] manifests itself in a number of ways. First, there is a tendency for connections between different events to be omitted; Flaubert favours the use of asyndetic constructions which, as Barthes's comments on their use in *Bouvard et Pécuchet* suggest, have a powerfully subversive effect.[34] Secondly, motives are not uniformly or consistently explained. Thirdly, there are numerous gaps or silences in the narrative account when insufficient or scanty information is provided about an aspect of a character's experience that seems to be of potential interest or relevance. Although in the plans for the novel, Flaubert had painstakingly established plausible motives for the main actions of most of the characters and although he had also specified the links connecting the various events, when it came to preparing the final version, he seems to have sought to render motives opaque and to suppress explicit indications of causality.[35] Last-minute corrections of the manuscript copy frequently consist in the removal of explicit connections.[36] The effect of these various features of the novel for many readers is one of fragmentariness, each event seeming to be isolated from the rest, each experience seeming to be devoid of meaningful connection with other experiences, with the result that the novel as a whole verges perilously on incoherence. It has been argued, however, that the effect of the suppressions and omissions in the narrative account is not automatically to produce a breakdown of causality at the level of *histoire*. According to W. Moser, an involuntary reflex leads the reader to seek to reconstitute a logical, causally-connected sequence of events.[37] Moser arguably underestimates the difficulty experienced by the reader in working out possible causal links, connections and motives, but his approach is a useful reminder that, as far as causality is concerned, what is true of *discours* is not necessarily true of *histoire*.[38]

If the reader experiences a certain degree of bewilderment when confronted by the at times incomplete account which is given of experience, it is in no small measure the result of the extent to which that account defers to the limited vision and understanding of Frédéric. Flaubert's use of point of view technique will be examined in the next chapter but at this stage it can be pointed out that frequently the information relayed to the reader is deliberately restricted to what is perceived or understood by Frédéric. Consequently, the connections between events, the identity of certain figures who appear in the narrative and the feelings and motives of other characters may often be blurred or obscured on account of the defective perception of the protagonist. In a way which is puzzling for the reader, the identity of the old lady seen at Rosanette's (p.134) and also that of the woman seen at Madame Dambreuse's (p.302) is never made clear. It is also common for the past lives of characters known to Frédéric to be left in complete or partial obscurity. Rosanette gives Frédéric some account of her early years but it is not necessarily fully reliable and, as has been pointed out,[39] we learn very little about Madame Arnoux's attitude to her husband in the early days of her marriage. But it is not just the lives of the characters before the main action of the novel begins which is left undefined. The precise nature of the relations between Rosanette and La Vatnaz, of the relations between Rosanette and her various protectors, Oudry, Delmar and the Prince, the nature of the association between Arnoux and Regimbart, and of that between Madame Dambreuse and Martinon are all unclear. In all of these cases, the uncertainty of the reader is not necessarily profoundly disturbing, however, since it is simultaneously indicative of Frédéric's own bewilderment.[40]

On several occasions, the element of uncertainty, corresponding to Frédéric's limited vision, is finally removed. Flaubert will often defer a full explanation, in some cases by several hundred pages. Thus we are not told until page 332 that it was Rosanette who was at the theatre with Arnoux on page 25. The reason for Madame Dambreuse's hostile treatment of Cécile, described on page 364, is only made clear on page 378 and an explanation of La Vatnaz's concern for Dussardier on page 338 is only provided on page 398. These and similar examples of cleavage between action and motivation[41] have often been felt to possess subversive force. Is it, however, a question of a deliberate dislocation, designed to heighten the impression that the narrative account is rejecting or postponing to the latest possible moment the demands of narrative coherence, or is it, rather, a question of Flaubert's wishing, once again, to respect the limitations of Frédéric's point of view?[42] In most cases, it is to be noted, the explanation is provided indirectly by the character concerned rather than by the narrator: the placing of these deferred 'motivations' is often itself motivated by a logic based upon occurrence within the experience of the protagonist. At times, however, Flaubert is straining against the very limits of acceptability. The elucidation of the brothel episode, for instance, occurs so long after the episode itself that the psychological justification – it is only at this late stage in their lives that Frédéric and Deslauriers focus their attention upon their youthful escapade – is not altogether convincing and Gleize may well be right in interpreting the repeatedly deferred explanation of the 'tête de veau' as a parody of a textual strategy which is in danger of being overworked.[43]

The reader may also be able to infer attitudes and motives which are obscure or misconstrued by Frédéric. It is not uncommon for there to be a clear discrepancy between the character's understanding and the narrator's, with the latter spelling out what is misunderstood by Frédéric.[44] More frequently however, the narrator does not explicitly correct or clarify, leaving the reader to make the appropriate inferences from the behavioural cues provided. For instance, when Frédéric visits Arnoux (pp.63–4) in the summer of 1841, there are clear indications – Arnoux's physical appearance, his brusque tone, the two glasses on the table, his 'singulier sourire' when Frédéric apologises for breaking Madame Arnoux's sunshade – that Arnoux has been disturbed in the midst of illicit love-making, yet Frédéric makes the wholly inappropriate request to see Madame Arnoux. Similarly, although we are not *told* that the paper in which Arnoux wraps the bouquet presented to his wife on her birthday is the note carried by Frédéric from La Vatnaz, the reaction of Madame Arnoux suggests that she has been given evidence of her husband's infidelity. It is clear to the reader, but not to Frédéric, that Rosanette is hoping to be taken to the races by someone else (p.203), that she has been bribed by Cisy to spend the night with him (p.214), that Madame Dambreuse has prevented Cécile from seeing her father when he is dying (p.379). In all these cases the non-specification of motives poses no problem, but rather serves to underline the blinkered nature of Frédéric's vision. It is noticeable, in fact, how often the failure to understand or perceive is located at the level of Frédéric's awareness rather than the reader's understanding. As a result of the way in which the text is littered with clues and hints, which are communicated over Frédéric's head, as it were, the reader is at times more likely to experience a sense of knowing superiority over Frédéric rather than the confusion and disorientation that some critics have stressed.

For the reader to make appropriate inferences a certain amount of material needs to be provided. There are, however, times when the narrative account dries up, preventing the reader from making the kind of shrewd guesses and reasonable assumptions we have been discussing. The 'silence' which is inaugurated by the withholding of essential or potentially relevant information threatens to create a gap in the reader's understanding. Thus, we are told tantalisingly little of Frédéric's visit to the brothel with Cisy:

> Alors le gentilhomme battit la campagne; il parla de Mlle Vatnaz, de l'Andalouse, et de toutes les autres. Enfin, avec beaucoup de périphrases, il exposa le but de sa visite: se fiant à la discrétion de son ami, il venait pour qu'il l'assistât dans une démarche, après laquelle il se regarderait définitivement comme un homme; Frédéric ne le refusa pas. Il conta l'histoire à Deslauriers, sans dire la vérité sur ce qui le concernait personnellement. (p.77)

With a certain coyness, the narrative refrains from describing a visit which, in the context of a novel which pays close attention to Frédéric's relations with women, might have been expected to assume more importance. Instead, only by implication does it exempt Frédéric from the charge of having 'betrayed' Madame Arnoux, the 'truth' as far as Frédéric is concerned being rather different from what Deslauriers takes it to be.[45] Different in kind are the gaps that open up when a considerable period of time is dismissed in a short textual space (see above). In the most famous of these (III vii) sixteen years of Frédéric's life are passed over in virtual silence. It would be wrong, however, to argue that such gaps are totally lacking in expressive value. The very absence of information, in fact, tells the reader a good deal about the uneventfulness of Frédéric's existence during the specified time.

The plot-structure of *L'Éducation sentimentale* is not threatened solely by the uncertainties, gaps and silences so far discussed. At times, it has been claimed, when Flaubert does give a specific reason for an action, the explanation is flimsy and unconvincing, making the reader aware of the artificiality of the combination of events contrived by the author. At the beginning of Part II Frédéric makes a series of rapid visits to various women and friends, allowing a wide range of milieux to be depicted. Rather than suggest that he moves from one to another in a totally haphazard fashion, the text attempts to motivate his comings and goings. Thus the stilted atmosphere of the Dambreuse salon leads to a desire for less affected surroundings ('et par besoin d'un milieu moins artificiel', p.132), while the pleasure experienced with Rosanette precipitates a longing for Madame Arnoux ('ce désir en éveilla un autre', p.135). For J. Gleize, 'ces motivations soulignent plutôt qu'elle ne suppriment l'absence de lien logique entre les actions successives, mises en rapport d'équivalence ...; ces séquences se suivent moins parce qu'elles découlent les unes des autres que parce qu'elles se ressemblent ou s'opposent'.[46] There can be little doubt that Flaubert sought to create a network of oppositions between the three visits but does this mean that there can be no logical nexus linking them? It could be argued that it is precisely because there are important differences of an 'aesthetic' order between the three milieux that it becomes feasible that Frédéric is drawn from one to another. Aesthetic pattern and psychological motivation need not necessarily be opposed.

The artificiality of the narrative line adopted is, however, exposed in a way few will be inclined to dispute by the extensive use made of chance encounters and coincidences. Although, as J. Proust has argued,[47] chance encounters and appearances may belong to hidden causal chains, their impact is to instate the fortuitous firmly in the narrative line followed by the novel, to some extent threatening the impression of necessary connection between events established in other ways. Characters in *L'Éducation sentimentale* often appear and disappear suddenly, a fact which endows them with a surreal, dream-like quality. The irruption of Rosanette into the orbit of Madame Arnoux in Part III, echoing the earlier scene at the races where their paths cross for the first time, is typical of the highly artificial, even implausible manner in which characters materialise on occasion – unannounced, unexpected, and with startling rapidity. The thematic implications of chance-encounters will be considered in a subsequent chapter; at this stage it is their role in problematizing the underlying causality of the plot which is important. As a result of the extent to which unlikely encounters and coincidences are used, we are made aware of 'plot' as an artificial, ultimately arbitrary combination of events, whose real 'logic' is connected with the novelist's artistic ends;[48] whether, however, this 'modernist' admission necessarily undermines all notion of an 'external' causality or subverts the psychological postulates of work is debatable. It is arguable that two different types of causality coexist and that the novel as a whole sets up a dual perspective.

Although the narrative text of *L'Éducation sentimentale* may be shorn of the regular indications of causal connection which help to establish in the reader's mind the idea of necessary and logical continuity between the various events which make up the plot, it does not follow that the novel is totally lacking in coherence. Moser is perhaps overstating the case when he speaks of 'les chaînons d'une seule ligne de succession déterministe qui relie les événements du roman',[49] but the sequence of states through which Frédéric Moreau passes does not emerge as totally haphazard but rather appears to be endowed with a kind of logical necessity. This is not to say that he exemplifies a 'classical' consistency, repeatedly confirming through his actions a clearly defined 'identity' attributed to him at the beginning of the novel.[50] Indeed, on the face of it, Frédéric is totally lacking in a sense of purpose, moves aimlessly from one shallow aim to another, never sustains his attention or devotion to anyone or anything. In the course of the novel he becomes preoccupied with four different women, turns to a wide variety of friends and takes up a series of different projects, artistic, financial and political. However, a novel which purports to detail the life of an inconsequential character need not itself be inconsequential. What, then, forms the basis for the coherence and logical continuity which are being claimed for the plot of the novel?

One possibility is suggested by the claims made by Frédéric that Madame Arnoux has always been at the centre of his life. The bald assertion, '"Je n'ai jamais aimé qu'elle"' (p.412) is amplified in the rhetorical declaration, '"vous êtes mon occupation exclusive, toute ma fortune, le but, le centre de mon existence, de mes pensées"' (p.270) and the conviction that 'elle faisait comme la substance de son cœur, le fond même de sa vie' (p.405). For Madame Arnoux too his reticence suggests ' "un hommage involontaire et continu" ' (p.422) and the narrator informs us that even when Frédéric appears completely bound up with Rosanette and Madame Dambreuse 'il y en avait une troisième toujours présente à sa pensée' (p.390). It is, however, difficult for the reader to accept at face value the various claims made on behalf of Frédéric's love for Madame Arnoux and few readers now would regard it as a golden thread upon which his indifferent, mediocre life is strung, if only because it initially almost peters out ('sa grande passion pour Mme Arnoux commençait à s'éteindre', p.26), rests subsequently on insubstantial foundations and is finally, to all practical purposes, eclipsed. Quite clearly the romantic myth of undying love does not correspond to the shifting reality of Frédéric's life as presented to the reader. This is not, however, to dismiss the possibility of a continuity related in some way to Madame Arnoux. Provided the terms in which it is viewed are modified, it is feasible to argue that the idealised image of Madame Arnoux provides the basis for the coherence and continuity of Frédéric's life, acting as a kind of lodestar around which his whole mental world revolves. Given an underlying and compulsive dependency operating at an unconscious level upon this idealised image, Frédéric's behaviour begins to take on a certain shape. In the welter of fragmented scenes and apparently disparate experiences, it is possible to trace a connecting thread. At the heart of each of his main actions lies a specific aim or intention vis-à-vis the idealised image enshrined in a kind of inner sanctuary. Frédéric's life – reduced to its bare outline – consists in a series of adjustments, made at an unconscious level more often than not, designed to placate or profane the 'psychic constellation connected with the mother'. Frédéric's contact with Madame Arnoux in Part I is minimal but the fact that for three years she is almost always absent does not prevent his life from being organised around her saintly image. In Part II his time is divided between Madame Arnoux and Rosanette, but his attitude to the latter seems to be largely dictated by her antithetical relationship to Madame Arnoux. Frédéric's relationship with Rosanette is a kind of prolongation of his relationship with Madame Arnoux which allows a gap – the gap separating Madame Arnoux and the idealised image nurtured by Frédéric – to be closed. Frédéric's final act in Part II clearly illustrates the way in which Madame Arnoux's presence is never more strongly felt than when she is physically absent. In Part III, the contact with Madame Arnoux is substantially reduced, yet even here, there is a strong sense of lingering obsession, expressing itself in both the problematic prolongation of his relationship with Rosanette, the sacrilegious raiding of the past to fuel the flagging feelings of the present and, perhaps most important of all, an ineradicable sense of falling off. If Frédéric's life in Part III loses much of its charge and is registered by him as a kind of decline, this is because he has largely ceased to minister to the commanding figure whose influence continues to be felt *in absentia*. From this point of view, the final meeting with Madame Arnoux confirms the postulate of an underlying continuity; if this occasion is worthy of discrimination, while the previous sixteen years had been elided in a few lines, it is because what ensures the coherence of the narrative – an abiding obsession with an idealised image – resurfaces.

Although it is possible to make out a case for the plot of *L'Éducation sentimentale* not being as disconnected as might appear at first sight, the problem of what overall meaning it supports remains. What is most profoundly disturbing about a novel whose title hints at lessons to be learnt and experiences from which the characters will emerge chastened, is that it is extremely difficult to extract from it any clear, unequivocal 'message', on account of what has been described as Flaubert's refusal 'to structure the story according to the demands of its explicit theme'.[51] Flaubert's choice of protagonist and of subject-matter have often perplexed critics but, in themselves, a mediocre hero and a dismal record of failure do not necessarily lead to a novel whose overall meaning eludes the reader, as the example of Balzac's *Un Début dans la vie* shows. While Balzac shows his tactless hero finally adjusting to the demands of society, having learnt the lessons of his initial mistakes,[52] Flaubert blocks any anticipated *Bildung* both by equivocating over the causes of Frédéric's failure and by leaving Frédéric little wiser at the end of the novel than at the beginning, with the result that the thematic implications of the hero's mediocrity remain problematic, as Culler has suggested: 'Frédéric's mediocrity poses an obstacle to intelligibility ... if his mediocrity explains his behaviour, it does so in a way that closes rather than opens thematic perspectives'.[53]

The reasons for the failure of the story of *L'Éducation sentimentale* to support clear thematic conclusions are varied. Inherent in the decision to portray the development of Frédéric Moreau over a prolonged period of time is the risk of monotony. Given the somewhat colourless character of the protagonist and the uneventful nature of much of his experience, it is perhaps inevitable that the account of his life will appear to meander in a rather inconsequential manner from one meaningless episode to the next. The plot of the novel continues rather than advances, lacking any apparent impetus to reach a clearly defined thematic goal. This apparent aimlessness of the story-line is compounded by a strong tendency towards repetition, underlining a problematic sameness in Frédéric's experience. While repetition in *Madame Bovary* helps to sustain the major oppositions of the novel, in *L'Éducation sentimentale* it works in a more subversive manner, according to J. Gleize: 'la répétition est ici organisatrice de l'histoire elle-même, une même conduite d'échec se répétant de façon compulsionnelle tout au long du roman; la linéarité du récit n'est ni progressive, ni dramatique, mais répétitive, statique'.[54] Although Flaubert frequently makes a character remember an earlier occasion which is being repeated, using the device he calls a 'rappel', the ultimately arbitrary nature of the narrative line is not concealed:

> La fréquence du processus de rémémoration par lequel Frédéric évoque le passé nous semble cependant moins importante pour la qualification psychologique du personnage que pour la caractérisation du récit, qui avoue ici que l'histoire est répétition d'elle-même, que sa progression n'est qu' apparente. La motivation psychologique ne 'naturalise' pas l'histoire, mais en désigne le caractère construit, et finalement arbitraire.[55]

Although the self-reflexive nature of repetition may not be as marked as Gleize suggests, there can be little doubt that the large number of occasions where one event recalls another, such as the two trips down the Champs-Elysées, while almost invariably marking a deterioration of one kind or another, does create the impression that the plot is getting bogged down. Although the reader may be able to perceive differences and variations between the separate occasions described, he is also aware of a problematic sameness which undermines any sense of meaningful development.

Although the repetition of similar events and reactions produces a sense of dreary sameness, the novel repeatedly shakes the reader out of the apathy this might give rise to by generating tension through the expectation that something significant is about to happen. The sense of expectation is whipped up most frequently in the context of Frédéric's relationship with Madame Arnoux. On several occasions Frédéric is shown desperately seeking her out, confident that the welcome she will

extend will be warmer. The actual encounter is delayed by the introduction of various kinds of difficulties designed to increase both
Frédéric's impatience and the reader's sense of expectation. Finally,
when it takes place, Frédéric's hopes are dashed and the reader, too, is
disappointed at the failure of Frédéric's relationship to progress as
anticipated. But, as the *scénarios* have shown, it is not just here that
Flaubert sets out to create a false sense of expectation.[56] In other
spheres, too, we are led into believing that Frédéric is about to make
headway, only to witness another setback, another rebuff. Frédéric's
various enterprises – business, artistic, intellectual – all come to nought,
in spite of the high hopes invested in him at the beginning of the novel,
and for different reasons he is unable to make any kind of progress with
Rosanette throughout most of Part II, while in Part III it is the expected
break which is long delayed. At times the reader is made to feel obscurely
let down by the text which perversely refuses to yield the meaning it
repeatedly promises. In this respect the reader's position in the experience of reading duplicates that of Frédéric in the experience of life.

The most critical point, the one at which the reader's expectations of
thematic resolution intensify, is the ending of the novel and it is at this
juncture that *L'Éducation sentimentale* becomes most elusive, most
resistant to the demands of traditional meaning. Madame Arnoux's final
visit, occurring as it does so many years later, raises a last flicker of hope
in the reader that Frédéric's fictional existence may yet end on a more
positive note and his relationship with Madame Arnoux be pushed to a
definitive conclusion. What takes place is not devoid of significance –
indeed it casts light retrospectively upon the whole course of their
relationship, as will be seen in a subsequent chapter – but in terms of the
reader's expectations, it is no different from what precedes. Once again,
Flaubert leads the reader to believe that the relationship is about to be
consummated,[57] only to defer fulfilment indefinitely. The value to be
placed upon Frédéric's definitive renunciation is not, however, clear and
the reader is left in an uncertain state of mind. Once again the reader's
experience runs parallel to the protagonist's; the withering 'Et ce fut
tout' conveys both Frédéric's disappointment at the way his 'grande
passion' has been reduced to such modest proportions and, at the same
time, can be read as an expression of narratorial dismay at the way a
potentially rich flow of experience has shrunk to such a derisory trickle.
The ambiguity of the ending of *L'Éducation sentimentale* is com-

pounded by the inclusion of an additional chapter which, as well as dividing the reader's interest,[58] breaks the symmetry of the novel in two ways: first, it means that Part III has a total of seven chapters while the other two Parts have six and secondly, placed at the very end of the novel, it prevents the novel beginning and ending with a scene involving Madame Arnoux.[59] The conversation that takes place between Frédéric and Deslauriers is disconcerting for a number of reasons and it is not altogether surprising that it baffled contemporary readers. Although, as will be seen in a subsequent chapter, there may be some useful distinctions made in the course of the discussion of the reasons for their failure, the main impression created is of an inability to understand or come to terms with their own inadequacies. The opposition between Frédéric and Deslauriers is not one which is immediately meaningful and the diagnosis of failure itself fails to convince the reader that either character has learnt much from his experience. Much more devastating, however, is the final gleeful evocation of the brothel episode, a daring compositional choice on Flaubert's part. Whichever way one interprets the final assessment of this episode, it has the effect of undermining the novel as a whole. If it is taken seriously, it detracts from the significance – for Frédéric and also for the reader – of the relationship with Madame Arnoux which had occupied a central place in his life, raising the question of why so much of the novel has been devoted to what is now declared to have been less rewarding than the visit to the brothel.[60] If, on the other hand, it is dismissed as a cynical comment which does not reflect the real views of the characters concerned, it throws into doubt the authority of a narrative account which ends on what may be a totally misleading and inaccurate assessment of experience, albeit that of the characters. What is perhaps most bizarre about the conclusion is that it places considerable thematic weight on an episode which not only took place before the main action of the novel begins but which also has been only briefly alluded to and then hundreds of pages earlier.[61]

The final chapter of *L'Éducation sentimentale* possesses a self-depreciatory, self-derogatory quality that works on several levels, systematically devaluing the experiences described in the novel, the characters who make the disabused assessment and the narrative account which gives such prominence to such an episode. The privileging of the brothel incident constitutes a profanatory dismissal of Frédéric's love for Madame Arnoux and a general disparagement of his relationships with other women. What possible reason, the reader wonders, is there for highlighting such an abortive incident? Is it because the two adolescents, without appreciating their good fortune, escaped the clutches of members of a now despised sex? Is it on account of the poetry of non-fulfilment? Is it because, for once, heart and senses are not opposed? Is it perhaps as much for the quite unjustified opprobrium that is brought down upon them? It is perhaps significant that there is no obvious explanation, but what does none the less emerge strongly is a powerful feeling of disillusionment on their part when considering what life has had to offer them. Of course, the fact that Frédéric and Deslauriers take such a disabused view is itself a comment upon them. As one critic puts it, the characters 'achieve no wisdom and rather than learning from the past, compulsively relive it in memory'.[62] To think so highly of such an incident points, it might be felt, to an ineradicable immaturity, an inability to progress beyond an essentially adolescent attitude to the opposite sex. In many ways, Frédéric regresses rather than progresses and his final fixation upon a scene from his late childhood suggests that he has never been able to grow up. Most damagingly, however, the last episode constitutes a bleakly despairing assessment of the novel itself which has chosen to concentrate on such unrewarding lives and such undistinguished characters.

It would be foolish to underestimate the challenge posed by Flaubert's manipulation of the events which make up the plot of L'Éducation sentimentale. The idea that he has simply done away with time, continuity, coherence and thematic significance needs, however, to be queried. It should not be assumed that simply because a novelist departs decisively from the traditional type of plot he is necessarily seeking to eliminate its basic ingredients. There is much that is problematic about the plot of L'Éducation sentimentale, as has been seen, and Flaubert makes few concessions to easy readability. Yet, at the level of histoire, certain features are preserved; time does seem to flow monotonously on; it is possible to connect the various phases through which Frédéric passes and, in spite of the gaps at the level of discours, it is possible to postulate a continuity and a coherence in his evolution. The reader may be at a loss over what to make of the ending of the novel but it is clearly not completely senseless; the puzzling and problematic element does not preclude a number of psychologically suggestive interpretations which will be discussed in a subsequent chapter. It might be noted, too, that the problematization of plot is bound up with the vivifying attempt at allowing the reader to enter and share Frédéric's subjective awareness to an unprecedented extent. Within the often distorted, limited and trivial perspective imposed by Frédéric's consciousness time, causality and coherence all begin to disintegrate; Flaubert's reliance upon this perspective is not so great, however, as will be seen in the next chapter, that it is not possible for the reader to correct the defects of his point of view and in so doing begin to restore what had been eroded by the choice of such a dim register of experience.

IV

Narrative Techniques

If *L'Éducation sentimentale* is a baffling novel, it is in no small part on account of the new narrative techniques employed by Flaubert. Flaubert's originality in this sphere has long been recognised; the various innovations associated with him together constitute what has been aptly termed a 'mutation' in the novel form.[1] The single, most far-reaching of these innovations is, of course, the technique of impersonality, which consists, essentially, in removing from the narrative account all traces of a recognisable personality. But he also developed the technique of point of view, presenting the world not from the 'objective' standpoint of an omniscient narrator, but from the 'subjective' viewpoint of one of the characters involved in the action. Lastly, he is responsible for the development of a whole range of devices, the controlled use of parallels and oppositions, an intensive system of internal reference, a highly suggestive symbolism, which enhance the expressive possibilities of the form and allow meaning to be communicated obliquely rather than being stated directly. It would be misleading to suggest that these various techniques were all totally new; what characterises the Flaubertian novel is a more systematic, self-conscious deployment of devices which had previously been used in a more spasmodic, less intensive manner. Flaubert's elaboration of a new narrative practice was not without its problems. The *Correspondance* testifies to the agonised questioning and endless difficulties experienced by him as he sought to reconcile contradictory needs and demands. It has already been seen that Flaubert was drawn both to analysis and synthesis, which he struggled to reconcile through the practice of 'hidden psychology'. But there are other conflicts –' between, for instance, a strong mimetic urge and an equally strong non-figurative tendency,[2] between an enduring quest for 'le mot juste' and a despairing sense of the inadequacy of language as a means of conveying experience, between a strong drive to alienate a bourgeois reading public and a desire to appeal to a select few, from Sainte-Beuve to George Sand. Such contradictions and tensions should lead us to expect not a perfectly consistent narrative practice, but rather divisions, internal conflicts and hesitations in the way the story is told. The narrative account offered by Flaubert is, as it were, traversed by different modes, pulled in different directions, swayed towards an experimental 'modernist' mode, held back by the constraints of traditional narrative practice.

Before examining the narrative techniques employed in *L'Éducation sentimentale*, it is necessary to establish some kind of 'model' of the way narrative works. The first and central assumption that can be made is that all narratives presuppose a narrator even though one may not be readily apparent, just as every utterance or record of an utterance presupposes a speaker even though the speaker may not be readily apparent. Although the notion that all narratives imply a narrator has been contested in certain quarters, the arguments in favour of accepting it seem overwhelming.[3] In some cases, of course, there can be no possible doubt; in many narratives the narrator is clearly characterised. But even in 'third-person' narratives, in which no explicit reference is made to the narrator and in which the novel might seem to be approximating to 'pure' or narrator-less narration, the very availability of the narrative can only be accounted for by the postulate of a narrator. In addition, although the narrator may not refer to himself directly, his existence may still be apparent in certain types of expression which fall into the category of what linguists call 'discours'[4] and in certain functions that he assumes, such as the analysis of the inner life of characters.[5] The importance of the concept of the narrator is that it prevents the narrative account from being regarded as the direct expression of the 'author'. The voice that appears to be speaking in the narrative should not be equated with that of the actual person who wrote the novel. This is easy to accept in the case of so-called 'first-person' narratives, but is less obvious in the case of 'third-person' narratives where the narrator is often assumed to be the author. A strict narratological approach, however, insists on the distinction between the narrator who, inasmuch as he appears to be speaking the narrative account, can be considered to be an aspect of narrative discourse and the author who, although ultimately responsible for the creation of the novel, inhabits a different sphere beyond the novel.

Narrators can be classified in various ways, according to whether they participate in the action, develop a distinct personality, reveal all that they know, have access to the minds of the characters and so forth.[6] One of the most striking attributes of certain narrators is the omniscient ability to move freely in time and space, to penetrate into the recesses of the characters' minds. This type of 'omniscient narrator' enjoys a very special prerogative, an immunity to a certain kind of question: 'It is a peculiar property of fiction that the narrator is not necessarily subject to the question "How do you know?" when describing the inner world of characters.'[7] The exercise of this prerogative does not depend upon the narrator assuming a recognisable personality. Thus, even where a narrator is made to keep a low profile, his existence is incontrovertibly attested by the ready access to the inner world of characters which is provided. It should also be noted that omniscience docs not necessarily presuppose omnicommunicativeness.[8] A narrator may be assumed to know everything that takes place in the characters' minds and also to know what the future outcome of events will be, without being under an obligation to communicate that knowledge. As a story-teller he is thought to be entitled to withhold information in the interests of narrative suspense.

Endowed with the attribute of omniscience, the narrator has considerable powers and can be credited with a good deal of the information provided in the narrative account. There is, however, a limit to what can feasibly be attributed to him. Primarily a voice, the narrator's jurisdiction extends over what is made explicit in the narrative account but not over the way in which the account is organised. In order to explain the way in which a narrative may convey more than is actually stated by the narrator, it is necessary to adduce the concept of the implied author. Originally coined by Wayne Booth, this term has taken on a very specific meaning in recent narrative theory. Not so much the 'author's second self' or an extension of the author in the work, it is first and foremost a textual construct in the definition proposed by Rimmon-Kenan: 'the implied author must be seen as a construct inferred and assembled by the reader from all the components of the text. Indeed, speaking of the implied author as a construct based on the text seems to me far safer than imagining it as a personified "consciousness" or "second self".'[9] The distinction between the implied author and the narrator is clearly outlined by Seymour Chatman:

> Unlike the narrator, the implied author can *tell* us nothing. He, or better, *it* has no voice, no direct means of communicating. It instructs us silently,

through the design as a whole, with all the voices, by all the means it has chosen to let us learn.[10]

Whether or not it is appropriate to think of the implied author as involved, like the narrator, in the narrative transaction is the subject of debate; Chatman and others place the implied author between the real author and the narrator within what has now become a widely accepted model of communication, but there is some force to Rimmon-Kenan's objection that the implied author, since by definition he is voiceless and silent, 'cannot literally be a participant in the narrative communication situation'.[11]

It is generally agreed, however, that the implied author, whether or not he can meaningfully be considered as engaged in communication with an implied reader, functions as a necessary peg upon which to hang norms and values that differ from those of the narrator. In the case of many 'first-person' narratives the values of the narrator are not those which are promoted by the work as a whole. In the case of 'third-person' narratives the narrator is less likely to be 'unreliable' but this does not necessarily mean that the values which emerge can be automatically attributed to him. Much that serves to create the meaning of the work – structural contrasts, symbolism etc. – cannot be viewed as the product of the narrator's activity, falling rather within the purview of the implied author. The way in which the work is organised, the compositional choices which have been made, the type of narration adopted can all be attributed to the implied author. No more than the narrator, the implied author cannot be equated with the real author, the flesh-and-blood creature who actually composed the work. That there is a close relationship between implied author and real author cannot be doubted but to insist on a distinction between the two is not just splitting narratological hairs. The implied author, belonging to the domain of fiction, is a textual construct and, as such, different in kind from the real author.[12]

If we bear these distinctions in mind when examining Flaubert's narrative technique, we will be in a better position to grasp its contradictory quality. Impersonality, as understood by Flaubert, consists in the suppression of the author's feelings and opinions leading to the apparent elimination of the novelist from the novel. In narratological terms, however, it is achieved primarily by preventing the narrator from assuming a recognisable personality. Debarred from expressing opinions or passing judgments on the characters, the Flaubertian narrator is scarcely perceptible and does not constitute himself as a recognisable figure. However, although he is not allowed to grow to the proportions of the expansive Balzacian narrator, he cannot be said to have been completely eliminated. The narrator's inconspicuousness becomes his defining feature; he must be postulated if someone is to assume the mantle of objectivity. It is also necessary to adduce the notion of the narrator in order to account for the omniscient insight which is repeatedly granted into the lives of the characters. It can only be the narrator who knows the important things that have happened to them, who can follow their fortunes over the years, who can see into their minds, who can understand their motives and their feelings. The omniscience of the Flaubertian narrator is, as we shall see, restricted in various ways but omniscience as an attribute is indivisible, with the result that the various restrictions imposed do not detract from the potential capacity which is an indisputable mark of the narrator's existence.

Although the narrator may be prevented from expressing opinions, it cannot be said that no values emerge from the novel. Flaubert did not wish to block all communication between himself and the reader as the following statements makes clear:

> Je ne crois même pas que le romancier doive exprimer *son* opinion sur les choses de ce monde. Il peut la communiquer, mais je n'aime pas à ce qu'il la dise.

> Quelle forme faut-il prendre pour exprimer parfois son opinion sur les choses de ce monde, sans risquer de passer, plus tard, pour un imbécile? Cela est un rude problème.[13]

Although the narrator is not allowed to express his opinions, certain opinions may, none the less, be conveyed to the reader. One way of explaining this paradox is provided by the notion of the implied author. If the text does communicate certain opinions in spite of the silencing of the narrator, it is a result of the good offices of the implied author. Flaubert's repeated assimilation of the novelist's presence in his work to that of God in creation can be interpreted in narratological terms; the narrator, 'visible nulle part', is subjected to a process of compression, while the implied author, 'présent partout', undergoes the opposite process of expansion.[14]

Other functions of the vanishing narrator are taken over by character. To an unprecedented degree, Flaubert chooses to present the inner thoughts, feelings and perceptions of his characters, allowing the world and other characters to be filtered through the medium of Emma's or Frédéric's consciousness. Rather than give the narrator's 'objective' view of events, Flaubert often prefers to present the character's 'subjective' view in a fully focalised account. We see the world through the eyes of Emma and, to an even greater extent, through the eyes of Frédéric. The extent to which character takes over the functions of the narrator when point of view technique is used should not be overstated. As Genette points out, a crucial distinction needs to be made between 'qui voit' and 'qui parle'; although it may be the character's view of events which is recorded, it is the narrator who is ultimately responsible for putting this view into words and conveying it to the reader.[15]

The redistribution of functions between narrator, implied author and character is responsible for much that is disconcerting in *L'Éducation sentimentale*. Narratorial effacement produces an impression of blankness; the fictional world, which is rarely explained or valorised by the narrator, takes on a gratuitous and opaque quality. Deferring to the awareness of Frédéric, with its multiple deficiencies and blindspots leads to a radical subjectivisation and destabilisation of the external world and other characters. What is seen through Frédéric's eyes is blurred, partially registered, misconstrued, fragmented. The world becomes a sliding décor ('et les deux berges . . . filèrent', p.3), an unreal 'spectacle' (p.290), a meaningless fantasmagoria of fleeting impressions and fantasised fulfilment. The effect of the off-loading of narratorial functions is to require a much greater effort on the part of the reader who must attempt to 'correct' Frédéric's distorted impressions and pick up the far fainter signals coming from the implied author. The reader is engaged in a double task – that of reconstructing from the fragmented impressions of Frédéric a coherent fictional world and, at the same time, that of making some kind of sense, with the help of the implied author, of the long-drawn-out and apparently desultory development of the protagonist.

Although it depicts in some detail the historical events of 1840–51, the main emphasis in *L'Éducation sentimentale* falls upon the inconsequential thoughts, hesitant feelings, mixed motives and ineffectual responses of Frédéric Moreau. It is principally, but by no means exclusively, his life and development which are depicted, his impressions which are relayed and his 'case' which is regarded as profoundly symptomatic. A wide variety of methods lend depth and variety to the protagonist's inner life. Within a broadly omniscient account, Flaubert ranges from explicit analysis to an extremely subtle art of suggestion. For much of the time Frédéric's thoughts and impressions are conveyed in full using various techniques, the most famous of which is *style indirect libre*; this means that for much of the time he is a subject with whom both narrator and reader coincide. An important part of Flaubert's technique, however, is the systematic if intermittent dissection of his hero's feelings and motives which turns him into an object of psychological investigation to be observed by a dispassionate narrator and attentive reader.[16] But even in the process of practising his dissective art, Flaubert will allow the scalpel to falter or be hurriedly laid aside. It is at such moments that the implied author comes into his own. Where there is a gap or silence in the narrator's account, where the reader is left uncertain about what Frédéric is feeling, another relationship comes into play. In order to complement a defective narratorial account the reader seeks information elsewhere, information whose dispersal throughout the text is organised by the implied author. The suggestive possibilities latent in the symbolism and the aesthetic patterning of the work are limitless; one of the reasons why *L'Éducation sentimentale* yields itself so readily to re-reading is that on one level there is much that is left unsaid but at another level there is a vast amount of material and a considerable combinatorial potential which facilitate a process of divination, of plumbing hidden depths, of grasping fine shades of feeling.

Whatever Flaubert's reluctance to allow the narrator to become too prominent in the text, he was not willing to expunge statements of an analytic nature altogether. Indeed, passages of omniscient analysis are surprisingly numerous. The most conspicuous of these passages are the extended dissections of Frédéric's underlying psychological state over a prolonged period of time. A good example of this type of sustained 'analyse morale' is the following:

> Bien qu'il connût Mme Arnoux davantage (à cause de cela, peut-être), il était encore plus lâche qu'autrefois. Chaque matin, il se jurait d'être hardi. Une invincible pudeur l'en empêchait; et il ne pouvait se guider d'après aucun exemple, puisque celle-là différait des autres. Par la force de ses rêves, il l'avait posée en dehors des conditions humaines. Il se sentait, à côté

d'elle, moins important sur la terre que les brindilles de soie s'échappant de ses ciseaux. (p.172)

The narrator, in this passage, focuses his attention not on Frédéric's reactions on a specific occasion but on his habitual responses to Madame Arnoux, the underlying causality of which is clearly brought out. Although there is a possibility that we are occasionally being given Frédéric's rationalisation of his own hesitancy ('et il ne pouvait se guider d'après aucun exemple . . . '), the reader has little doubt about attributing the bulk of the analysis to the narrator since it offers an iterative account of Frédéric's behaviour and a central insight ('Par la force de ces rêves, il l'avait posée en dehors des conditions humaines') which, had Frédéric been able to arrive at it, would have made him behave differently. Similar examples of sustained psychological analysis are common in the 'panoramic' sections of the novel; Flaubert has no compunction about allowing the narrator to adopt an overtly explanatory tone with regard to the underlying motivation of recurrent behaviour.[17]

In a number of important passages the narrator has considerable success in his attempts at disentangling mixed, multiple or conflicting reactions. Sometimes the analysis builds up gradually to the specification of the motive which is most difficult to define:

et il resta là, jusqu'à minuit, sans savoir pourquoi, par lâcheté, par bêtise, dans l'espérance confuse d'un événement quelconque favorable à son amour. (p.66)

Or the struggle between conflicting tendencies may be carefully recorded:

il se mit en route, se substituant à Frédéric et s'imaginant presque être lui, par une singulière évolution intellectuelle où il y avait à la fois de la vengeance et de la sympathie, de l'imitation et de l'audace. (p.246)

But the scrupulous determination to identify all the component motives is best illustrated by the sustained scrutiny of a crucial reaction – Frédéric's final renunciation of Madame Arnoux:

Cependant, il sentait quelque chose d'inexprimable, une répulsion, et comme l'effroi d'un inceste. Une autre crainte l'arrêta, celle d'en avoir dégoût plus tard. D'ailleurs, quel embarras ce serait! – et tout à la fois par

> prudence et pour ne pas dégrader son idéal, il tourna sur ses talons et se mit à faire une cigarette. (p.423)

The analysis here moves with ease from the realm of obscure inhibition, of which Frédéric himself has little knowledge, through less deep-seated reaction and considerations to the brief snippet of *style indirect libre* which articulates the most superficial and disreputable element in Frédéric's rejection, blending conscious and unconscious, basely practical and persistently idealistic strands into a rich and persuasive whole.

Fairly common also are shorter passages in which the motives of characters at specific moments are examined. The most frequent form used to present motives is the construction with 'par' followed by an abstract noun, as in the following examples:

> L'après-midi, par desœuvrement, elle découpait des fleurs dans un morceau de toile perse . . . ; (p.145)

> Frédéric conservait ses projets littéraires, par une sorte de point d'honneur vis-à-vis de lui-même; (p.147)

> Par l'exercice d'un tel mensonge, leur sensibilité s'exaspéra; (p.273)

> Pas esprit de domination, elle voulut que Frédéric l'accompagnât le dimanche à l'Église. (p.391)

There are over fifty examples of this construction being used by the narrator in rapid identifications of the motives, usually straightforward, of a wide range of characters. The brief and confident ascription of motives signals the availability of the minds of all the characters for omniscient inspection; the fact that in many cases we are not told much more about the inner life of the character does not betoken ignorance on the part of the narrator but rather reflects his desire to give preferential treatment to Frédéric.

Causal constructions, usually introduced by 'car', are found comparatively infrequently. In some cases the nature of what is being explained is trivial or superficial but there are occasions when important insights are conveyed:

> Aucun misérable ne passait; et sa velléité de dévouement s'évanouit, car il n'était pas homme à en chercher au loin les occasions; (p.137)

> et ses progrès furent rapides, car il les abordait avec des forces jeunes et dans l'orgueil d'une intelligence qui s'affranchit; (p.14)

Bien qu'on l'aimât tout à l'heure, on le haïssait maintenant, car il représentait l'Autorité; (p.29)

Deslauriers ... dissimula son dépit, – car il conservait par obstination quelque espérance encore du côté de Mme Arnoux. (p.261)

The reactions of characters here are rooted in personal qualities of which they themselves can hardly be thought to be aware, making it possible to attribute the explanation that is given to the narrator.

'Pour' and 'afin de', on the other hand, are used on several occasions to describe the intention underlying a given course of behaviour:

Alors, par un raffinement de haine, pour mieux outrager en son âme Mme Arnoux, il l'emmena jusqu'à l'hôtel de la rue Tronchet; (p.284)

pour faire au défunt une sorte de réparation, il s'offrit à le veiller lui-même; (p.379)

Pour lui cacher cette déception, il se posa par terre à ses genoux; (p.422)

Et, comme il cherchait son regard, Mme Arnoux, afin de l'éviter, prit sur une console des boulettes de pâte ... ; (p.197)

An even less conspicuous way of indicating motives is the frequent use of participles:

Mais, le voyant loin des théories de Sénécal, il était plein d'indulgence; (p.179)

N'ayant plus rien à attendre du capitaliste, il lâchait son protégé; (p.389)

Mais, sa passion devenant plus forte, elle avait exigé une rupture; (p.390)

Il ne parla pas d'elle, retenu par une pudeur; (p.15)

mais il la déchira, et ne fit rien, ne tenta rien, – immobilisé par la peur de l'insuccès; (p.23)

Elle acceptait ces caresses, figée par la surprise et par le ravissement. (p.269)

Equally unobtrusive are phrases designating a state of mind which precipitates a course of action:

il ne dit rien de l'héritage, – dans la peur de nuire à son passé; (p.110)

Mais il n'osait faire sa réclamation, – par mauvaise honte, et dans la crainte qu'elle ne fût inutile; (p.185)

A la nouvelle de sa blessure, elle était accourue chez lui dans l'intention de la reprendre. (p.398)

The commonest form of omniscient statement concerning the inner life is the rapid identification of the emotion a character experiences, with little attempt to refine or qualify what is meant by the single abstract noun used. In this type of presentation emotions seem to be overtaking the characters. Sometimes neutral formulae, often using the verb 'éprouver', are used,[18] but it is far more common for the narrator to employ expressions which imply that the character has no choice but to be swamped by a given emotion. Frequently the emotion in question is the subject of the sentence and is coupled with a verb such as 'envahir', 'saisir', 'gagner' or 'prendre':

Une lâcheté immense envahit l'amoureux de Mme Arnoux; (p.261)
Une haine l'envahit contre les riches; (p.186)
Une sorte de jalousie l'envahit; (p.393)

une joie l'avait saisi; (p.62)
une peur l'avait saisi; (p.253)

Puis une torpeur la gagna; (p.402)
Cet enthousaisme le gagnait; (p.180)
une angoisse intolérable le gagnait; (p.279)

Un remords le prit; (p.24)
une grande hésitation le prit; (p.63)
une pitié le prit; (p.362)
une pudeur le prit. (p.379)

Passive constructions with the same verbs are also repeatedly found:

Il fut saisi par un de ces frissons de l'âme . . . ; (p.49)
Frédéric fut saisi par l'étonnement. . . ; (p.76)
Frédéric fut saisi d'une espèce de remords; (p.217)

Deslauriers . . . , gagné par le délire du cancan . . . ; (p.71)
Frédéric . . . , fut gagné par la démence universelle; (p.302)

il fut pris de tendresse pour cette homme; (p.42)
il fut pris d'attendrissement; (p.48)
il fut pris par une angoisse. (p.191)

The frequency of this type of expression contributes powerfully to the strong impression of a generation of men with little or no control over their own emotions.

Lastly, a steady omniscient gaze is focused upon inter-personal relations; the narrator repeatedly defines the impact of one character upon another in a confident, economical manner. The relations between Frédéric and Deslauriers, in particular, are examined in an extremely succinct fashion:

L'amertume de son ami avait ramené sa tristesse.(p.17)
Frédéric s'était senti troublé par l'amertume de Deslauriers. (p.114)

But the impact of the various women in Frédéric's life is also conveyed at times through rapid analysis:

lassé, énervé, vaincu enfin par la terrible force de la douceur . . . ; (p.92)

la contemplation de cette femme l'énervait; (p.67)

toute sa personne avait quelque chose d'insolent, d'ivre et de noyé qui exaspérait Frédéric . . . ; (p.213)

Cette certitude anticipée de ce qu'il regardait comme une belle action déplut au jeune homme. (p.386)

As one might expect, it is almost invariably Frédéric's reactions to others which are outlined, there being few occasions when the impact of his behaviour on them is recorded.[19] The predominance of the former stems partly from the fact that he is the main character, partly from his passivity; Frédéric is someone who is acted upon by others rather than someone who acts upon others.

Although there are a substantial number of occasions when the narrator makes statements of an analytic nature, the overall impression given by the novel is not one of confident dissection. In spite of the existence of analytic passages, the reader does not have the sense that Frédéric's reactions are being clearly and firmly anatomised, as Raitt points out: 'La mobilité de l'analyse qui caractérise le roman est particulièrement apparente dans le flux et le reflux des sentiments de

Frédéric qui se noient dans l'incertitude et l'ambivalence'.[20] But why, if
the narrator does engage in intermittent analysis, is the reader left with
the impression that nothing is being clearly defined? The answer lies, in
part, in the way in which the narrator practises analysis, in particular in
the problematic introduction of a note of uncertainty in analytic passages. The narrator often appears to be reflecting on various possibilities,
speaking of the character's inner motivation as if it were something
inherently obscure or extremely complex. This dubitative tone atten-
uates the narrator's omniscience, without, however, dissolving it completely. Frequently the narrator continues to enjoy total omniscience
with respect to what a character experiences while enjoying only limited
omniscience with respect to why he experiences it. Although he may
appear momentarily to be interpreting motives from the outside, normally he presents the flow of experience from within. It has also been
argued that the dubitative tone suggests the narrator's lack of solidarity
with his own account.[21] Such an impression inevitably conflicts with the
customarily close and attentive attitude of the narrator to his material.
What emerges most strongly, however, is the sense that the narrator
himself is experiencing the limits of his omniscience; Flaubert's narrator,
at the critical point of his analytical investigation, when the reader
expects him to proceed with surgical confidence in the examination of the
reactions of his character, appears to experience a debilitating loss of
nerve which makes him unable to complete his dissection with the
requisite degree of aplomb.

The commonest way in which the narrator expresses an element of
doubt is by inserting 'peut-être' or 'sans doute' into his account. This may
be in connection with thoughts or feelings but may equally well be
associated with motives:

Frédéric s' excitait intérieurement à le mépriser encore plus, pour bannir,
peut-être, l'espèce d'envie qu'il lui portait; (p.123)

il se lança même jusqu'à faire *Prudhomme sur une barricade*, peut-être par
l'effet d'une jalousie naïve contre ces bourgeois qui avaient bien dîné;
(p.348)

et Frédéric (cela tenait sans doute à des ressemblances profondes) éprouvait
un certain entraînement pour sa personne; (p.173)

Mme Dambreuse, pour l'en distraire sans doute, redoublait d'attentions.
(p.413)

It is also common for alternative possibilities to be suggested:

> M. de Cisy, pour s'éclairer sans doute, ou donner de lui une bonne opinion, se mit à dire doucement . . . ; (p.139)

> Sénécal, par sentiment du devoir ou besoin de despotisme, s'écria de loin . . . ; (p.198)

> Martinon, ne croyant pas que cela fût vrai, ou trop avancé pour se dédire, ou par un de ces entêtements d'idiot qui sont des actes de génie, répondit que . . . . (p.368)

The narrator will also add another possible motive as if it were an afterthought:

> et puis il aimait mieux Frédéric dans la médiocrité. (p.267)

> et puis le charme de sa personne lui troublait le cœur plus que les sens; (p.273)

> Et puis il craignait peut-être d'en trop apprendre. (p.391)

Lastly, the use of 'une sorte de' is used to suggest the difficulty the narrator has in defining the precise nature of the motive in question:

> Elle n'aimait pas à entendre blâmer le Gouvernement, par une sorte de prudence anticipée; (p.11)

> Il était empêché, d'ailleurs, par une sorte de crainte religieuse; (p.200)

> Quelquefois une sorte de pudeur sexuelle les faisait rougir l'une devant l'autre. (p.273)

Although such passages, in which an element of uncertainty is apparent, may cast doubt on the extent of the narrator's omniscient powers, they also help to create the impression that there is a whole domain of psychological reality where complexity is of the essence.

Another of the most unsettling aspects of Flaubert's use of the analytic mode is the frequent uncertainty over who is analysing. On occasion it is quite clear that the character is engaging in deliberation. The following passage conveys Deslauriers's suspect calculations about Madame Arnoux's likely behaviour: 'Par vengeance ou besoin d'affection, elle se réfugierait vers lui' (p.169). Or it may be quite clearly the narrator who is engaging in analytic activity, as has been seen above. But it is far from uncommon for there to be a real ambiguity; the reader is left wondering whether it is Frédéric or the narrator who is engaging in analytic speculation in the following passages:

> Pour se venger de son maître, sans doute, le garçon se contenta de sourire; (p.108)

> elle caressait les floches rouges d'un écran japonais, pour faire valoir ses mains, sans doute . . . . (p.131)

On many occasions the issue is trivial but the ambiguity at times extends to central questions about the nature of Frédéric's attachment to Madame Arnoux:

> Il souhaitait connaître les meubles de sa chambre, toutes les robes qu'elle avait portées, les gens qu'elle fréquentait; et le désir de la possession physique même disparaissait sous une envie plus profonde, dans une curiosité douloureuse qui n'avait pas de limites. (p.6–7)

This passage can be read either as accurate narratorial analysis of Frédéric's tendency to sublimate desire or as the character's deluded view of his own response.[22] Similarly, the analysis of Frédéric's religious responses is ambiguous:

> Ce n'était pas la vanité qui le poussait à faire cette aumône devant elle, mais une pensée de bénédiction où il l'associait, un mouvement de cœur presque religieux. (p.8)

Once again it is critical whether it is the narrator or the character himself who is making the point; if it is the former, then we are given a strong impression of a love which, transcending the physical, fulfils something akin to a religious need. If, however, it is the latter, we are more aware of the essentially bogus nature of Frédéric's feelings and of his inability to come to terms with their true nature. Different readers will be inclined to interpret these passages in different ways but there is nothing in the text itself which allows either one or the other to be declared indisputably 'correct'. Indeed, it may well be that the only solution is a dual reading which keeps both possibilities alive, playing one off against the other.

The last and arguably most disconcerting aspect of the use of the analytic mode is the complete suppression of analysis at a juncture when it would normally be expected to be operative. The failure to provide any explanation of motives at key junctures is likely to strike the reader as capricious in view of the existence of analysis elsewhere. Generally speaking, Frédéric's motives and inner states are made clear. The explicit analysis of his 'case' is, however, taken only so far. Repeatedly Frédéric's sexual inhibitions and hesitancy are made clear but there is little attempt to account for them. The omniscient narrator has a limited competence in the sphere of unconscious motivation. It is, however, the behaviour of other characters which is analysed in a disconcertingly intermittent manner. The narrator may at times give a firm omniscient account of the motives of minor characters, as has been seen, but when he keeps close to Frédéric's point of view, the behaviour of minor characters is often shorn of explanation with the result that at times it takes on an abrupt or puzzling quality.[23]

In spite of the uncertainty which characterises the analytic mode, the assertion made by one critic that Frédéric's consciousness is 'largely opaque as an object',[24] is questionable. The nature of our knowledge of Frédéric's inner life has changed significantly, has become more tentative, but it has not ceased altogether to possess an analytic dimension. It would, however, be wrong to suggest that there is a preponderance of analysis in the presentation of the inner life; the most frequent strategy is for consciousness to be presented rather than analysed, with the aid of a range of methods. When he wishes to give prominence to a particular thought or impression, Flaubert makes use of direct 'speech' or quotation, even where the thought is clearly unspoken:

'Cependant, il aime la sienne!' songeait Frédéric; (p.232)

Frédéric l'attira sur ses genoux et il se dit: 'Quelle canaille je fais!' en s'applaudissant de sa perversité; (p.373)

Mais il eut honte de cette perfidie, et, une minute après: 'Bah! est-ce que j'ai peur?' (p.245)

In some cases the phrase introducing the direct speech is suppressed and the context alone determines to whom the reflection belongs:

C'était comme une désertion immense.
'Il va se marier! est-ce possible!'
Et un tremblement nerveux la saisit. (p.248)

Une angoisse abominable le saisit à l'idée d'avoir peur sur le terrain.

'Si j'étais tué, cependant? Mon père est mort de la même façon. Oui, je serai tué.' (p.227)

In this type of construction consciousness is represented with the absolute minimum of narratorial interference; the words used are exactly the ones which the character would use. But precisely for this reason it is employed sparingly by Flaubert, since what can be articulated is restricted by the degree of awareness and linguistic skill of the character.

Indirect speech, similarly, is subject to the constraints of the verbal skill of the character in question but the change of pronouns and the back-shifting of tenses involves a certain amount of narratorial interference. Examples of indirect speech being used to present consciousness can be found but they are comparatively rare,[25] Flaubert generally preferring the form of presentation which is closely associated with his writing, *style indirect libre*. *Style indirect libre* is to indirect speech as the second type of direct quotation of thoughts (i.e. with the *inquit* clause suppressed) is to the first type. It has been the subject of a vast amount of critical investigation, both as a general device and as a characteristic form of Flaubertian intervention in the thought-processes of his characters.[26] What follows is inevitably a brief and selective account of a subject about which much more could be said. The grammatical characteristics are easy to define; narratorial manipulation is reflected in the change of first-person to third-person pronouns and in the back-shifting of tenses while the character's perspective is apparent in the use of deictics,[27] the appearance of definite articles and pronouns without antecedents and the use of emotional and descriptive terms. It has been argued by a minority of critics that *style indirect libre* is a type of discourse without a narrator,[28] but the generally held view is that the narrator is merely effacing himself or merging with the character.[29] One of the best characterisations is provided by R. Pascal: 'It reproduces the inner processes of character, expressed in the same syntactic form as objective narration and embedded firmly within the narratorial account, but evoking the vivacity, tone and gestures, of the characters.'[30] The disappearance of the narrator can, in fact, be only a passing illusion, since the character cannot be deemed responsible for the narrative account: 'the narrator appears to withdraw from the scene and thus present an illusion of a character's acting out his mental state in an immediate relation with the reader'.[31]

Logically, the narrator must be assumed to be operating in *style indirect libre* – albeit with a minimum of interference – for the words on the page are never those the character would use; the change of person and the back-shifting of tenses constitute an incontrovertible grammatical indication of the role of the narrator in articulating the awareness of character. This is not to say that there is no fusion or confusion of voices; as Genette puts it 'le narrateur assume le discours du personnage, ou si l'on préfère, le personnage parle par la voix du narrateur, et les deux instances sont alors confondues'.[32] *Style indirect libre* is an inherently ambiguous and mixed mode and has proved to be an extremely versatile tool. It lends itself to the representation of all types of awareness, ranging from the lucid and fully verbalised, through confused states of rêverie, dreams and hallucinations, to levels of awareness below the verbal; it can also be used as a vehicle for rendering a wide range of perceptions in what has been called 'substitutionary perception' or 'vision by proxy'; while appearing to defer to the perspective of character, it allows narratorial attitudes (sympathy, irony) to be insinuated.[33]

Style indirect libre is a central feature of Flaubert's narrative strategy. Alison Fairlie suggests that it 'helps to solve the problem of how to convey with savour and precision the experience of characters who have themselves little command over words, for the author can move almost imperceptibly between their semi-inarticulate conceptions and his own more exact and heightened expression of them.'[34] It has also been pointed out that *style indirect libre* is the most obvious way in which Flaubert achieves imaginative self-submergence in the experiences of his characters.[35] But perhaps the most important advantage of *style indirect libre* is that it allows Flaubert to be simultaneously involved and detached, treading the perilous tightrope that is suspended over clinical remoteness on the one hand and total immersion on the other. *Style indirect libre* allows the narrator to get close to character but not so close that the vitalising process of implicit denunciation and necessary omniscient distantiation are suspended. Lastly, it is the systematic use of *style indirect libre* which allows Flaubert to fulfil his central aim, which is to 'représenter un état psychologique'; *style indirect libre* is an essential vehicle of psychological penetration.[36]

There are occasions when *style indirect libre* is used in a sustained way but, as a rule, it is interwoven with other modes and usually of short duration. The following passage is typical:

'Comme vouz voudrez', dit Frédéric qui, affaissé dans le coin de la berline, regardait à l'horizon le milord disparaître, sentant qu'une chose irréparable venait de se faire et qu'il avait perdu son grand amour. Et l'autre était là, près de lui, l'amour joyeux et facile! Mais, lassé, plein de désirs contradict-oires et ne sachant même plus ce qu'il voulait, il éprouvait une tristesse démesurée, une envie de mourir. (p.208)

The transition from dialogue to narrative is smoothly affected and the focus shifts from physical posture indicative of despair to the inner feelings of Frédéric, which are clearly summarised, paving the way for the brief snippet of *style indirect libre* ('Et l'autre était là . . . '). Only for a brief moment do narrator and reader coincide with Frédéric's conscious-ness, as the last sentence immediately presents him not as a subject but as an object, whose confused state of mind and emotional reactions are meticulously described. Flaubert often builds up gradually to *style indirect libre*, reserving it to articulate a precise thought or impression:

En effet, le duel dont Rosanette se croyait la cause avait flatté son amour-propre. Puis elle s'était fort étonnée qu'il n'accourût pas se prévaloir de son action; et, pour le contraindre à revenir, elle avait imaginé ce besoin de cinq cents francs. Comment se faisait-il que Frédéric ne demandait pas en retour un peu de tendresse! C'était un raffinement qui l'émerveillait, et, dans un élan de cœur, elle lui dit: 'Voulez-vous venir avec nous aux bains de mer?' (p.259)

This passage begins with a rapid account of the reactions of Rosanette to the duel and Frédéric's delay in capitalising on it; there is no need to go into any detail in establishing her mistaken beliefs and readiness to complete her side of a non-existent bargain. But what is fully articulated in *style indirect libre* is the thought ('Comment se faisait-il . . . ') which richly reflects puzzlement, readiness to please, a disabused view of male expectations, generosity and admiration. 'Un peu de tendresse', could be narratorial euphemism or represent Rosanette's own wish to stress the emotional rather than the physical element in her relationship with Frédéric. The effect of this misplaced admiration upon her is then recorded, propelling her to the less than satisfactory (from Frédéric's point of view) proposition she makes in direct speech, which neatly pairs impractical and impulsive generosity with the muddled reflection con-veyed earlier.

Many more similar examples could be quoted. The important point to note is that Flaubert makes constant but sparing use of *style indirect libre*. Although for much of the novel he adopts Frédéric's point of view, he constantly changes his mode of presentation of this point of view, shifting rapidly, sometimes in mid-sentence, from *style indirect libre* to indirect speech or summary or analysis. The single piece of *style indirect libre* constitutes the point of greatest proximity between narrator and character but his momentary coinciding with the consciousness of the character appears to be a form of privileged and sympathetic delving only because it is surrounded by statements of a more detached or analytic cast. The characters whose inner thoughts are conveyed in *style indirect libre* belong to a different category from the rest, seeming on the whole more familiar. Thus Madame Arnoux is seen from the inside but her husband is not, in spite of the fact that he figures prominently in the narrative. Deslauriers stands out in the circle of Frédéric's friends not just because their friendship goes back to childhood days but also because his are the only thoughts rendered in *style indirect libre*. Thus, although a large number of characters remain relatively remote, though not, it must be stressed, totally opaque, a select few are more richly endowed with an inner life which analysis cannot fully dissect or Frédéric's consciousness distort.

There are, of course, other modes of presenting the inner life which are intermediate between the incisiveness of omniscient analysis and the intimacy of *style indirect libre*. The narrator will often describe an emotional state or summarise the content of mental activity. Such passages are close to, but distinguishable from, *style indirect libre*, as can be seen in the following example:

> Frédéric était resté seul. Il pensait à ses amis, et sentait entre eux et lui un grand fossé plein d'ombre qui les séparait. Il leur avait tendu la main cependant . . . . (p.143)

After the indicator of incipient reflection, the narrator conveys the broad impression that Frédéric arrives at as he thinks about his friends. At no moment, however, would Frédéric actually think or feel precisely what is recorded in the second sentence. The last sentence, however, gives a specific thought which is formulated in his mind. A large number of statements relating to Frédéric's inner life are not rewritable in the first person and hence cannot be regarded as representing the character's own interpretation according to the formula proposed by Barthes.[37] Verbs like 'sembler' or 'éprouver' mark narratorial summary:

Chaque mot qui sortait de sa bouche semblait à Frédéric être une chose nouvelle . . . ; (p.48)

Rosanette semblait un être si délicat, inconscient et endolori . . . qu'il se rapprocha d'elle . . . ; (p.315)

Frédéric n'osait retourner chez Mme Arnoux. Il lui semblait l'avoir trahie; (p.357)

le partage de ces reliques . . . lui semblait une atrocité; (p.414)

Jamais elle ne lui avait paru si captivante . . . ; (p.169)

et il éprouvait une sorte d'angoisse, comme ceux qui reviennent après de longs voyages; (p.243)

Cependant il éprouvait un plaisir de vanité immense; (p.350)

Et Frédéric s'applaudissait de son indépendance, comme s'il eût refusé un service à M. Dambreuse. (p.182)

While the gap separating the narrator's and the character's perspective and powers of verbal performance is often minimal in *style indirect libre*, in passages such as those above the narrator condenses and puts into words a perception, impression or experience that the character has but does not himself formulate. The character is, on the other hand, more than just an object of investigation as in analytic statements, since there is no probing beyond the terms in which the character himself apprehends his experience.

It would be wrong to suggest that the reader is given uninterrupted access to the inner life of Frédéric, either in the form of analysis, or in the form of the rendering or summarising of his impressions. There are moments when the narrative account becomes voluntarily restricted, confining itself to the description of physical gestures and facial expressions or the recording of brief utterances. This is not to say, however, that the reader is left completely in the dark about what the character is feeling. Intense emotion is repeatedly indicated by means of physical pointers such as trembling or loss of colour, often establishing ironic parallels between the anguish of different characters at different moments. Louise's trembling on discovering Frédéric's absence from Paris anticipates Madame Arnoux's on hearing he spends the night with Rosanette. But trembling is also the index of bliss: 'Mme Arnoux se mit à trembler de tous ses membres' (p.270). In some cases the echo is very strong:

> Le milord reparut, c'était Mme Arnoux. Elle pâlit extraordinairement; (p.208)

> Frédéric pâlit extraordinairement. (p.407)

In each case the character experiences a sense of irretrievable loss, Madame Arnoux when she sees Frédéric with Rosanette, Frédéric when he learns of the departure of the Arnoux. Among other emotions or attitudes unequivocally signalled by physical posture are sexual submissiveness ('Elle y restait, la taille en arrière, la bouche entr'ouverte, les yeux levés', p.423), impatience ('Frédéric fit deux ou trois tours dans la chambre. Il haletait, se mordait les lèvres . . .', p.404), availability ('Et posée sur une seule hanche, l'autre genou un peu rentrée, en caressant de la main gauche le pommeau de nacre de son epée, elle le considéra pendant une minute', p.118). Gestures, on occasion, are used to convey significant changes of heart; in the factory at Creil Madame Arnoux at first refuses to take Frédéric's arm (p.198) but after his spirited attack on Sénécal's treatment of the workers she takes it (p.199)

Attitudes are often clearly expressed in the form of direct utterances, from Madame Arnoux's telling ' "les rêves ne se réalisent pas toujours" ' (p.195) to Louise's ' "Est-ce que je peux vivre sans toi!" ' (p.253). The duel provokes Arnoux's revealing expression of affection ' "Ah, cher enfant!" ' (p.231) and Louise's sensuality is powerfully expressed in her appreciation of 'l'existence des poissons': ' "Ça doit être si doux de se rouler là-dedans, à son aise, de se sentir caressé partout." ' (p.252) Word and gesture combine in the factory to indicate that Madame Arnoux has her feet firmly on the ground:

> 'Ce sont les patouillards', dit-elle. Il trouva le mot grotesque, et comme inconvenant dans sa bouche; (p.196)

> Et, comme il cherchait son regard, Mme Arnoux, afin de l'éviter, prit sur une console des boulettes de pâte, provenant des rajustages manqués, les aplatit en une galette, et imprima dessus sa main. (p.197)

Or the way something is said can be more important than what is said:

> Et, zézayant à la manière des nourrices:
> 'Avons pas toujours été bien sage! Avons fait dodo avec sa femme!' (p.333)

Baby-talk points not only to Rosanette's immaturity but also to Frédéric's childlike dependency on women. Although Frédéric may often have a distorted impression of appearances, it is to be assumed that his hearing is sound. Dialogue is an essential vehicle for overcoming the limitations of his point of view.

The sudden drying up of information has a powerful appeal for certain critics who delight in the text's reluctance to spell things out, which is seen as constituting as essential part of the 'modernity' of the novel.[38] The effect of 'focalisation externe', is however, extremely variable, depending on whether it is possible to make inferences from the seen to the unseen. It is by no means always the case that the reader is left as much in the dark as Frédéric. It is worthy of note that each Part of the novel culminates in a scene in which words and gestures alone are finally used. In each case a strong, even violent emotional reaction is shown rather than stated or analysed. The reader is not in any doubt about the nature of this reaction, largely because it is the natural conclusion of a process to which direct access has been given earlier on. Louise's desperate sobbing follows a full evocation of her growing attachment to Frédéric; Frédéric's tears and his false explanation of them are to be read in the context of the drama of profanation which has just taken place, while Madame Arnoux's brutal cutting of her hair, which is the equivalent of the earlier tears, expresses a different kind of frustration. The omission of information can have a paradoxically reassuring function, making the reader think that he 'knows' the characters sufficiently well to be able to imagine what they feel. In each of these scenes Frédéric fails to reciprocate the woman's feeling and in each case the reader is aware of an indifference on his part to the woman he is with, which the woman herself fails to perceive. Similarly, at the end of II ii Arnoux's fulsome tribute to Frédéric ('"Vous êtes bon, vous!"') is underscored by the reader's realisation that the true reason for his apparent solicitude for Madame Arnoux is that he does not wish Arnoux to risk quarrelling with Rosanette on finding her with another man.

It may not, however, always be apparent what a character is feeling. After Frédéric has lent money to Arnoux he is visited by his wife who explains why she has come:

'Mon mari', reprit-elle avec effort, 'm'a engagé à venir chez vous, n'osant faire cette démarche lui-même.' (p.187)

The cause of Madame Arnoux's discomfort, indicated by the phrase 'avec effort', is not immediately clear, though the reader is in a position to engage in intelligent speculation. There is the possibility that she does not like asking favours, or that she is aware of her husband's short-comings, or that she is embarrassed by a dubious complicity with him. Similarly, when Frédéric visits Madame Arnoux at Creil, the account given is tantalisingly incomplete:

> Il appela très haut. On ne répondit pas; sans doute, la cuisinière était sortie, la bonne aussi; enfin, parvenu au second étage, il poussa une porte. Mme Arnoux était seule, devant une armoire à glace. La ceinture de sa robe de chambre entr'ouverte pendait le long de ses hanches. Tout un côté de ses cheveux lui faisait un flot noir sur l'épaule droite; et elle avait les deux bras levés, retenant d'une main son chignon, tandis que l'autre y enfonçait une épingle. Elle jeta un cri, et disparut. (pp.194–5)

It may well be, of course, that Madame Arnoux has simply not heard Frédéric's loud announcement of his presence and is genuinely shocked by his arrival. Such an explanation does not completely dispel the sneaking suspicion that she may, almost without realising, have allowed herself to be seen in a different state. Even if such an interpretation is rejected, the description of Madame's Arnoux's state points possibly to another, more problematic, aspect of her activity. Nothing, however, is certain and the episode raises more questions than it answers. On two separate occasions Madame Arnoux emits a burst of manic laughter:

> Elle partit d'un éclat de rire, un rire aigu, désespérant, atroce; (p.248)

> et un rire aigu, déchirant, tomba sur eux, du haut de l'escalier. (p.361)

Beneath the surface of virtuous resignation runs a vein of intense frustration which manifests itself in these demented outbursts. In both cases the full extent of her emotional deprivation is brought home by a farcical substitution, Deslauriers for Frédéric, Rosanette for herself. While the exact nature of Emma's impression when she laughs in a similar way[39] is conveyed, the reader must attempt to deduce precisely what is passing through Madame Arnoux's mind, whether it is a bitter reflection on the irony of fate which brings the wrong people together at the wrong time or the anguished recognition of her own self-imposed inaccessibility. A certain amount of uncertainty can work productively to stimulate the reader to engage in purposeful reflection on the character's predicament.

The use of externals as pointers to inner states depends to a large extent upon a conventional gestural code. What can be expressed tends to be rather limited; frequently gestures or postures are used at moments of strong emotion which do not require much elucidation. If the gestures and postures described are thoroughly conventional *signifiants*, their *signifiés* belong to a range of commonly accepted or universally recognised emotional states. More complex effects are generated by the large number of objects which take on a symbolic meaning of which neither character or narrator is aware. The use of symbolism is a good deal less extensive and obvious than in *Madame Bovary* but there are, none the less, a not insignificant number of occasions when the reader has the impression that an object has an ulterior meaning. A good example is the Renaissance 'coffret' which appears at four crucial points in the novel. In the first scene it is a token of Arnoux's affection for his wife, an affection which both partners feel the need to seal publicly:

> Elle alla chercher dans son boudoir le coffret à fermoirs d'argent qu'il avait remarqué sur la cheminée. C'était un cadeau de son mari, un ouvrage de la Renaissance. Les amis d'Arnoux le complimentèrent, sa femme le remerciait; il fut pris d'attendrissement, et lui donna devant le monde un baiser. (pp.7–8)

The symbolic meaning of the casket is complex. It constitutes a public expression of Arnoux's affection and wealth, the two being closely associated. The 'attendrissement' which Arnoux experiences reflects his appreciation of his wife's devotion which he receives in return for his gift. But, although it is associated with the public display of marital harmony, the casket is also a private object; it belongs both to the 'public' 'cheminée' and the 'private' 'boudoir' and its precious 'fermoirs d'argent' ensure that its contents are sealed from the public gaze. It is also associated, therefore, with a hidden realm, a kind of forbidden underside of marriage, glimpsed at this stage by Frédéric as an innocent bystander. In the next scene the casket loses its aura as both public and private symbol of marital harmony for it contains incontrovertible evidence of Arnoux's infidelity:

> Elle le regarda en face, sans rien dire; puis allongea la main, prit le coffret d'argent sur la cheminée, et lui tendit une facture grande ouverte. (p.167)

At the heart of bourgeois marriage lies the deception associated with adultery. The bill for another 'cadeau', this time a shawl for his mistress, Rosanette, stands for the sexual and financial profligacy which is both generated by and subverts the peaceful harmony of bourgeois domesticity. Once again Frédéric is a witness, but this time he is not altogether blameless, both because he has been instrumental in the purchase of the shawl and because in his own way he too has betrayed Madame Arnoux with Rosanette.

On the third appearance the casket has been transferred from its domestic orbit, for Arnoux has, as is his wont, made a present of it to Rosanette:

> C'était celui de Mme Arnoux! Alors, il éprouva un attendrissement, et en même temps comme le scandale d'une profanation. Il avait envie d'y porter les mains, de l'ouvrir. Il eut peur d'être aperçu, et s'en alla. (p.260)

The casket is now associated with Madame Arnoux herself, and more specifically with her sexuality. The conflicting reactions it provokes in Frédéric duplicate those that she herself generates in him. Frédéric is struck between dread and devotion on the one hand, desire and determination on the other. His first reaction, 'attendrissement', an ironic echo of Arnoux's, is accompanied by an obscure sense of profanation, which provokes the clearly sexual 'envie d'y porter les mains, de l'ouvrir'. Significantly, however, the sexual response is immediately repressed on account of fear of detection by the father-figure, Arnoux, to whom both Madame Arnoux and Rosanette belong. The container which had previously contained evidence of Arnoux's involvement with Rosanette is now itself contained within her world where it takes on a new aura. It is as if the image of woman located in Frédéric's unconscious is undergoing a drastic modification, as the sexual reality of Madame Arnoux is brought home to him. The casket has proleptic force; the rue Tronchet assignation represents an abortive attempt on Frédéric's part to seize the forbidden object.

The casket undergoes a different kind of profanation when it is put up for auction and bought by Madame Dambreuse. In spite of its peripatetic existence it remains the focus of Frédéric's memories and desires:

> souvent, pendant leurs conversations, ses yeux le rencontraient; il était lié à ses souvenirs les plus chers, et son âme se fondait d'attendrissement, quand Mme Dambreuse dit tout à coup: 'Tiens! je vais l'acheter.' (p.415)

The 'atrophie sentimentale' which characterises the end of Frédéric's 'éducation sentimentale' is not yet total; the tarnished casket ('"Avec un peu de blanc d'Espagne, ça brillera"') still retains a magic ability to resuscitate the past, but the intervention of Madame Dambreuse leads to a sacrilegious appropriation ('on lui envoya le coffret. Elle le plongea dans son manchon') of an object which has become almost as sacred in Frédéric's mind as the veil of Tanit is in *Salammbô*. But if money can profane, it does not have the power to purchase affection; Madame Dambreuse hurries into her carriage 'comme un voleur' but she is not followed by Frédéric. 'Attendrissement' is not a transferable asset; Madame Arnoux's hegemony remains intact.

The chest is not the only object to change place and in doing so take on a symbolic meaning. Transferred to Rosanette's apartment, the 'lustre en vieux saxe', first seen in the office of *L'Art industriel* (p.21), is comically endangered by Arnoux's antics:

> Les danses s'arrêtèrent, et il y eut des applaudissements, un vacarme de joie, à la vue d'Arnoux s'avançant avec son panier sur la tête; les victuailles faisaient bosse au milieu. 'Gare au lustre!' Frédéric leva les yeux: c'était le lustre en vieux saxe qui ornait la boutique de l'*Art industriel*. (p.116)

A sort of 'confusion' is established between Madame Arnoux and Rosanette by Arnoux's feckless shunting of objects backwards and forwards between wife and mistress. A troubling sameness between the two women is created in spite of Frédéric's strenuous attempts at keeping them apart. A similar pattern of confusion is created by the numerous gifts and presents – bracelets, sunshades, shawls – which are duplicated. On several occasions Frédéric's gaze is caught by the sudden appearance of a bracelet, the token of the 'ownership', permanent or temporary, of the woman in question. Madame Arnoux's shawl, which Frédéric rescues when it is about to fall into the water, derives in his rêverie a privileged status from physical proximity: 'Elle avait dû bien des fois, au milieu de la mer, durant des soirs humides, en envelopper sa taille, s'en couvrir les pieds, dormir dedans!' (p.7) Rescuing the shawl takes on a complex symbolic meaning; a metonymic substitute for Madame Arnoux, it is associated with the fantasy of rescuing the mother, but its restoration also suggests that, at this stage, Frédéric is anxious both to protect and cover the saintly figure of Madame Arnoux. There is, however, another 'châle' (p.169) or rather two more, the two 'cachemires', one belonging to Madame Arnoux and the other given to Rosanette by Arnoux at Frédéric's suggestion. Madame Arnoux discovers Arnoux's infidelity partly on account of the disturbing similarity between the two shawls:

> 'Oh! c'est bien simple: j'ai été pour faire réparer mon cachemire, et un chef de rayon m'a appris qu'on venait d'en expédier un autre pareil chez Mme Arnoux.' (p.167)

Arnoux envelops wife and mistress in a common affection, although the fact that his wife's shawl is the worse for wear and Rosanette's is brand-new points to different degrees of attentiveness, while Rosanette's final selling of the shawl (p.176) suggests a lower valuation of his affection than Madame Arnoux's attempts at preservation. Frédéric's encouragement of Arnoux's infidelity leads to the purchase of the shawl and it is not surprising that he feels guilty (p.166) about its repercussions. The earlier rescue of a shawl, which represented a kind of consolidation of Madame Arnoux's security within marriage, has been followed by an act of subversion, since the discovery of the 'cachemire' drives the wedge even further between Madame Arnoux and her husband. Another of Madame Arnoux's possessions which is duplicated is the sunshade to which Frédéric draws near when he first meets her ('il se planta tout près de son ombrelle, posée contre le banc', p.6). Later he accidentally breaks the ivory handle of a sunshade lying on a chair at the Arnoux's, which he mistakenly thinks belongs to Madame Arnoux. Attempting to compensate for his clumsiness, he later offers a similar but more expensive sunshade to Madame Arnoux on her birthday, much to Arnoux's annoyance. The overtones of the sunshade are complex: closely associated with femininity, the sunshade evokes a common or joint fragility. Frédéric's failure to differentiate is a mark of his inexperience but the breaking of the sunshade also suggests an attempted rejection of the 'false' Madame Arnoux while the 'real' Madame Arnoux becomes the beneficiary of a deep-seated restorative urge.

Flowers, too, form a richly suggestive pattern. A telling opposition is established between the two occasions when Madame Arnoux is offered flowers. On the first, her birthday, her husband gathers roses in the garden ('Arnoux descendit dans le jardin, pour cueillir des roses', pp.83–4) but commits the double offence of wrapping them carelessly so that Madame Arnoux pricks herself on the 'grosse épingle, sottement mise', and of using the letter brought by Frédéric from Paris to wrap them up. Conjugal devotion comes thus heavily contaminated. Frédéric's corresponding token may be more modest ('il cueillit une rose, la seule du jardin', p.188) but it comes without incriminating packaging. While Madame Arnoux pricks herself on Arnoux's bouquet, she playfully twirls Frédéric's rose and while she throws Arnoux's out of the carriage window, she promises to keep Frédéric's, pointing to different reactions on her part to husband and young admirer. Flower imagery extends beyond these two isolated examples, however. Roses are associated with Rosanette in numerous ways – through her name, through explicit comparisons ('sa figure ressemblait ... à une rose épanouie', p.152) and through her playful enticements ('elle posa un pétale de fleur entre ses lèvres, et le lui tendit à becqueter', p.211), endowing them with strong sexual overtones, as opposed to the religious overtones they assume on occasion in connection with Madame Arnoux ('ce nom-là ... qui semblait contenir ... des jonchées de roses', p.273). The symbolism of roses and flowers is particularly complex and central to the presentation of relations between the sexes. The 'gros bouquet' which Frédéric presents both pathetically and poetically 'comme un amoureux a sa fiancée' (p.428) is the first of several gifts and tributes which testify to the frequently wildly inappropriate expectations he entertains of the opposite sex.

One of the most striking features of *L'Éducation sentimentale* is the insistent presence of the river Seine. The river's state, constantly varying, often appears to correspond to the inner state of the protagonist. At times the link is explicit, as in the description of Frédéric's euphoria after the first dinner with Madame Arnoux:

> Il s'était arrêté au milieu de Pont-Neuf, et, tête nue, poitrine ouverte, il aspirait l'air. Cependant, il sentait monter du fond de lui-même quelque chose d'intarissable, un afflux de tendresse qui l'énervait, comme le mouvement des ondes sous ses yeux. (p.49)

At other times the connection is not so obvious. The gradual rundown of Frédéric's activity towards the end of his first year in Paris, for instance, may be reflected in the description of the river:

> Les becs de gaz s'allumaient; et la Seine, verdâtre dans toute son étendue, se déchiraient en moires d'argent contre les piles des ponts. (p.24)

At other times the extended description of water tantalises the reader with the promise of symbolic meaning which is never fully fulfilled. At

Nogent, for instance, the Seine flows over a weir in a movement which does not quite succeed in corresponding to a pattern of unity in variety in Frédéric's life:

> Cela formait ensuite des bouillonnements, des tourbillons, mille courants opposés, et qui finissaient par se confondre en une seule nappe limpide. (p.252)

The flowing of the river parallels the constant outpouring of emotional energy in the novel. One of the most basic needs of the characters in *L'Éducation sentimentale* is to 's'épancher'. At times the river facilitates sentimental effusion: 'Le plaisir . . . d'une excursion maritime facilitait les épanchements' (p.4). Frequently it provokes a kind of liquid release of emotion in which the self becomes submerged. The imagery of submergence effectively conveys a total immersion in emotion, a wallowing in sentimentality. But what, one might ask, is the precise information value of the water imagery? Does it add anything to our understanding of what the characters are experiencing? If it is the correlative of a state, already described, it might be thought that its information is redundant; if, on the other hand, no explicit reference is made to an emotional state to which it is equivalent, there is not enough basis for attempting a symbolic recuperation. There is, however, a possibility, half-way between these two extremes. Descriptions of water may help to amplify what we have already been told a character is experiencing. In addition they establish a predominant atmosphere, of deliquescence and dissolution, part pleasurable, part disagreeable, which is symbolically appropriate, consonant with the general pattern of behaviour in the novel.

Not all critics accept the view that symbolic details contribute to our understanding of character. Jeanne Bem, for instance, suggests that the symbolism may develop independently and that the 'characters' are forced to conform to its constraints. Noting the way in which the letter delivered by Frédéric to Arnoux at Saint-Cloud circulates from one character to another she writes:

> Il est clair . . . que ce ne sont pas les personnages qui se déterminent, mais que c'est la lettre qui s'entête à leur faire jouer un rôle précis, celui du messager qui s'ignore. Cette insistance et cette ignorance représentent assez bien les contraintes du symbolique.[40]

The view that there is a kind of autonomous symbolic logic at work in the novel is, however, no more persuasive than the more traditional idea that symbolic details contribute to the understanding of character. What seems to characterise the symbolism of *L'Éducation sentimentale* is the uncertainty that surrounds it; the intricate web of symbolism which strikes the reader of *Madame Bovary* so forcibly gives way in Flaubert's second novel of modern life to more muted and sporadic symbolic effects.

The wide range of narrative techniques employed by Flaubert all contribute in their different ways to what has been defined as his central artistic purpose – the construction of the mental world of his characters.[41] The difficulty of elaborating appropriate methods for the presentation of the inner life was not underestimated by Flaubert:

> Peut-être les formes plastiques ont-elles été toutes décrites, redites; c'était la part des premiers. Ce qui nous reste, c'est l'intérieur de l'homme, plus complexe, mais qui échappe bien davantage aux conditions de la *forme*. Aussi je crois que le roman ne fait que de naître, il attend son Homère.[42]

In his pioneering attempt to find an adequate way of evoking the inner world of Frédéric Moreau, Flaubert employs a mixture of methods, some well-tried, some disconcertingly new. *L'Éducation sentimentale* bears the marks of a residual attachment to a traditional analytic mode; however, a characteristic uncertainty frequently introduced into analytic passages often undermines the security of the omniscient position adopted by the narrator. Paradoxically, the loss of nerve betrayed in the hesitations, gaps and silences of the narrator's account work productively, stimulating the reader to participate more actively in the process of constructing and understanding the reactions of Frédéric. To a radically new extent in a third-person narrative, however, Flaubert sought to present rather than analyse Frédéric's thoughts and feelings and he developed to this end techniques such as *style indirect libre* which have far-reaching repercussions on the form of the novel, leading to the effacement of the narrator, who seems almost to merge with character. In spite of the prevalence of *style indirect libre* and related techniques for presenting the flow of Frédéric's consciousness, Frédéric is not consistently viewed from within. On the many occasions when Frédéric and other characters are viewed from the outside we are rarely left in a state of complete uncertainty over what they are experiencing. It is a general characteristic of all narratives that their full meaning far exceeds the sum of the explicit statements they contain, as Genette points out: 'Le récit en dit toujours moins qu'il en sait, mais il en fait souvent savoir plus qu'il n'en dit.'[43] In the case of *L'Éducation sentimentale*, the narrative may not directly specify a character's reaction but none the less convey it through the provision of a wide range of behavioural cues and symbolic pointers. Thus, although the narrator may in various ways have been displaced from his traditional stronghold, the effect on the psychological element is not necessarily detrimental, since the faltering of the narrator allows the implied author to light up the psychological sphere in new and more subtle ways.

V

Motive Forces

One of the strongest expectations of readers of fiction is that the novelist will provide a satisfactory explanation of why characters develop in a certain way and why their fictional lives possess the overall shape they do; the way in which different formative experiences, different types of character, different approaches to life all produce different results, success or failure, happiness or unhappiness, frustration or fulfilment, is something most novelists attend closely to. Speculation about crucial determinants is particularly likely to arise in novels in which the destinies of two characters, similar in certain respects, dissimilar in others, are plotted. The pressure to offer a clear and convincing account of why characters turn out as they do in this type of novel can be very strong, as Flaubert's comments on his own novel, the first *Éducation sentimentale*, completed in 1845, show:

> Il faudrait pour l'*Éducation* ... écrire un chapitre qui manque, où l'on montrerait comment fatalement le même tronc a dû se bifurquer, c'est-à-dire pourquoi telle action a amené ce résultat dans ce personnage plutôt que telle autre. Les causes sont montrées, les résultats aussi; mais l'enchaînement de la cause à l'effet ne l'est point. Voilà le vice du livre, et comment il ment à son titre.[1]

The presentation of the divergent destinies of Jules and Henry, each subjected to a particular formative experience, is deemed unsatisfactory precisely because the final outcome, the choice of way of life, be it that of the artist or that of the careerist, is not felt to be the necessary outcome of the combination of a certain type of character and a given set of experiences. There is some uncertainty over whether the two main characters are fundamentally the same ('le même tronc') or whether they may be capable of responding differently to various influences. Such a hesitation over the identity of the characters leads to an element of equivocation when attempting to determine how crucial certain experiences are. Flaubert, even at this very early stage in his development as a novelist, displays a characteristic awareness of the baffling complexity of the factors underlying life stories.

Whether he felt under the same obligation as in 1845 and whether he was any more successful in meeting it when writing the major version of *L'Éducation sentimentale* are both debatable questions. On the one hand, there is a stronger opposition between the 'characters' of Frédéric and Deslauriers; on the other, they experience a common failure. What is perhaps most significant, however, is the abandonment of the earlier narrative mode which permitted sweeping statements relating to the overall course of the lives of fictional characters. If anyone is going to speculate about the causes of failure in *L'Éducation sentimentale* (1869), it will have to be the characters themselves and there is perhaps no more reason to expect them to succeed in this final task which is imposed upon them than in any of their other activities:

> Et ils résumèrent leur vie.
>
> Ils l'avaient manquée tous les deux, celui qui avait rêvé l'amour, celui qui avait rêvé le pouvoir. Quelle en était la raison?
>
> 'C'est peut-être le défaut de ligne droite', dit Frédéric.
>
> 'Pour toi, cela se peut. Moi, au contraire, j'ai péché par excès de rectitude, sans tenir compte de mille choses secondaires, plus fortes que tout. J'avais trop de logique, et toi de sentiment.'
>
> Puis ils accusèrent le hasard, les circonstances, l'époque où ils étaient nés. (pp. 426–7)

It has been argued that this discussion is largely misleading and that Frédéric and Deslauriers have learnt nothing. Deslauriers's life is not obviously a failure, particularly after 1851, he cannot be accused of excessive logic and the various factors adduced in the last sentence are virtually synonymous.[2] The reader, as a result, is left in a quandary over the whole question of why the two central characters fail: 'There is no attempt to adjudicate between fate and error as possible causes: statements of either position are displayed as stupidities.'[3] There is indeed something painfully and comically inadequate about the reductive and oversimplified explanation that each character offers, particularly when presented so baldly, and each might seem to cancel the other out. No sooner has an element of personal responsibility been recognised than the blame is shuffled off onto external factors, suggesting an inability to come to terms with failure. This is not to say, however, that the whole discussion should be dismissed as totally irrelevant. In a plan for the last chapter Flaubert wrote 'font eux-mêmes *La Morale du livre*, se disent pourquoi (peut-être) ils n'ont pas atteint leur but'.[4] There may well be an element of irony suggested in the underlining of *La Morale du livre* but it is not necessarily sufficiently powerful to invalidate totally what the characters propose by way of explanation of where they went wrong.

Although at first sight the discussion might seem rather too cut and dried, it proves on closer examination to be less straightforward. There is agreement that both characters have made a failure of their life, but it is not clear whether the abortive pursuit of a mistaken ideal in itself constitutes failure or rather is adduced as the cause of failure. This ambiguity is particularly crucial in the case of Frédéric, who can as reasonably be seen as having failed *in* as *through* his adoration of Madame Arnoux. It is by no means certain that either character has finally emerged from his experience of life sufficiently chastened to renounce his initial ideal. Any impression of bogus certainty is also defused by the element of doubt both characters express ('peut-être', 'cela se peut') about Frédéric's failure, if not about Deslauriers's. Frédéric, perhaps significantly, is the first to offer an explanation, one which loses some of its authority by being indiscriminately advanced as applicable to both of them. In his case, the reason for failure may be clearer, or, alternatively he may more obviously bear a measure of responsibility for it. Frédéric's explanation of the disappointing course of his life can be related to the Balzacian model that haunts the novel. Deslauriers's encouragement of Frédéric at the beginning of the novel (' "Rappelle-toi Rastignac dans *la Comédie humaine*! Tu réussiras, j'en suis sûr" ', p. 18) is a reminder for the reader of the advice given by Vautrin to his protégé: ' "Il faut entrer dans cette masse d'hommes comme un boulet de canon. Vous, si vous êtes un homme supérieur, allez *en droite ligne* et la tête haute." '[5] Frédéric's explanation reflects, therefore, a lingering adherence to what might seem in his case a totally inappropriate set of prescriptions for social success. It can also be related to the romantic ideal of sustained devotion which Flaubert professed to admire: 'J'aime les passions longues et qui traversent patiemment et *en droite ligne* tous les courants de la vie.'[6] These two different interpretations of what is implied by a direct course may not seem equally plausible but each has some validity as Frédéric strives for conflicting goals in more than one sphere. The diametrically opposed trajectory adduced by Deslauriers as the reason for his failure also takes on extra resonances in the context of his over-reliance upon Balzacian precedent; only at this late stage does he recognise that the Vautrin prescription of a resolutely unswerving course leads to a fatal neglect of contingent factors in any social situation. The Balzacian formula, to which Frédéric belatedly and half-heartedly turns, is finally rejected by Deslauriers as unworkable.

In neither case is the failure to follow the right course felt to be the only significant factor at work. Deslauriers's diagnosis of the causes of failure identifies for each of them a corresponding condition, one which is defined in terms of being burdened by too much rationality or too much sentimentality. This is the point at which the maximum degree of personal responsibility is accepted; Deslauriers is here identifying a characteristic imbalance, amounting to a personal failing, as the crucial determinant. While Deslauriers, with his more analytic mind, is made to offer the most trenchant assessment, the final invocation of external factors is made by both characters, who are now seen in an undifferentiated way as equally subject to the vagaries of the outer world. Are, however, the various factors referred to synonymous, as Culler claims? 'Le hasard' stands for the apparently contingent realm, the chance meeting, the coincidental development; 'les circonstances', in contrast, designate the social and financial circumstances in which characters find themselves, that is to say something more enduring than 'le hasard'; finally 'l'époque' stands for the historical, political and cultural situation in which the characters are enmeshed. The brief summary of the final stage of the discussion marks a kind of progress in the thinking of the two characters, therefore, the various factors being arranged in ascending order of importance. To have listed the three factors in reverse order would have produced a very different effect.

The mental juggling with a variety of potential causes of failure by the two principal characters concerned cannot but, given its strategic placing, encourage similar speculation on the reader's part. A series of strong, almost schematic, oppositions between the careers and characters of Frédéric and Deslauriers provide support for an overview which coincides in certain respects with that of the characters themselves. If Frédéric has been disappointed in the pursuit of his ideal it is in part

because he has not been sufficiently direct or forceful in his approach to
Madame Arnoux; Deslauriers, on the other hand, in making a Balzacian
bee-line for wealth and power has failed to take adequate stock of the
hidden obstacles standing in the way of his progress. More resolution, in
one case, more circumspection in the other, might indeed have brought a
greater measure of success. Deslauriers's linking of a wrong approach to
life with a characteristic one-sidedness likewise possesses a certain
validity. Throughout, Frédéric is swayed by emotion rather than reason,
generous impulses rather than self-interest, an idealistic view of the
opposite sex rather than a realistic one, all of which leads him to
squander his time and energy in the unproductive worship of an
unattainable ideal. Deslauriers, on the other hand, has erred in the
opposite direction, activated as he is by reason rather than emotion, a
narrow self-interest rather than any real concern for others, a realistic
rather than an idealistic analysis of the political situation, all of which
leads him to concentrate his time and energy on what turns out to be an
equally unproductive pursuit of an unattainable ideal. In addition, a
strong opposition between the 'characters' of Frédéric and Deslauriers is
established; the former is vacillating, weak-willed, irresolute, soft-
hearted, while the latter is single-minded, strong-willed, determined,
hard-headed. In Frédéric's case there seems to be a clear connection
between character, trajectory and final outcome. In Deslauriers's case,
however, there is no such obvious connection; on the contrary, in many
respects he might appear to possess the right kind of character and
approach for the successful pursuit of power. It is at this point that the
limitations of the characters' understanding become apparent and the
reader may be inclined to differentiate between them with respect to the
importance of external factors.

Although external factors are blamed by both characters, they seem
more relevant to Deslauriers than to Frédéric. In particular, Flaubert has
set up a strong contrast between the financial circumstances of the two
characters. While fortune in the shape of a substantial inheritance smiles
on Frédéric, Deslauriers is constantly bedevilled by his penurious
condition. A striking opposition develops, as a result of this strong
contrast, between the two characters, when it comes to the reasons for
failure. In Frédéric's case, the crucial factor would appear to be psychological: he fails to make much progress with Madame Arnoux on account
of a problematic 'lâcheté' or lack of true determination, and, in a more

general way, he fails in life, artistically, socially, politically, on account of his spinelessness, rather than on account of any serious external obstacles. Deslauriers on the other hand, seems to fail in the pursuit of his chosen goal above all on account of his lack of means, repeatedly finding himself forced to abandon his ambitious and self-seeking projects. Unlike Frédéric, Deslauriers cannot be accused of failing for want of trying. It is not a little paradoxical that, beneath the common failure which constitutes such a neat parallel, diametrically opposed factors appear to be at work.

It would be wrong, however, to suggest that external and internal factors carry equal weight in the context of the overall impact made by the novel. Although Deslauriers figures prominently in the crucially important opening and closing sequences, he is only intermittently present in the main body of the work. It is, therefore, the behaviour of Frédéric which dominates the reader's attention and as a result it is the importance of the psychological factor which comes over more forcibly. There is, however, a marked difference between *L'Éducation sentimentale* and *Madame Bovary*, in which an inner determinism is heavily emphasised and a strong impression of inevitability created.[7] This is to a large extent on account of the fact that *L'Éducation sentimentale* is a good deal less explicit when it comes to the presentation of motives.[8] There are good grounds, none the less, for considering that the underlying assumptions relating to the rigidly determined nature of human behaviour have not undergone substantial change.

At an early stage in his development Flaubert came to the belief that each man behaves in accordance with the dictates of his 'nature'. Since nobody is in a position to choose their own nature ('Es-tu le créateur de ta constitution physique et morale?'),[9] the freedom of human beings is an illusion[10] and the notion of responsibility problematic.[11] Flaubert appears to have retained this early belief in the inevitability of much of human behaviour, insisting that 'chacun suit sa voie, en dépit de sa propre volonté'.[12] Similarly, he does not waver in his view that the fundamental determinant of a person's behaviour is a genetically determined 'tempérament' which produces a characteristic pattern of responses. Discussing his own special case Flaubert claimed in 1846: 'Je marchais avec la rectitude d'un système particulier fait pour un cas spécial.'[13] The importance of this 'système' constructed by the individual in response to the promptings of his 'temperament' continues to be stressed in 1861, but in more general terms: 'On se fait un système d'après son tempérament ... on ne choisit pas son tempérament.'[14] Flaubert's belief in the importance of what is intrinsic to the individual subsequently led him to challenge the brand of determinism put forward by Taine; 'Il y a le milieu, d'abord, puis la race (que vous pouvez moins préciser que le milieu), puis l'*ingenium* de chaque individu, que vous ne pouvez pas définir.'[15] Flaubert is clearly inclined to attach far more importance to individual genetic inheritance, while recognising the difficulty of defining it: 'Bien des choses s'expliqueraient si nous pouvions connaître notre généalogie véritable ... l'hérédité est un principe juste qui a été mal appliqué.'[16]

Apart from the brief but telling comment that Frédéric and Deslauriers at the end of the novel are once again, 'réunis par la fatalité de leur nature' (p. 424), there is no explicit statement in the novel itself which reflects Flaubert's continuing belief that behaviour is determined to a large extent by a person's innate characteristics. Although Frédéric and Deslauriers, as has been seen, come close at one point to accepting a degree of personal responsibility for their failure, they are still a long way off recognising the full importance of the internal factor, in spite of the fact that, arguably, it is precisely this factor which is uppermost in the presentation of the development of Frédéric.[17] From the outset Frédéric's passive nature gives rise to a characteristically rigid set of responses. Superficially, his reactions may appear inconsequential, unmotivated and inconsistent, but the reader gradually comes to realise that they are all manifestations of an underlying 'système' constructed on the basis of his constitutional passivity. Indeed, it is possible to diagnose 'excès de rectitude' rather than 'défaut de ligne droite', at a deeper level, as the fundamental cause of Frédéric's problems. In psychoanalytic terms, a persuasive rigidity of thought and response in which an inner, unconscious necessity determines patterns of behaviour which are frequently damaging to one's self is the defining feature of neurosis; this condition appears to afflict Frédéric for much of the time and it is in this sense that his behaviour frequently appears to be rigidly determined.

Frédéric's constitutional passivity is immediately apparent in the opening scene where he moves naturally from inconsequential daydreaming, through dubious assumptions ('il trouvait que le bonheur mérité par l'excellence de son âme tardait à venir', p. 4) and sub-romantic posturing, to a position of instant dependency upon Arnoux and his wife. As for the actual process of falling in love, it is presented not so much as a bolt from the blue – though for Frédéric it has all the suddenness of such an occurrence – as an intentional act on his part, the result of a deep-seated need to sink into a submissive posture of adoration. Several impulses are evident in this initial encounter – a readiness to undergo a kind of psychic dazzlement, a compulsive need to worship, an automatic avoidance of eye-contact, a desire for detached contemplation from a distance –, all dictated not by the kind of person Madame Arnoux is but by prior inner propensities. What we witness here is the first appearance of the 'système' which constitutes Frédéric's way of coming to terms with the world.

A full examination of Frédéric's relationship with Madame Arnoux will be found in a subsequent chapter; at this point it is enough to note that his infatuation consumes a vast amount of time and energy, displacing not only worldly ambition and artistic projects but also his relationships with other men and women. Other aspects of his life are always subsidiary to or a function of his lingering devotion to an idealised figure of perfection, which structures and pervades his whole fictional existence. Frédéric, it can be said, defines himself in and through his adoration of Madame Arnoux, organising his life and his self around the worship of her saintly image. This is not to say that he is at ease or content with his chosen way of behaving; there are repeated moments of angry rejection and attempted extrication but the superficiality of such responses, their profound inability to 'dent' the 'système' into which all his psychic energy is channelled are frequently demonstrated by his ready resumption of a posture of drooling wonderment on the slightest pretext. The image which seems to evoke most accurately the impossibility of stepping outside the 'système' he has devised is that of the prison: 'et incapable d'action, maudissant Dieu et s'accusant d'être lâche, il tournait dans son désir, comme un prisonnier dans son cachot' (p. 69). A powerful inner determinism ensures that Frédéric serves his time in a prison of his own making.

The fact that Madame Arnoux is married and a mother and therefore less likely to be able to reciprocate his feelings does not act as a disincentive precisely because, it is suggested, he has opted at an unconscious level for attachment without involvement. Although part of him gradually comes to desire Madame Arnoux in a conventional

manner, his love for her is essentially one which outstrips the physical
and renders 'action', defined in sexual terms, problematic:

> L'action, pour certains hommes, est d'autant plus impraticable que le désir
> est plus fort. La méfiance d'eux-mêmes les embarrasse, la crainte de
> déplaire les épouvante; d'ailleurs, les affections profondes ressemblent aux
> honnêtes femmes; elles ont peur d'être découvertes, et passent dans la vie
> les yeux baissés. (p. 172)

Frédéric's reluctance to make a more determined bid to secure Madame
Arnoux's affection stems from the fact that he is incapacitated by the
very strength of his desire and restrained by a fundamental lack of
confidence in himself. His feeling for her does not need to be exteriorised
or communicated; it is enough for him simply to experience a sense of
rapturous wonderment without it being a prelude to declaration. What
this means, however, is that to a large extent feeling is contained within
the self rather than expressed; Frédéric substitutes a private, narcissistic
dalliance with an idealised mental image for a more direct contact with
Madame Arnoux herself. As he recognises in his final equivocal tribute
to her, he has not sought to possess her in person because an internalized
image of her attractions suffices: 'Est-ce que j'y pensais seulement'.
puisque j'avais toujours au fond de moi-même la musique de votre voix
et la splendeur de vos yeux!' (p. 423)

The same compulsive avoidance of 'action' is apparent in Frédéric's
marked propensity towards daydreaming in which Madame Arnoux's
image can be shaped according to his desire. Such is the strength of
Frédéric's feeling that his imaginings often take on the force of an
hallucination, blocking out external reality:

> cette contemplation était si profonde que les objets extérieurs avaient
> disparu; (p. 101)
> Et sa rêverie devint tellement profonde qu'il eut une sorte d'hallucination.
> (p. 362)

Frédéric's daydreaming invariably concerns himself and Madame
Arnoux; typically his mind generates images of conventional bliss in a
variety of minutely visualised settings, with himself enjoying the
modicum of physical contact denied to him in reality, or frozen in a highly
stylised posture of adoration. Madame Arnoux's eyes, which in reality he
is often afraid to look at, play a prominent part in his rêverie. The

incongruity and improbability of his imaginings are frequently stressed; at a time when she appears to the reader totally indifferent to Frédéric, he has visions of her committing herself to him; when she is clearly the virtuous wife, he pictures her in a harem; when envisaging the reciprocation of his desire, he is unable to exclude Arnoux from his visions of bliss ('il *les* recevrait chez lui', p. 98) and, even more contradictory, in the hallucinatory scenario mapped out on the assumption of Arnoux's death, he still sees himself 'chez *eux*, dans leur maison' (p. 316). In his mind's eye he cannot prise Madame Arnoux away from the husband to whom part of him insists she belongs.

Many of Frédéric's hallucinatory imaginings seem to be shaped by desires and compulsions over which he has no control. Certain unconscious needs – the urge to abase himself, the dependency upon the father-figure, Arnoux, a profanatory impulse – all appear to find expression in the images of fantasised fulfilment Frédéric repeatedly conjures up. Even more direct access to the shadowy depths of Frédéric's unconscious seems to be afforded by the melodramatic dream he has after attending Rosanette's ball:

> il lui semblait qu'il était attelé près d'Arnoux, au timon d'un fiacre, et que la Maréchale, à califourchon sur lui, l'éventrait avec ses éperons d'or. (p. 129)

The complex image of Frédéric teamed up with Arnoux possesses multiple meanings; if the manifest meaning relates fairly obviously to a fear of financial exploitation by Rosanette, the latent meaning seems to be bound up with an instant readiness to extend his association with Arnoux in new directions and a willing acceptance of the passive role in relation to women with strong masochistic overtones. Frédéric, one is led to believe, does not find his newly-acquired equine role too nightmarish.

But it is not just dreams and hallucinations which demonstrate Frédéric's passivity. An essential corollary of the impulse to adore is the instinctive tendency towards self-abasement which manifests itself in the opening scene: 'En même temps qu'il passait, elle leva la tête; il fléchit involontairement les épaules.' (p. 6) The slightest of pretexts is liable to trigger Frédéric's need to lower himself or his gaze: 'Les paroles rappelèrent à Frédéric celles que chantaient l'homme en haillons . . . Ses yeux s'attachaient involontairement sur le bas de la robe étalée devant lui.' (p. 72) An essential side-effect of the adoration Frédéric bestows upon Madame Arnoux is that he 'se sentait moins important sur la terre que les brindilles de soie s'échappant de ses ciseaux' (p. 173). Frédéric's natural posture, fantasised in daydreams and adopted in reality is that of kneeling: ' "Je ne vous offenserai pas! . . . je vous le jure." Et il se laissa tomber sur les genoux, malgré lui, s'affaissant sous un poids intérieur trop lourd.' (p. 270) The involuntary nature of these responses is stressed; self-abasement has something of the quality of a conditioned reflex.

Equally, there is something almost automatic about Frédéric's 'pudeur', his strong, irresistible urge to suspend or repress his desire, which repeatedly holds him back: 'Chaque matin, il se jurait d'être hardi. Une invincible pudeur l'en empêchait' (p. 172). Self-restraint is not the result of moral deliberation but of obscure compulsion, the product of a characteristic turning away from sexual experience. It does not appear, on the whole, that Frédéric could behave in any other way than he does, activated as he is by needs of various kinds, ranging from the frivolous to the deep-seated.[18] Emotions typically take over his whole being, a phenomenon frequently conveyed by the imagery of submergence:

Et les flots d'une infinie tendresse le submergeaient; (p. 189)

il sentit une ivresse le submerger. (p. 100)

Frédéric invariably succumbs to these needs, powerful feelings and inhibitions 'malgré lui';[19] for much of the time he appears to be at the mercy of promptings of which he is only dimly aware. It is not altogether surprising, therefore, that he fails to identify the underlying causes of his failure at the end of the novel.

Although Frédéric's behaviour seems to be determined to a large extent by an inner 'système' over which he has little control, external factors are far from being excluded. Indeed, it has been claimed that, beneath the appearance of psychological determinism, L'Éducation sentimentale is really 'le roman du hasard'.[20] It is certainly the case that there are many chance encounters and a remarkably high number of coincidences but this does not in itself mean that chance is presented as the key determinant or eclipses the inner determinism at work,[21] any more than the importance assumed by a 'fatalité subjective' means that the intervention of chance constitutes no more than a 'pseudo-explication' of Frédéric's failure to consummate his love.[22] Although, as Jacques Proust has pointed out, Flaubert's determinism implies a denial

of the purely contingent,[23] from the standpoint of the characters themselves the importance of the element of chance cannot be easily discounted, since the causal chains to which chance elements in theory
belong remain completely hidden. But since the reader's perspective is
not necessarily that of the character, the importance attached to chance
does not necessarily displace or invalidate the idea of inner determinism.

In the first place, the attitudes of the characters to chance are
psychologically revealing. Frédéric, weak and ineffectual as he is, is often
prepared to rely upon chance to make or break his links with various
women,[24] allows chance to pre-empt his own decision-making[25] or
further his ends.[26] In contrast, Deslauriers, strong-willed and self-
reliant, 'croyait . . . aux docilités du hasard sous la main des forts' (p. 78).
Chance may be used in attempts at covering up disloyalty[27] or as a
pretext for meetings.[28] Events which are categorized by characters as
fortuitous are often clearly the result of concerted action. But, although
the attitudes to chance adopted by the characters are often suspect, there
are none the less many events which are, at least from their point of view,
genuinely fortuitous. Such events frequently act as a catalyst, provoking
a reaction which is totally predictable. Simultaneous invitations or
demands upon his financial resources allow the more pressing commitment to Madame Arnoux to be shown taking precedence over worldly
ambition or friendship. Although the incidence of coincidental timing is
remarkably high, installing the fortuitous firmly in the plot-structure, it
invariably serves to underline the prior dependence of Frédéric upon
Madame Arnoux's idealised image, which dictates how he will respond
to the alternative courses of action presented to him.

A particularly intricate network of chance encounters furthers or
thwarts the progress of Frédéric's relationships with a wide range of
characters. The circumstances in which he first happens to meet each of
the four women with whom he becomes involved are carefully contrasted
and each fortuitous encounter produces a varying degree of response
from Frédéric. Encounters between the women themselves, often
appearingly highly contrived, none the less play an essential part in
exposing Frédéric's confused feelings and divided loyalties. Coincidences are often manipulated in order to highlight the disparity between
the fortunes or feelings of various characters. The fact that Frédéric
should be dallying with Louise in Nogent at the very moment that
Madame Arnoux takes stock of her love for him is a bitter reminder of

the impossibility of synchronising feeling. The element of chance twice plays a crucial role in Frédéric's relationship with Madame Arnoux: when the moment is ripe for the consummation of their love, Madame Arnoux's child falls ill, preventing her from attending the rendezvous at the rue Tronchet and when a reconciliation later creates an atmosphere of expectation Rosanette enters, seemingly by chance. It is as if, when all else has failed, Flaubert has to turn to chance in order to block fulfilment. Ironically, the very flimsiness of the pretext creates the impression of a higher ban being imposed, exposing an ultimately arbitrary narrative line and leaving the reader feeling obscurely but exhilaratingly let down. It is not a question of chance displacing the psychological factor but rather of their pulling in the same direction. In both cases, chance events have a disjunctional effect in the context of a continued wavering, between a mother's duty and love for Frédéric in one case, between the rival claims of mother-figure and woman of easy virtue in the other. In both cases the element of chance is the means to a psychologically satisfying outcome. From the outset to the final version, chance is just one of several factors at work in a complex multi-faceted situation, a necessary but not sufficient cause of Frédéric's failure to consummate his love. Chance and inner determinism need to be seen as complementary rather than mutually exclusive in Flaubert's scheme of things.[29]

While the role of chance is undoubtedly problematic, the role of 'les circonstances', which are particularly important in the case of Deslauriers, seems comparatively straightforward. Frédéric's failure can be attributed mainly to his own indifference: once he has inherited, he has ample financial means but lacks the appropriate motivation to make use of them; Deslauriers, on the other hand, is constantly hampered by financial constraints. At first unable to join Frédéric in Paris because his father refuses to pay his fees, it is only when he has wrested from him the sum of 7000 francs, which represents his share of his mother's estate, that he is able to pursue his studies in Paris, but this sum is less than is available to Frédéric, off whom he sponges in order to survive. In Part II the gap between them widens when Frédéric inherits and the differences between the comfortable life and elegant dress of the one and the shabby appearance and meagre fare of the other are repeatedly stressed. Deslauriers is no longer able to draw upon Frédéric's funds and his project of a newspaper flounders because Frédéric fails to provide the promised 15,000 francs. In Part III his financial position remains precarious, partly on account of his failure to hold any of the posts he obtains. Deslauriers's career would seem, therefore, to lend substance to his assertions at the beginning of the novel:

> 'Mais pour entreprendre n'importe quoi, il faut de l'argent! Quelle malédiction que d'être le fils d'un cabaretier et de perdre sa jeunesse à la quête de son pain.' (pp.16–17)

However hard one strives, whatever one's personal qualities, a certain amount of money is essential if one is to succeed, in the way Deslauriers wishes at least. The Balzacian myth of a rapid rise from rags to riches by dint of energy, resourcefulness, compromise and protection is punctured.

Not that the personal factors are completely discounted in his case. Deslauriers himself diagnoses 'excès de rectitude' and 'trop de logique' as the main causes of his failure. Endowed with a quarrelsome, irascible, self-assertive nature, Deslauriers's principal ambition is to 's'affirmer'; he seeks power over others and desires wealth first and foremost 'comme moyen de puissance sur les hommes'. His dreams betray a strong streak of megalomania:

> Il aurait voulu remuer beaucoup de monde, faire beaucoup de bruit, avoir trois secrétaires sous ses ordres . . .' (p.54)
> Deslauriers touchait à son vieux rêve, une rédaction en chef, c'est-à-dire, au bonheur inexprimable de diriger les autres, de tailler en plein dans leurs articles, d'en commander, d'en refuser; (pp.179–80)
> il ambitionnait toujours de constituer une phalange dont il serait le chef. (p.267)

Deslauriers's failure to fulfil his ambitions stems in part from the inherent falsity and naiveté of his expectations, in part from his lack of money, but also in part, as he rightly perceives, from his tendency to make a head-on, frontal assault ('excès de rectitude') and from a failure to take account of the illogicalities, vagaries and sectional interests of the world around him. Deslauriers is always convinced he is right and seeks to assert the rightness of his views with a degree of tenacity that amounts to pig-headness. His attitude to the legal question of Limitations is so unbending that he fails the 'agrégation' examination (p.112) and when his golden opportunity comes in 1848, though by dint of harrassment he obtains a post of 'commissaire' in the provinces (p.294), he shows a characteristic tactlessness:

> Comme il prêchait la fraternité aux conservateurs et le respect des lois aux socialistes, les uns lui avaient tiré des coups de fusil, les autres apporté une corde pour le pendre. (p.370)

His combative temperament and over-assertive manner repeatedly lead Deslauriers into confrontations; when he is sent to London after being involved in a plot to overthrow the Government, he even ends up exchanging blows ('il s'était flanqué des gifles avec ses frères', p.370). It is altogether appropriate, therefore, that he should lose his post as a *préfet* after 1851 'par excès de zèle gouvernemental' (p.425). In spite of his powerful intellect, in spite of his shrewd political analyses, in spite of his unbounded energy and determination, Deslauriers fails because 'on se méfiait de lui' (p.370), because he is too single-minded, unwavering and dogmatic in his unremitting and insensitive pursuit of power. Once again, therefore, there is a balance between internal and external factors, though it is weighted towards the latter. It is no more true in Deslauriers's case than in Frédéric's that 'Flaubert denies us the consolation of understanding failure',[30] unless to suggest a combination of causal factors is to be guilty of obfuscation.

Deslauriers is not, of course, the only impecunious character in the book. But, except in so far as it is a contributory factor helping to explain their political outlook, poverty does not act as a crucial determinant in the case of Dussardier and Sénécal, two other notably impoverished characters. This is in part due to the fact that neither works for his own personal advancement but rather for a political deal, while for Deslauriers political concern is always subordinate to ambition ('il attendait . . . un bouleversement où il comptait bien faire son trou avoir sa place, p.137). Thus Dussardier does not find his modest means a serious restriction, even rejecting La Vatnaz partly because 'elle était trop riche' (p.398). He is opposed not so much to the class system as such as to 'le Pouvoir' which he sees as the source of injustice. Sénécal, on the other hand is hostile to the system itself ('sa misère s'augmentant, il s'en prenait à l'ordre social, maudissait les riches', p.86). He feels the pinch of his straitened circumstances more keenly: 'ses études comme ses souffrances avivant chaque jour sa haine essentielle de toute distinction quelconque' (p.138). His austere lifestyle and scorn for all forms of pleasure-seeking, however, render him relatively immune to financial hardship, with the result that his own personal 'circonstances' do not assume the importance they do in Deslauriers's case. Although he is constantly losing his job as a result of aggressive behaviour or doctrinaire views, his poverty does not impinge upon his activity or directly determine his actions.

The third variable to which Frédéric and Deslauriers refer, the epoch or times in which they live, represents an area of overlap between several spheres, historical, political and cultural. *L'Éducation sentimentale* charts the contrasting trajectories of a cross-section of young men through a particularly turbulent period of history, characterised by a series of political upheavals and the spread of utopian theories. The impact of both political events and ideology depends, clearly, upon the temperament, circumstances and antecedents of the individual affected. Within an overall pattern of similarity, differences can be observed and characters may diverge or converge in their evolution. At no point wholly or solely responsible for the way a character acts, political pressures are always mediated by personal circumstances or psychological factors. Two characters, however, stand out, as being more directly affected by the political changes which characterise 'l'époque'. Dussardier and Sénécal put politics at the forefront of their lives, pursuing their political ideals with an unrivalled degree of commitment. Although not without personal feelings, they owe their place in the novel primarily to their functions as representatives of political attitudes.

Both have deprived backgrounds, Sénécal as the son of a 'contremaî-tre' from Lyons, Dussardier as an illegitimate child, and both have formative experiences which mark them out for a political role. Both are ardent Republicans and are active participants in the February Revolution. But there the similarity ends. Temperamentally they are opposed; Dussardier is warm, affectionate, loyal, Sénécal cold, hard, mathematical, dogmatic, each seemingly epitomizing the hypertrophy of a single organ, 'cœur' or 'tête'. Dussardier is attracted to the ideal of republicanism because he is instinctively opposed to injustice, Sénécal because it will bring about a more rational organisation of society. Though both pit themselves against a common enemy, they do so in different ways, Dussardier bravely leaping to the defence of what appears to him to be the innocent victim of an unjustly brutal authority, Sénécal physically attacking the son of an aristocrat. Dussardier's reading is limited, Sénécal's extensive, but since he constantly seeks 'de quoi justifier ses rêves' it does not necessarily make him any the wiser.

Dussardier is not the least envious when he learns of Frédéric's windfall
('"Vous êtes donc riche maintenant? Ah! tant mieux"', p.138), while
Sénécal's reaction is one of surly resentment.

The critical point in both characters' lives comes in February 1848.
Dussardier is exultant: '"La République est proclamée! on sera heureux
maintenant! ... Toute la terre libre"' (p.295); Sénécal 'était de ceux qui,
le 25 février, avaient voulu l'organisation immédiate du travail; le
lendemain, au Prado, il s'était prononcé pour qu'on attaquât l'hôtel de
ville' (p.305). Although at this point they are fighting on the same side,
there is already a significant difference between the type of action they
engage in. Dussardier wishes to liberate prisoners ('"Les forts sont
occupés. Il faut que j'y aille!"', p.296) and throws himself selflessly into
heroic activity, believing that the world is about to change; Sénécal, on
the other hand, demands that a specific programme be implemented,
that society be regimented, without actually risking his life in direct
action, as far as we know. Subsequently, Sénécal, by virtue of his clearer
commitment to a specific programme, is more directly involved in
politics, acting as president of the political club Frédéric visits and
revelling in his power as a demagogue (p.310). In June, Dussardier, as a
member of the National Guard, fights to defend the Republic, though he
is by no means certain that he has followed the right course: 'Peut-être
qu'il aurait dû se mettre de l'autre bord, avec les blouses; car enfin on
leur avait promis un tas de choses qu'on n'avait pas tenues' (p.339).
Sénécal, on the other hand, has participated in the insurrection and is
imprisoned in the 'terrasse du bord de l'eau', unaffected by the kind of
doubts that afflict Dussardier, before being deported to Belle-Isle. Later,
although both characters lose some of their revolutionary fervour, they
diverge markedly, the one defending the Republic to the last, the other
entering the future emperor's police force on the grounds that 'la
dictature est quelquefois indispensable' (p.376). While Dussardier inter-
venes heroically to save the life of a political opponent on the barricade in
June, Sénécal has no compunction about running through the last loyal
defender of the Republic, concerned as he is with the masses rather than
with the individual.

Although they represent opposing tendencies within republicanism,
naive idealism and socialist authoritarianism, though one shows 'trop de
sentiment' and the other 'trop de logique', while one finally sacrifices
himself in his enthusiastic but simplistic commitment to the Republican

ideal, which fails to discriminate between a good and a bad Republic, and the other survives because his latent belief in authority accords with the general reactionary swing, both lead lives in which a changing political situation acts as a crucial determinant. Investing all their hopes and emotional energies in the attainment of a specific form of political organisation, their fulfilment depends almost entirely upon the progress of politics between 1848 and 1851.

Changes of political regime have a less dramatic impact on the development of other characters in the novel on account of their lack of commitment, although new possibilities are opened for Deslauriers in February 1848 and after the *coup d'état* of 1851. The cynical detachment of Hussonnet, the prudent adaptability of Martinon, the immersion in his art of Pellerin, the perpetual grumbling of Regimbart all grant a relative immunity to fluctuations in the political sphere. Frédéric, however, is not impervious to political developments, experiencing a change of mood prior to the February Revolution ('" Je suis la mode, je me réforme"', p.283) which is partly instrumental in bringing about the substitution of Rosanette for Madame Arnoux and later becoming infected with the general mood of relaxed frivolity which pervades Paris. But the direct influence of political developments upon his life is extremely restricted; indeed, one of the points that Flaubert is making is that it is possible to live through a series of major political upheavals yet still remain almost totally immersed in one's own private affairs. It is not simply the need to prevent the colourful historical element overshadowing the psychological element which leads Flaubert to intensify Frédéric's emotional life at each of the turning-points of history but rather the desire to present a certain model of human motivation in which psychological needs and chance together act as a counterbalance to the impact of political change.

The meaning of 'l'époque' might, however, be extended to cover not just the political changes that take place but also the cultural pressures and ideological influences to which the characters are exposed and in this case there is scarcely any character who is unaffected by it. Although the political situation is clearly outlined and dramatically affects two characters at least, it is arguably less important as a determinant than the central cultural phenomenon of the age which Flaubert defined as a preference for sentiment, associated with Rousseau, as opposed to reason, associated with Voltaire:

si nous sommes tellement bas moralement et politiquement, c'est qu'au lieu de suivre la grande route de M. de Voltaire, c'est-a-dire celle de la Justice et du Droit, on a pris les sentiers de Rousseau, qui, par le sentiment, nous ont ramenés au catholicisme;[31]
Si on avait continué par la grande route de M. de Voltaire, au lieu de prendre par Jean-Jacques, le néo-catholicisme, le gothique et la fraternité, nous n'en serions pas là.[32]

For Flaubert the ideals promoted by the 'queue de Rousseau',[33] in particular the ideal of equality, are suspect and entail a neglect of the more important ideals of freedom and equity:

Qu'est-ce donc que l'Égalité si ce n'est pas la négation de toute liberté, de toute supériorité et de la nature elle-meme? L'Égalité, c'est l'esclavage;[34] Si on avait eu souci de l'Équité et non de la Fraternité, nous serions haut![35]

The baleful consequences of the adoption of a sentimental approach to politics are, in Flaubert's view, most apparent in the ideology of the Utopian Socialists, who are frequently berated both in the *Correspondance* and in the novel itself. Socialists are accused of denying individual freedom, of seeking to impose in a rigidly authoritarian manner a regimented way of life, or exhibiting a mentality characteristic of the Middle Ages.[36] Flaubert insisted that there was a strong religious element in Socialism: 'Ce que je trouve de christianisme dans le socialisme est énorme'[37] and regarded Socialism and Catholicism as two sides of the same coin:

le socialisme est une face du passé, comme le jésuitisme une autre;[38]
Le néo-catholicisme d'une part et le socialisme de l'autre ont abêti la France. Tout se meurt entre l'Immaculée-Conception et les gamelles ouvrières.[39]

Socialists, he believed were fixated upon an impossible, ideal society, one which they had no hope of achieving: 'O Socialistes! C'est là votre ulcère: l'idéal vous manque et cette matière même, que vous poursuivez, vous échappe des mains'.[40] This preoccupation with the ideal entailed a fatal neglect of reality, of 'l'évolution fatale des choses',[41] or of what Flaubert described as 'l'organisation essentielle de l'histoire',[42] resulting in a failure to have any purchase upon reality.

One of the main implications of *L'Éducation sentimentale* is that the generation of 1848 necessarily fails because it has mistakenly followed 'les sentiers de Rousseau'. That the widespread sentimentality of the responses and attitudes of the characters is less a matter of individual choice than of cultural conditioning is for Flaubert axiomatic, taking, as he does, the view that human beings are penetrated, or as we might now say, interpellated, by the cultural values of their age.[43] The fact remains, however, that the characters in the novel are far from sharing an identical outlook and that in certain cases a clear polarisation of attitude is being presented. Under the umbrella of a hegemonic sentimentalism there is a gradation in the political sphere from the hard-headed, doctrinaire Socialism of a Sénécal to the naive, instinctive Republicanism of a Dussardier, just as in the private sphere there is a spectrum ranging from the practical, no-nonsense approach to women of Deslauriers to the reverential attitude of Frédéric. It is not so much a question of certain characters being impervious to the conditioning of the age but rather of the contradictions inherent in the culture being dramatised in the full range of characters. Thus Sénécal, as will be seen, embodies an authoritarian tendency latent in the Socialism which, according to Flaubert's analysis, is the result of having followed Rousseau's direction, but remains, on the whole, unemotional in his unbending pursuit of the millenium. Dussardier, on the other hand, is full of generous impulses and strong feeling and manifests a touching faith in the possibilities that a Republic would open up, but his views never crystallise into the clear, but ultimately sentimental dogma of Sénécal. In spite of their differences, both characters are seen as being tarred with the same cultural brush.

Alberto Cento's account of Flaubert's documentation for *L'Éducation sentimentale* reveals that there is a source for every statement made by Sénécal; the outlook of Sénécal and the development of his views are the product of a process of highly selective quotation from a wide range of Socialist tracts and papers. Thus, his 'idéal de démocratie vertueuse', incoherent and contradictory as it is, is assembled on the basis of a reading – his and Flaubert's – of representative and influential Utopian Socialists, as the narrator explains and Cento demonstrates.[44] Likewise, his adoption of a hard-line approach prior to the *coup d'état* (' "La fin des choses les rend légitimes. La dictature est quelquefois indispensable" ', p.376) is not simply the result of Flaubert's wish to score a point against Utopian Socialism or prove the equation 'Communisme = dictature'[45] but, once again, evidence of Sénécal's ideological permeability for, as

Cento has found, such views were commonly expressed in clandestine Jacobin papers, such as *Le Moniteur républicain*, before the February Revolution and in the *Annuaire Lesur* in 1849.[46] Flaubert may not have fully understood the historical reasons which help to explain Socialism and its demand for equality,[47] but he had read more than enough Socialist works to form an accurate picture of the impact Socialism could make on someone of a certain kind of sensibility and background.

It was not, however, Flaubert's belief that anyone in an under-privileged position in society but endowed with energy and a certain amount of intelligence would become an embodiment of 'la démocratie envieuse et *tyrannique*'.[48] Deslauriers, of similar background to Sénécal, reacts in the opposite way to the same cultural influences, rejecting with Flaubertian panache 'l'idolâtrie imbécile de l'autorité' prevalent in Utopian Socialism. The sources for Deslauriers's famous plea for a scientific approach to politics are, Cento lamely recognises, the *Dossier* and the *Correspondance* of Flaubert himself and to a certain extent the lawyer acts as a mouthpiece for Flaubert's own views on political matters – though his attitude as a whole is not without certain deliberately established contradictions –[49] but his negative response, contrasting with Sénécal's positive reaction, serves to stress the unavoidability of Utopian Socialism. Even if the reaction it generates is one of enraged rejection, it is something that leaves a mark on a person's sensibility.

Dussardier's attitude in political matters, in contrast, is largely instinc-tive and clearly rooted in his own personal experience but even he is not totally protected from the distorting effect of a certain cultural tradition: 'En face, ... une petite bibliothèque en acajou contenait les *Fables* de Lachambeaudie, *les Mystères de Paris*, le *Napoléon* de Norvins et, au milieu de l'alcôve, souriait, dans un cadre de palissandre, le visage de Béranger!' (p.386) Dussardier does not, however, have any clear idea about the kind of society he would like to see come into existence, childishly cherishing the Republic simply because 'elle signifait ... affranchissement et bonheur universel' (p.233) His emotions are strongest when confronted with examples of the brutality of 'le Pouvoir' or victimisation of the underdog.[50] As long as there is an oppressive régime in power, Dussardier's course of action is to seek the liberation of the oppressed but, faced with the ambiguous situation of June 1848, his sentimental Republicanism is found wanting. Responding characteristically to a generous impulse, he goes to the rescue of an urchin who has challenged the National Guards to shoot him but is himself wounded in the process. The fact remains, however, that he has fought against the insurrectionists and this may have been in the interests of oppression: 'le brave garçon était torturé par cette idée qu'il pouvait avoir combattu la justice.'

The divergent tendencies of Sénécal and Dussardier are taken to their logical conclusion at the end of the novel in the former's killing of the latter. Sénécal, who has always had authoritarian tendencies, finally aligns himself with the principle of Authority, for which he has declared his support by becoming a kind of Imperialist policeman. Imbued with 'l'idolâtrie imbécile de l'Autorité', an 'homme de théories' who is not concerned with individuals, he takes the life of the person who in the past has not just struggled valiantly for a common cause but has also rescued him from the hands of a brutal 'Autorité', all in the interests of a higher political good. Dussardier, on the other hand, has become so emotionally fixated on the ideal of the Republic, which for him is a kind of living repository of the hopes and aspirations of his generation (*'notre république'*, p.399), that when its demise is imminent, he is compelled to lay down his life in a last futile gesture. Previously, in June, Sénécal and Dussardier had fought on different sides but now they are placed face to face, locked in an opposition which reflects the contradictory attitudes to the principle of Authority prevalent in the culture to which the two characters are exposed. What the two share, however, is the illusion that it is possible to impose a superior form of political organisation upon humanity, irrespective of vested interests and 'l'organisation essentielle de l'histoire'.

It is, of course, not just in the political sphere that the Rousseauistic legacy is apparent. Frédéric's worshipping attitude towards Madame Arnoux both reflects and is rooted in a general revival of the Catholic religion, the cult of the Gothic and, more specifically, the poeticisation of woman associated with the cult of the Virgin Mary.[51] Frédéric's 'grande passion' is also clearly mediated by literary models, Romantic in the main,[52] while readiness to be lulled into a state of passive expectancy is a clear manifestation of 'le mal du siècle' which has been described as first and foremost 'le mal de l'avenir'.[53] As with Emma Bovary, however, the line separating cultural conditioning and individual characteristics is difficult to draw. Although, as will be seen in a later chapter, there is a strong parallelism between what happens in the political sphere and what happens in the private sphere, and although Frédéric and Dussardier follow a very similar evolution as the ideal upon which they are fixated gradually recedes, suggesting that 'une causalité globale'[54] is shaping the reactions of a wide range of characters, it is none the less the case that in the private sphere, such is the thoroughness with which the antecedents and temperament of characters are presented, the predominant impression created is that of cultural influences reinforcing rather than regulating the 'système' which determines individual responses. Although Flaubert is sensitive to all forms of cultural conditioning and makes Frédéric, like Emma, ideologically permeable, he is working with a notion of the self as individuated in a meaningful way prior to cultural determination.

There are grounds, therefore, for querying the view that as well as denying the characters themselves any 'compensatory understanding', Flaubert also denies the reader 'the consolation of understanding failure'.[55] On one level it might seem that the discussion between Frédéric and Deslauriers is designed to display the comical inability of the human mind to reach any kind of understanding of the past, come to terms with personal inadequacy or perceive any convincing overall pattern in experience. The attempts of the two men at reaching some general conclusion are in many ways ridiculously perfunctory and astonishingly naive. Yet it is characteristic of Flaubert to combine the utterly stupid and the unexpectedly perceptive and we should guard against automatic disqualification of whatever the characters say. Frédéric and Deslauriers achieve a nascent awareness – albeit at an age when they are unlikely to benefit from it – of the complexity of factors at work in their lives and theirs is not an education in which nothing whatever is learnt. What is more critical, however, is the degree of understanding which the reader achieves. It is certainly the case that there is something peculiarly elusive about the novel, which makes it difficult for the reader to say with any confidence where Frédéric and Deslauriers 'go wrong'. Does this mean, however, that the fictional world of *L'Éducation sentimentale* 'refuses to be composed'?[56] Comparing and contrasting the characters and destinies of Frédéric and Deslauriers in the light of the variables isolated in their discussion is not a totally futile or fruitless exercise. It is even possible to extract from the novel an overall conclusion to the effect that, however important external obstacles standing in the way of the fulfilment of aspirations might seem, in Frédéric's case, which is the case that carries the most weight, the critical factor which repeatedly accounts for the way he reacts is the way he is made, an altogether more difficult obstacle to overcome.

VI

Love

L'Éducation sentimentale devotes a considerable amount of space to relations between the sexes, presenting a wide spectrum of male attitudes to women ranging from the reverential to the exploitative and showing the powerful influence exerted by the simplified sexual stereotypes of virtuous woman, *lorette*, *grande dame* and provincial innocent. Undertaken in a critical spirit, Flaubert's presentation of modern love emphasises the inadequate nature of the responses of men to women and the untenable narrowness of the stereotypes upon which they are based. Through Frédéric, Flaubert seeks to 'montrer que le plus honnête homme, en matière de femmes, est un misérable'.[1] It is as if the development of Frédéric and his contemporaries has somehow been arrested at the stage of puberty. The final celebration of the brothel episode carries multiple resonances but one of the most striking is the suggestion that the apparently fundamental differences in attitude displayed by Frédéric and Deslauriers in the course of the novel are rooted in a common, seemingly ineradicable, immaturity. Whether revered or exploited, woman remains for both characters essentially a sexual object and the fact that 'nothing' happens in the brothel suggests that, however great the expenditure of time and energy, neither character has, in effect, succeeded in fully engaging with the opposite sex.

However fallible and misguided male attitudes to women, in general, may be shown to be, there is nothing simple or straightforward about Frédéric's 'grand amour'. 'Je ne vois de simplicité nulle part dans le monde moderne', Flaubert declared,[2] and it is above all Frédéric's strangely self-defeating, contradictory and problematic passion for Madame Arnoux that illustrates the complexity of modern man's responses. Flaubert's presentation of a familiar type of idealising love, already explored in depth by Balzac and Sainte-Beuve, though less overtly analytic, displays a more sophisticated awareness of the problems and contradictions inherent in the passion which is both selfless and

152

selfish, pointless and poetic, fulfilling and frustrating, and which seeks both to elevate and degrade its object.[3] Flaubert's account anticipates in its richness and subtlety subsequent analyses, in particular, those of Freud, Proust and Barthes.[4]

In *Mémoires d'un fou* Flaubert had already presented – albeit a good deal less dispassionately – a rudimentary form of the early idealising love undergone by Frédéric. The adolescent hero of this early work experiences 'une sensation toute mystique en quelque sorte, toute volupté à part' after encountering Maria.[5] Like Frédéric in the initial phase of his relationship with Madame Arnoux, he can only adore from afar since the object of his devotion remains confined within the circle of maternal duties and finally resorts to a very different kind of woman for the profanatory expression of his love: 'Oh! Maria, j'avais été traîner dans la fange l'amour que ton regard avait créé'.[6] In a striking manner, the central problem of the poeticisation of woman – the impossibility of making contact with the object of one's adoration – is outlined. *Mémoires d'un fou* also highlights the importance of what Freud called the 'psychical constellation connected with the mother'[7] in directing and shaping the idealising urge. In a vivid dream the hero pictures his mother drowning and himself powerless to come to her aid, while subsequently he is able to rescue Maria's shawl from the encroaching tide.[8] The symbolic significance of these incidents seems clear: the shawl can be seen as a metonymic substitute for Maria herself and the fact that it is rescued from the water in which the mother has drowned suggests that the finding of a love-object is to a large extent a refinding, as Freud later insisted.[9] The implication is that, underlying the idealisation of woman and rendered problematic by it, is the infantile fixation of tender feelings upon the mother.[10]

Madame Arnoux is first and foremost an idealised mother-figure and it is altogether appropriate that she should bestow her parting kiss upon Frédéric 'comme une mère'. The person to whom Frédéric devotes most of his time and energy is a mature, married woman, with at first one, then two, children, confined most of the time to a domestic orbit where she exhibits the maternal virtues of gentleness, loving care, patience, moral rectitude. From the outset her status as a mother is apparent to Frédéric but in no way detracts from her appeal. In his final tribute Frédéric celebrates precisely those characteristics which have put her out of his reach: 'C'était Mme Arnoux telle que vous étiez, avec ses deux enfants, tendre, sérieuse, belle à éblouir, et si bonne!' (p.423) Ironically, while in the first chapter Madame Arnoux's maternal qualities help to explain the strength of her appeal, at the end of the novel they constitute a powerful source of embarrassment. The woman who has been revered as a mother-figure is finally rejected for the same reason. Frédéric's retraction is the result of a complex variety of motives but uppermost is 'l'effroi d'un inceste' (p.423). Flaubert hints at what Freud made explicit: the obstacle raised against incest inevitably leads to the inhibition of sexual desire for anyone who recalls the incestuous figure.[11] Although on one notable occasion[12] the images of Madame Arnoux and his own mother become confused in his mind, and although in an earlier version Madame Moreau is made to kiss her son on the brow in an identical manner to Madame Arnoux at the end of the novel,[13] Flaubert does not wish to imply that Frédéric's adoration of Madame Arnoux is exclusively based upon his relationship with his mother. Frédéric's family circumstances – brought up by his mother alone after the death of his father in a duel before he is born – point to a strong attachment to his mother, who is shown to have a lasting influence over her weak-willed son,[14] but the value attached to the figure of the mother depends also upon cultural factors. 'Le culte de la mère', against which Flaubert railed,[15] the revival of the Marial cult and literary models such as Goethe's *Sorrows of the Young Werther*, explicitly referred to in the novel,[16] all help to establish motherhood as the pinnacle of female desirability, making it impossible to disentangle the familial from the broader cultural factor in the motivation of Frédéric's fixation on the mother-figure.

Following in the footsteps of Werther, the literary figure he most closely resembles, Frédéric's love for Madame Arnoux is at first purely subjective, hopelessly narcissistic, gratuitously reverential. In the opening encounter on the river steamer he can be seen setting in motion the wheels of a cumbersome mental process, mounting the time-honoured private production evoked by Barthes in connection with Goethe's novel:

> Charlotte est bien fade; c'est le piètre personnage d'une mise en scène forte, tourmentée, flamboyante, montée par le sujet Werther; par une décision gracieuse de ce sujet, un objet falot est placé au centre de la scène, et là adoré, encensé, *pris à partie*, couvert de discours, d'oraisons . . .[17]

Remorselessly, undiscriminatingly, the idealising gaze invests everything connected with the object of adoration – even that most banal of objects, the work-basket – with momentous significance, oblivious to the prosaic, even sordid, surroundings in which the 'apparition' takes place. It is not so much Frédéric's perceptions themselves, which are often sharp and detailed, that are called into question as the interpretation he puts upon them and the value he attaches to what he sees and hears. The details of the domestic situation Frédéric gradually makes out – the presence of the child, the affection of the husband ('Il chuchota dans son oreille une gracieuseté, sans doute, car elle sourit', p.8), the wife's Penelope-like absorption in embroidery – do not lead Frédéric to be less reverential or prevent him from dreaming of blissful happiness with Madame Arnoux. On the whole he remains passive, unrealistically hoping that she will say the first word, but there is a brief moment of action, rich in symbolic meaning, when he rescues the shawl that is about to fall in the water. If he is to enter her life, it will be in a restorative, protective rather than disruptive capacity.[18] What actually passes between Frédéric and Madame Arnoux – the utterly banal comment ('"Voilà bientôt l'hiver, la saison des bals et des dîners"') and the souful gaze ('un regard où il avait tâché de mettre toute son âme') – constitutes the minimal but sufficient basis for rapturous adoration. Frédéric's world has undergone a decisive change: 'L'univers venait tout à coup de s'élargir. Elle était le point lumineux où l'ensemble des choses convergeait' (p.10). From now on his existence will have a purpose and direction as a result of the opening up of the possibility of moving from the plane of everyday reality to a higher plane of 'sacred' love.[19]

At the end of his first year in Paris Frédéric has still not had a single opportunity of seeing Madame Arnoux; it is hardly surprising therefore that 'sa grande passion pour Mme Arnoux commençait à s'éteindre' (p.26). When he does meet her again, having overcome his dismay at discovering that the offices of *L'Art industriel* are not part of her normal orbit (p.40), he is immediately caught up in the same delusional system, doting on her every word ('Chaque mot qui sortait de sa bouche semblait à Frédéric être une chose nouvelle, une dépendance exclusive de sa personne' p.48) but not daring to look her in the eye. The routine musical performance produces a characteristically over-enthusiastic, inflated response in the vision of Madame Arnoux's reaction to a disembodied, air-borne lover ('son cou ... se renversait mollement sous des baisers aériens', p.49). Comically, a formal handshake opens up multiple interpretations ('Pourquoi cette main offerte? Était-ce un geste irréfléchi, ou un encouragement', p.49). Once again little is required to create a feeling of euphoria, releasing 'un afflux de tendresse qui l'énervait' (p.50). Love is primarily something that wells up inside Frédéric, given the slightest opportunity.

In the regular meetings which follow, Frédéric's contemplative gaze absorbs and animates the most insignificant details of appearance and setting but he makes little headway and receives scant reward for his long-suffering toleration of Arnoux. After a drab, empty summer spent in Paris and an outing in which he 'humait avec délices' the foul-smelling Parisian fog, Frédéric settles down into what becomes a full-time occupation:

> La contemplation de cette femme l'énervait, comme l'usage d'un parfum trop fort. Cela descendit dans les profondeurs de son tempérament, et devenait presque une manière générale de sentir, un mode nouveau d'exister. (p.67)

Madame Arnoux is the essential reference-point around which his metropolitan world is organised: 'Paris se rapportait à sa personne, et la grande ville, avec toutes ses voix, bruissait, comme un immense orchestre, autour d'elle.' (p.68) For all the intensity of his adoration, prudential considerations ('il préférait toutes les douleurs à l'horrible chance de ne plus la voir', p.69) and what he takes to be Madame Arnoux's natural modesty, combined with her clear warning not to overstep the mark, ensure the deadlock and 'angoisse permanente' of the moonsick lover (p.70). Contrasting with the frantic cavortings of his friends at L'Alhambra, Frédéric's version of Madame Arnoux sleeping 'tranquille comme une fleur endormie' (p.76), reminiscent of Félix de Vandenesse's image of Mme de Mortsauf as a lily 'toujours intact et droit sur sa tige',[20] projects upon the loved one a sexual quiescence which is a guarantee of moral superiority but requires the suppression of physical desire on his part. So the euphoria of the first dinner rapidly gives way to suicidal despair as the hopelessness of his situation and futility of his adoration are brought home to him.

As little is required to revive Frédéric's love as was needed to bring it into existence in the first place. Invited to Saint-Cloud for Madame Arnoux's birthday, Frédéric has his first 'serious' conversation, in which the 'droiture d'esprit' of Madame Arnoux is fully revealed. Feeling her looks penetrate him 'comme ces grands rayons de soleil qui descendent jusqu'au fond de l'eau' (p.84), his love becomes unconditional: 'il l'aimait sans arrière-pensée, sans espoir de retour, absolument' (p.83). Such unqualified devotion is marred, however, by Frédéric's complete lack of insight into the cause of Madame Arnoux's distress, of which he himself is the unwitting instrument. Having just received proof of her husband's infidelity, the last thing Madame Arnoux is likely to want to do is communicate with Frédéric through the medium of her child! But the inspiration Madame Arnoux provides is in no way dependent upon the actual encouragement she gives and for once the effect of Frédéric's devotion is not to enervate him: the admiration Madame Arnoux has expressed for orators gives rise to visions of courtroom notoriety and Frédéric displays a-characteristic application: 'Jusqu'au mois d'août, il s'enferma, et fut reçu à son dernier examen' (p.86). All to no avail, however, since his mother's precarious financial position abruptly removes him from the scene of his public triumphs for a period of three years.

The development of Frédéric's relationship with Madame Arnoux throughout Part II is rendered more complicated by an important new factor – the presence of Rosanette. The company of Rosanette, though a rival distraction, also serves to throw Frédéric back into the orbit of Madame Arnoux; when, for instance, he thinks Rosanette is about to become his mistress, he finds himself thinking of Madame Arnoux: 'Ce désir en éveilla un autre; et malgré l'espèce de rancune qu'il lui gardait, il eut envie de voir Mme Arnoux' (p.135). Frédéric struggles valiantly to maintain a distinction between the two women whom he sees in the stereotyped terms of his age as *femme vertueuse* and *lorette*, but they become confused precisely because he seeks to impose a clear-cut differentiation in his responses to them:

> La fréquentation de ces deux femmes faisait dans sa vie comme deux musiques: l'une folâtre, emportée, divertissante, l'autre grave et presque religieuse; et vibrant à la fois, elles augmentaient toujours, et peu à peu se mêlaient; – car, si Mme Arnoux venait à l'effleurer du doigt seulement, l'image de l'autre, tout de suite, se présentait à son désir, parce qu'il avait, de ce côté-là, une chance moins lointaine; – et, dans la compagnie de Rosanette, quand il lui arrivait d'avoir le cœur ému, il se rappelait immédiatement son grand amour. (p.146)

Increasingly interwoven, the two main strands in Frédéric's life are shown to be mutually supportive; Rosanette both compensates for the deficiencies of Madame Arnoux and enhances the appeal of her tranquillity. In other respects his attitude is unchanged; Frédéric continues to misinterpret words and gestures, to attach excessive importance to trivial utterances and to experience the urge to make sacrifices.

When Frédéric first meets Madame Arnoux again after his prolonged absence, her changed surroundings and domestic situation lead him to feel that she has undergone some kind of deterioration, while what he takes to be her indifference provokes the first of several incensed rejections. Significantly, it is only after he has made the acquaintance of Rosanette that he is 'ressaisi par un amour plus fort que jamais' (p.136) and almost immediately drawn into complicity with her (' "*Il* vous a mené au bal, n'est-ce pas?" '). Intimacy is achieved by suspect means – reporting on her husband's misdemeanours, sexual and financial: 'Il pouvait donc lui être utile. Le voilà qui entrait dans son existence, dans son cœur!' (p.144). While in Part I the strength of the affection uniting Madame Arnoux to her husband had been accepted by Frédéric as an essential part of her charm, in Part II he actively conspires to diminish her loyalty to Arnoux by encouraging his association with Rosanette, on the calculation that 'plus Arnoux serait détaché de sa femme, plus il aurait de chance auprès d'elle' (p.148). When the dissension becomes open – in the quarrel over the shawl – Frédéric experiences a mixture of guilt on account of his own encouragement of the purchase and exultation at the thought that 'par vengeance ou besoin d'affection, elle se refugierait vers lui' (p.169). It is the suffering of Madame Arnoux which raises his hopes and strengthens his love. As she dries her tears, Madame Arnoux appears more captivating and beautiful and for the first time Frédéric finds himself experiencing sexual desire for her: 'Malgré lui, il regardait la couche, au fond de l'alcôve, en imaginant sa tête sur l'oreiller; et il voyait cela si bien qu'il se retenait pour ne pas la saisir dans ses bras' (p.168). The addition of this element, combined with the complicity which develops between them, determines his exclusive concentration on Madame Arnoux after a long period of alternation between her and Rosanette.

Frédéric's hopes have, however, been raised prematurely; for all his parasitic clinging, the Arnoux marriage turns out to be frustratingly resilient. This is in part the result of Frédéric's own contradictory position. Concerned as he is for Madame Arnoux's well-being, he offers Arnoux substantial financial help and thereby refurbishes his image as breadwinner. More importantly, in spite of the intensification of his passion for Madame Arnoux, he becomes increasingly hesitant and inhibited:

> Bien qu'il connût Mme Arnoux davantage (à cause de cela peut-être), il était encore plus lâche qu'autrefois. Chaque matin, il se jurait d'etre hardi. Une invincible pudeur l'en empêchait; et il ne pouvait se guider d'après aucun exemple puisque celle-là différait des autres. Par la force de ses rêves, il l'avait posée en dehors des conditions humaines. (p.172)

But the obstacles are not purely internal. Although his financial support is rewarded with a visit which takes on a momentous importance ('ses talons se posèrent à des places différentes sur le tapis', p.188) and although Madame Arnoux accepts the rose which he offers her as a token of his affection, her reception of him at Creil, with its reasoned rejection of his advances, brings home to him 'l'inanité de son espoir'. Madame Arnoux's attitude is not, however, one of indifference – something Frédéric fails to appreciate – and his self-pity and angry dismissal do not completely obscure the fact that he takes flight from Madame Arnoux with almost as much precipitation as he has sought her out, suggesting that he is only too ready to accept humiliation as the price that has to be paid if her virtue is to be preserved.

The superficiality of Frédéric's rejection of Madame Arnoux is suggested by his half-hearted attempts at winning Rosanette, his anguished reaction when he is seen by Madame Arnoux in her company at the races ('sentant qu'une chose irréparable venait de se faire et qu'il avait perdu son grand amour', p.208) and by his instant resumption of his old posture of drooling wonderment on meeting Madame Arnoux in the street. As a result of Madame Arnoux's discovery of her love, Frédéric is allowed to make his first declarations and his first physical advances (p.269). While his fulsome tributes pour out unchecked, the amount of physical contact remains problematically restricted. On the first occasion he kisses her on the eyelids, which have temporarily veiled the source of the purity which paralyses him, but is interrupted by the accountant. On the next occasion he is more fervent but not more forceful, prefacing his declaration with the compulsive adoption of the reverential posture and emphasising in a conventionally euphemistic manner the spiritual quality of his love (' "Est-ce que vous ne sentez pas l'aspiration de mon âme monter vers la vôtre . . . " ', p.270). The possibility of Frédéric's elaborate tribute being backed up by appropriate deeds is precluded by his ready compliance with Madame Arnoux's plea – based, the reader suspects, more on the powerful physical effect produced upon her by Frédéric's words than on a realistic assessment of the likelihood of his making a move – that he should leave. Frédéric's failure to capitalise on the position of advantage in which he finds himself[21] can be attributed less to respect for Madame Arnoux's virtue than to the intensity of his desire which seeks self-preservation through self-denial.

In the subsequent idyllic meetings at Auteil the sexual element continues to be carefully contained: 'Il était bien entendu qu'ils ne devaient pas s'appartenir. Cette convention, qui les garantissait du péril, facilitait leurs épanchements' (p.271). There is something inherently artificial about such a repressive solution and growing intimacy produces increasing frustration: 'Toutes les précautions pour cacher leur amour le dévoilaient; plus il devenaient fort, plus leurs manières étaient contenues. Par l'exercice d'un tel mensonge, leur sensibilité s'exaspéra' (p. 273). Such an arrangement is not without its passing consolations, however; shared memories and shared dreams of 'une vie exclusivement amoureuse' (p.272), the simple open-air pursuits and aimless conversations of a leisured way of life, the way the most banal details of setting and appearance become charged with an individual meaning of their own, all contribute to 'une béatitude indéfinie, un tel enivrement qu'il en oubliait jusqu'à la possibilitié d'un bonheur absolu' (p.273), leaving unresolved the question of whether his forfeiting of what is euphemistically referred to as 'le bonheur absolu' is the cause or the effect of his experiencing 'une béatitude indéfinie'. The process of deferment cannot, however, continue indefinitely. Although Frédéric believes that Madame Arnoux appeals predominantly to the heart rather than the senses, he is consumed in her absence by 'des convoitises furieuses', finds himself beginning to hate her for her lack of responsiveness and finally elicits the promise of the meeting in the rue Tronchet which is synonymous with an agreement to consummate their love. How would Frédéric have reacted had Madame Arnoux not been detained? The pious nature of his preparations ('et plus dévotement que ceux qui font des reposoirs, il changea les meubles de place, etc.', p.276) suggests that even at this late stage desire has not completely displaced reverence and that, even if she had attended the rendezvous, he would have been no nearer to resolving the question of what he really wants of Madame Arnoux. But however confused and divided his expectations are, there can be no mistaking the intensity of his anguish when she fails to turn up (p.280).

As a result of the demands Rosanette and Madame Dambreuse make upon his time, there is little contact between Frédéric and Madame Arnoux in Part III. Three meetings, each with a distinct tonality, ensure, however, that the image of Madame Arnoux retains much of its power, in spite of the paucity of contact. At the first of these, the Dambreuse dinner, Frédéric is seen swinging from extravagant claims ('il jura qu'il n'avait pas vécu un seul jour sans être ravagé par son souvenir', p.345) to abrupt rejection (' "Eh bien, va te promener!" se dit Frédéric', p.345). Madame Arnoux's coldness is understandable, given both the public setting and his months of neglect, and Frédéric's impatience at the lack of instant response casts doubt on the validity of the earlier assertion 'et le vieil amour se réveilla' (p.344). A full explanation of the failure to attend the rendezvous is finally given in the second meeting and appears to revive Frédéric's love, but it is Madame Arnoux who makes the physical advances, stretching out her hand to him and opening her arms for him to embrace her, pointing to a deep-seated reluctance on his part to express his love in physical terms. That the real resistance comes from Frédéric is confirmed by the last encounter; Madame Arnoux has sought out Frédéric on the slender pretext that she wishes to repay her debts but really, it is made clear, in the hope that their relationship will be consummated. It is noticeable that it is Frédéric who is determined to confine their love to the past in the discussion of whether it was best for it to have remained unfulfilled. Madame Arnoux's use of the present tense ' "Cela vaut peut-être mieux" ') leaves possibilities open in spite of her apparently prudential attitude, while Frédéric's use of the conditional perfect (' "Non! Non! Quel bonheur nous aurions eu!" ') rules out such possibilities, in spite of what appears to be a vehement rejection of her cautiousness. Frédéric proceeds to conceal his violent dismay at the ravages wrought by time upon Madame Arnoux by sinking to his knees and delivering a moving, rhetorical tribute to the woman she once was but is no longer. But as she leans forward towards him and he experiences 'le contact indécis de tout son corps', Frédéric is overcome with emotion and arrests the movement towards physical union with the brief ' "La vue de votre pied me trouble" ', echoing her earlier plea ' "Laissez-moi! au nom du ciel!"'. Frédéric can proceed only so far in the demonstration of his love; when he embraces her, she is left suspended in a stereotyped posture of sexual receptivity: 'Elle y restait, la taille en arrière, la bouche entr'ouverte, les yeux levés' and finally pushes him aside in despair. Madame Arnoux's frank admission ('"J'aurais voulu vous rendre heureux"') provokes a last sudden burst of desire which is, however, rapidly stifled for a complex variety of motives – something akin to the obstacle set up against incest, practical and prudential considerations, and the desire that his ideal should not be degraded. This final renunciation, interpreted by Madame Arnoux as a sign of consideration, throws light retrospectively on the contradictory nature of his attitude to Madame Arnoux. What value is to be attached, one might ask, to an ideal which Frédéric shrinks from attaining? In avoiding physical expression of his love is Frédéric rising above the baseness of earth-bound sexuality or is his love for Madame Arnoux to be viewed as an alternative, hyper-civilised and self-deluding way of hoarding and regulating sexual energy through adoration. That sublimation should be a mark of modern man's debasement was the kind of paradox to appeal to Flaubert.

If Frédéric's attitude to Madame Arnoux is largely shaped by his perception of her as mother-figure, his response to Rosanette is determined by his narrow definition of her as the opposite of a mother-figure. While the presence of maternal characteristics leads him to look up to Madame Arnoux, their absence accounts for his tendency to look down on Rosanette. Diametrically opposed to the idealising urge which leads him to overvalue Madame Arnoux is the need to debase which makes him undervalue Rosanette. While idealisation renders the sexual element problematic, but makes for emotional release, debasement permits a freer expression of sensuality but is associated with a more inhibited emotional response. Once again personal and cultural factors are interwoven. The tendency to debasement can be derived from Frédéric's emotional fixation upon the ideal mother-figure which can be traced back to his childhood, but it also typifies the conventional attitude to women in nineteenth-century society. As Kate Millet puts it, 'patriarchal society tends to hold women in contempt, a contempt which is particularly intense in association with female sexuality.'[22] The exaggerated respect which is accorded to 'la femme vertueuse' coexists with a correspondingly extreme disrespect for the woman of easy virtue, sexual availability being taken as a sign of inferiority.

In spite of his view of her as a person of little worth, Frédéric's relationship with Rosanette does not follow the conventional pattern of rapid conquest and exploitation. Although in their first meeting she conforms to type in her blatant sexual provocation, Frédéric is reluctant to accept her invitation to dance (p.118) and subsequently, in his symbolic dream, expresses an unconscious fear of her sexuality ('il lui semblait qu'il etait attelé près d'Arnoux, au timon d'un fiacre, et que la Maréchale, à califourchon sur lui, l'éventrait avec ses éperons d'or', p.129). Further contact leads, however, to a more conventional response. In direct contrast to his adoption of a posture of respectful reserve with Madame Arnoux, Frédéric, automatically assuming that she is bound to become his mistress, accords himself a licence to make immediate physical contact with Rosanette, kissing her on the neck on her first visit (p.135) and making a more direct bid for her favours soon after (p.149). Adoption of a sexually acquisitive approach does not, however, produce the expected results. This is partly on account of a desire on Rosanette's part to be treated differently by Frédéric, partly on account of a certain half-heartedness in him which stems from his greater commitment to Madame Arnoux, and partly from a desire to avoid humiliating disappointment or interruption.

Frédéric's continuing relationship with a woman who resists his advances suggests that there is more to his response than the desire for sexual release. As with Madame Arnoux, it is Rosanette's lifestyle and entourage as much as the woman herself that appeals and he finds himself being won over by her lack of mercenary impulses ('Frédéric fut charmé par ce désintéressement', p.153) and amused by her impulsive, inventive, ebullient behaviour. Although he may wish to restrict his response to the physical, there are moments when 'il lui arrivait d'avoir le cœur ému', for instance the occasion in the Café Anglais when Rosanette places the petals of a flower between her lips and invites him to kiss her which 'attendrit Frédéric' (p.211). Here Frédéric's response spills over into one normally reserved for another kind of woman. Throughout Part II Frédéric's relationship with Rosanette constitutes an offshoot of his main relationship with Madame Arnoux; Rosanette is neglected when he makes headway with Madame Arnoux, cultivated when he seeks revenge. The seduction of Rosanette at the end of Part II, unflatteringly for her, is the direct result of his disappointment at Madame Arnoux's failure to attend the rendezvous.

While in Part II it takes a surprisingly long time for Frédéric to conquer Rosanette, in Part III, given his generally contemptuous attitude, it takes a surprisingly long time for him to break with her. From an early stage he is exasperated by 'l'ineptie de cette fille' (p.313) and he gradually becomes more and more irritated by her as he becomes aware of her poor taste, laziness and ignorance. His reasons for continuing the association are multiple. There is the joy of possession ('il éprouvait la joie d'un nouveau mari qui possède enfin une maison à lui', p.313) and conventional male pride at being able to protect a weaker being ('il fut heureux de ce qu'elle était faible et de se sentir assez fort pour la défendre', p.329); there is also his appreciation of the 'beauté toute nouvelle' which is revealed in Fontainebleau and of Rosanette's charming, childish ways; there is a strong sexual bond which finally degenerates into 'un goût des sens âpre et bestial' (p.393); lastly, there is a strong emotional element in his response which, though not allowed to develop, expresses itself in the need he feels in Fontainebleau to 'lui dire des tendresses' (p.330) and his feelings of pity on seeing how happy she is to be pregnant ('en le voyant si heureuse, une pitié le prit', p.362) or how upset after the quarrel with La Vatnaz (p.315). Frédéric is never able to match the intensity of Rosanette's emotions, however, particularly when she becomes a mother, just as he is unable to match the strength of Madame Arnoux's physical desire. For all his admiration of the maternal characteristics exhibited by Madame Arnoux, Rosanette's naively expressed maternal pride (p.387) fails to elicit from him a corresponding commitment. As Simone de Beauvoir aptly observes, 'C'est seulement dans le mariage que la mère est glorifiée, c'est-à-dire en tant qu'elle demeure subordonnée au mari'.[23]

Frédéric's affection for Rosanette is undermined by his involvement with Madame Dambreuse and his lingering attachment to Madame Arnoux. As a result of carefully timed coincidences Frédéric finds himself drawn away from Rosanette as she passes through all the major stages and crises of her life with him. Ironically, at the very moment Madame Dambreuse becomes his mistress, Rosanette resolves to give up all her other lovers (p.373). While in Part II Frédéric had been scandalised by any rapprochment between Madame Arnoux and Rosanette, in Part III he takes a perverse pleasure in alternating between Madame Dambreuse and Rosanette (p.371, p.390). The birth of Rosanette's child is overshadowed by the upheaval caused by the death of Monsieur

Dambreuse and his plans for marrying Madame Dambreuse. Although he has very little contact with Madame Arnoux her image is always at the back of his mind and largely responsible for his poor treatment of Rosanette and Mme Dambreuse: 'il y en avait une trosième toujours présente à sa pensée. L'impossibilité de l'avoir le justifiait de ses perfidies, qui avivaient le plaisir, en y mettant de l'alternance' (p.390). There are, however, two occasions where his preoccupation with Madame Arnoux proves particularly damaging for Rosanette. On the first, when Rosanette announces her pregnancy, he is still smarting from the humiliation of being plucked away from Madame Arnoux; instead of drawing closer to Rosanette on hearing the news, he ends up incongruously imagining that the child that is destined to be born will be his by Madame Arnoux not Rosanette (p.362). On the second occasion, the death of Rosanette's child, Frédéric's grief rapidly gives way to a more acute anguish over the 'malheur plus considérable' which the death of the child seems to him to foreshadow – the departure of Madame Arnoux – and at a time when he might have been expected to console Rosanette he is frantically trying to get together the money required to save another woman. Finally, the break with Rosanette which follows soon after is occasioned principally by what Frédéric incorrectly believes to be her vindictive treatment of Madame Arnoux (p.411). Earlier his adoration of Madame Arnoux had given Frédéric a sense of purpose in life; now his concern for her has become increasingly disruptive, making him increasingly and at times unjustly dissatisfied with Rosanette. The painfully inadequate nature of his responses to Rosanette in her various crises and the general deterioration of his treatment of her as he becomes more and more exasperated can be attributed to his residual and totally pointless attachment to a woman he has scarcely ever seen in recent times.

The way Madame Arnoux's departure coincides with the collapse of his relationship with Rosanette is consistent with a general pattern in which Frédéric's two loves are interwoven, giving rise to the suspicion that, at the level of his sensibility at least, they constitute 'les deux moitiés d'un seul amour'.[24] Although Frédéric attempts to establish a rigid opposition between the two women, they are in many respects complementary rather than antithetical figures. It is possible to interpret Frédéric's relationship with Rosanette as an attempt at completing his relationship with Madame Arnoux by supplying, as it were, the missing element of sexuality. When he makes love to Rosanette, it is as if she is an intermediary, a means of reaching Madame Arnoux who would otherwise have remained inaccessible. The strong feeling of profanation generated by the episode stems not just from his having insulted Madame Arnoux by substituting Rosanette for her but also from an obscure sense that the virtue of the virtuous woman has somehow been destroyed as a result of his contact with the woman of easy virtue. In his subsequent relationship with Rosanette, who represents a kind of extension of Madame Arnoux, Frédéric can be thought of as trying to grasp the ideal but, precisely because of his divided sensibility, failing to do so. One of the reasons why the schoolboy visit to the brothel is viewed with such affection may well be that it represents a kind of parting of the ways, a miraculous moment of fusion of conflicting attitudes to women. For once the worshipful attitude coexists unproblematically with sexual expectation. The brothel constitutes the original site of Frédéric's 'seul amour', a kind of sexual Eden which throws into relief the post-lapsarian dissociation of sensibility which afflicts him.

The latent identity of the two women is suggested by numerous parallels and similarities hidden beneath a central opposition. When asked when she first realised his love for her, Madame Arnoux recalls 'un soir que vous m'avez baisé le poignet entre le gant et la manchette' (p.422) but a similar – or perhaps identical – kiss is planted on Rosanette's wrist on the way to the races ('Et, lui tenant toujours le poignet, il appuya dessus ses lèvres, entre le gant et la manchette', p.20). The deliberate confusion over who receives the kiss has the effect of making the reader wonder whether the two women are not one body. Significantly, the kiss is given just before they are brought scandalously together (p.208), suggesting that what is done to one woman can somehow rub off on the other. The syntactic similarity of 'il sentait, à travers la batiste, les fermes contours de son corps' (p.149) and 'il sentait à travers la ouate du vêtement la forme de son bras' (p.67) is striking and suggests a physical identity beneath the very different kinds of clothing which the two women wear. While Frédéric pictures Madame Arnoux as being 'tranquille comme une fleur endormie' (p.76), Rosanette's face resembles in his eyes 'une rose épanouie entre ses feuilles' (p.152), suggesting that they constitute open and closed forms of a single entity.

A number of objects, charged with symbolic significance, are found in the orbits of both women. On entering the apartment of Rosanette, the casket, which is closely associated with Madame Arnoux, undergoes a kind of profanation. Frédéric's response ('Il avait envie d'y porter les mains, de l'ouvrir', p.260) takes on a clear sexual significance. It is as if Madame Arnoux's image, as a result of contamination with Rosanette, has shed some of its inaccessibility, inviting the more direct response Frédéric exhibits prior to the planned rendezvous in the rue Tronchet. Other objects exist in duplicate – the threadbare cashmere shawl as opposed to the brand-new one given to Rosanette, the broken sunshade as opposed to the exotic replacement offered by Frédéric to Madame Arnoux. The precise significance of these similarities is not always easy to establish. Flaubert may have delighted in establishing 'sardonic parallels'[25] between two very different kinds of woman without necessarily wishing to suggest a fundamental sameness. While clearly critical of the excessively simple opposition between the two women to which Frédéric clings and taking a perverse delight in setting up 'une égalité fâcheuse' (p.133) between them, he may still wish to stop short of a complete equation or conflation of *la femme vertueuse* and the *lorette*. What cannot be doubted, however, is the powerful repercussions in the psychological sphere of the assimilation – purely aesthetic in origin – of Madame Arnoux and Rosanette. Flaubert courts disaster by stripping away differential relations to reveal an underlying sameness and dismantling 'la barre de l'opposition, fondement de toute "pertinence"',[26] but in so doing he also makes a major contribution to our understanding of the complexities of male sexuality, and, in particular, of the hidden connection, established at an unconscious level, between idealised mother-figure and prostitute.[27]

Overshadowed by his preoccupation with Madame Arnoux and Rosanette, Frédéric's casual interest in the home-town sweetheart, Louis Roque, fails to develop into the kind of permanent attachment which, according to one critic,[28] would have afforded him lasting happiness. The freckled child who freely roams her father's garden attracts Frédéric in the first instance because of her resemblance to Marthe, Madame Arnoux's daughter, and his lifting her up to kiss her represents an attempted continuation of his recent physical contact with Marthe. During his long provincial exile, Louise comes to fill an emotional gap in his life ('Son cœur, privé d'amour, se rejeta sur cette amitié d'enfant', p.95) but, thinking of her as a child, he fails to appreciate either the intensity of her devotion in spite of its resemblance to his own adoration of Madame Arnoux, or her nascent sexuality and accompanying feelings of shame. When he returns to Nogent in Part II the intensity of feeling shown by the rapidly maturing Louise assuages his wounded pride and provokes mild euphoria: 'Pour la première fois de sa vie, Frédéric se sentait aimé; et ce plaisir nouveau, qui n'excédait pas l'ordre ses sentiments agréables, lui causait comme un gonflement intime' (p.251). Though attracted by her candour and youthful freshness, Frédéric is arrested in his response to Louise by the same instinctive fear of sexual contact as is apparent in his relationship with Madame Arnoux: 'devant cette vierge qui s'offrait, une peur l'avait saisi' (p.253). In spite of his undertakings, Frédéric makes little attempt at proceeding to marriage with Louise; though tempted by her fortune and admiring her frankness and spontaneity, he is put off by her lack of taste and social graces, which is glaringly exposed when she is placed in a Parisian environment ('ce peu d'élégance avait contribué sans doute au froid abord de Frédéric', p.345). It is only when all else has failed that his mind turns tentatively to Louise ('"Qui sait, cependant? ... plus tard, pourquoi pas?"', p.417), taking for granted, as erroneously as the hero of *Sylvie*, the readiness of the provincial standby to wait indefinitely.

   In contrast to Louise, Madame Dambreuse, the rich, fashionable wife of a Parisian banker, is regarded by Frédéric as a worthy conquest. If the provincial setting in which Louise finds herself lowers her in Frédéric's estimation, the high Parisian society in which Madame Dambreuse moves with such ease is an essential part of her complex charm. While Louise, the provincial standby can always be counted upon, however casual his treatment of her, Madame Dambreuse, with her social graces and puritanical manner, needs to be treated with infinite respect and tact 'comme une chose anormale et difficile' (p.367). If Frédéric's behaviour with Madame Arnoux is largely instinctive, his treatment of Madame Dambreuse, stemming as it does from naked social ambition ('Une maîtresse comme Mme Dambreuse le poserait', p.366), is constantly calculated, though, as it turns out, on the basis of a whole series of false assumptions. The ease of his conquest belies the sexual impregnability he has anticipated, while her attacks on her husband and Cécile and her domineering ways are a long way off 'les délicatesses de sentiment' (p.367) he expects of her. In spite of 'la désillusion de ses sens' (p.376) and his disappointment at the contraction of Madame Dambreuse's fortune, Frédéric continues to feel obliged to treat her with a greater degree of consideration and respect than Rosanette, even though the latter is having his child. With his preconceived ideas about 'le monde supérieur des adultèras patriciens' (p.369) he shows remarkable compliance, falling in with Madame Dambreuse's plans for them to marry and meekly accompanying her to church, though he does not give up Rosanette as instructed, as if wishing not to be taken over completely by her. It is not until he receives final proof of her brutal egoism when she pig-headedly insists on purchasing the treasured chest belonging to Madame Arnoux, that he is finally led to throw off her yoke. Significantly, the woman who seems least worthy of his attentions is the one he comes closest to marrying; the way in which he perseveres – even if he has to draw in a profanatory way upon the memory of Madame ·Arnoux – in a relationship which is in so many respects unrewarding, is evidence of his loss of powers of discrimination and general deterioration. If this is what the atrophy of sentiment leads to, sentiment cannot be all that bad.

For all the time and energy he lavishes upon the opposite sex, Frédéric fails to reach a viable attitude or experience lasting fulfilment with any of the four women he knows. Other characters, while not as constantly preoccupied with women, are hardly more successful. In some cases the problem does not arise, Sénécal recommending complete abstinence ('il valait mieux s'abstenir', p.58) and Pellerin, even more comically, preferring tigers (p.57). An alternative to sublimation is provided by Hussonnet's free and easy bohemian familarity and Deslauriers's no-nonsense approach ('"Est-ce que je vais m'empêtrer de femmes"', p.75). However, the brief account of the latter's relationship with Clémence Daviou suggests that the demands of women upon his time and attention cannot be so easily evaded. A clearly exploitative attitude is apparent in Martinon's association with a well-dressed but unattractive woman (p.74), his relationship with Madame Dambreuse and, possibly, too, in his apparent 'désintéressement imprévu' (p.368) in marrying Cécile. Following a well-defined Balzacian formula women are used as a means of social advancement. In contrast to such demeaning approaches are the respect Regimbart professes for 'les femmes vertueuses' (p.407), Dussardier's naive and unfulfilled desire to 'aimer la même, toujours' (p.57) and the extreme timorousness of Cisy ('M. de Cisy avait à leur endroit toute espèce de crainte', p.58). The implication of *L'Éducation sentimentale* is that for the generation of 1848 there is no happy medium between idealisation and debasement; women are either madonnas, to be placed on a pedestal and worshipped from afar, or instruments of sexual gratification or social ambition.

 The only character who comes near to avoiding a one-sided approach is Arnoux who, much to Frédéric's annoyance, gets the best of both worlds. Arnoux is both an inveterate philanderer and a devoted husband, who successfully avoids too reverential an attitude to his virtuous, long-suffering wife and too dismissive an attitude to his mistress, largely because he does not see them in the same stereotyped terms as Frédéric. Thus, he is unproblematically appreciative of his wife's physical charms, which bear comparison, as far as he is concerned, with those of Rosanette, and as a token of his affection thinks of taking her to a 'cabinet particulier', a treatment normally accorded to a different kind of woman (p.175). Rosanette, on the other hand, is more than just 'une bonne fille' but someone who needs to be treated with generosity and respect. The indulgence and affection shown by both women towards Arnoux stems from their realisation that within the traditional wife-and-mistress framework Arnoux is as attentive as is possible. This does not mean, however, that he is presented as a paragon; there is an element of thoughtlessness in his behaviour, apparent in the way he uses a note arranging for a new mistress to wrap round the bouquet he presents to his wife, in his constant transfer of objects from one woman to another and in his blurted-out praise of his wife's physique. Arnoux's attitude to his wife, Frédéric rightly feels, is muddled and inconsistent. None the less, Arnoux provides a useful foil to Frédéric's inability to love where he desires or desire where he loves.

 In addition to the close investigation of Frédéric's responses to women, Flaubert offers a sympathetic and penetrating account of various female responses to men. Although Frédéric's changing attitude to the four women in his life constitutes the principal narrative focus, there is sufficient information provided for the reader to reach a clear understanding of the nature of their responses to him. Paradoxically, the man who, on the face of things, might appear singularly unsuccessful with women, provokes feelings of unusual intensity in all four women, for each of whom, idealised as a person of exceptional thoughtfulness and sensitivity, he appears to open up the possibility of a kind of fulfilment so far denied. But although Frédéric does not altogether disappoint these expectations, allowing each woman to experience a brief release from the generally unrewarding conditions and frustrations of her life, he is unable to sustain his devotion and finally abandons each of them. In spite of marked differences in origin, position and temperament, the expectations of all four women converge in a remarkable manner upon a single figure who represents the poor best patriarchal society has to offer. The manner in which each woman responds to Frédéric belies the stereotype with which each is associated and allows a more complex character to emerge, Madame Arnoux revealing herself to be less self-sacrificing, Rosanette less flighty, Louise less long-suffering and Madame Dambreuse less straight-laced than might have been expected.

Flaubert's complaint that the cult of the Virgin Mary 'avait formulé et annulé à son profit toutes les aspirations féminines du temps'[29] is directly relevant to Madame Arnoux, whose story is that of a woman who has invested all her energies in the cares and responsibilities of motherhood. She is not, however, a static figure; much of the psychological interest of her character lies in the subtle changes brought about in her behaviour by the gradual erosion of her commitment to the maternal ideal, an ideal whose problems she lives, as it were, from within. As her husband's infidelities become more flagrant and his financial enterprises more reckless, as her children grow away from her and her material conditions deteriorate, the balance between her romantic idealism and her down-to-earth practicality is altered and prudential considerations give way to the urge to seek some kind of compensation for 'les chagrins, les inquiétudes, les humiliations' (p.360) which she endures as wife and mother. Ironically, however, Frédéric does not keep pace with this development and finally insists on restoring to her the maternal image she seeks to shed.

It is throughout Part I, when the reader has least access to the inner life of Madame Arnoux, that she seems happiest in the role of mother, ministering with loving care to the needs of her child, gracefully accepting the tribute of her husband's affection and deftly deflecting Frédéric's tentative advances. The first stirrings of dissatisfaction on discovery of Arnoux's infidelity, completely misunderstood by Frédéric, come at the end of Part I (p.85), only to be followed by her re-immersion in maternal cares (p.109) on the birth of a second child during Frédéric's long absence from Paris. Madame Arnoux displays a certain irritation with her husband's reckless treatment of the child and, while in Part I she had shown considerable affection for him, she makes no attempt in Part II to hide her antipathy for him from Frédéric, who enters into ambiguous complicity with Madame Arnoux as her husband's watchdog. Marital disharmony being a precondition of his own success, Frédéric is in the unfortunate position of wishing unhappiness upon the woman he loves; disturbingly, it is her suffering which facilitates his approach.

Yet, for all his faults, Madame Arnoux makes it clear when Frédéric visits her at Creil that she does not contemplate leaving her husband ('Mais, pour l'amour de ses enfants, jamais elle n'en viendrait à une telle extrêmité', p.172) and parries Frédéric's hesitant advances and clumsy overtures with repuditions of romantic passion ('tout cela ... était criminel ou factice', p.199) and common-sense, down-to-earth pronouncements ('"L'expérience est trop coûteuse"') which once would have been welcomed as evidence of her 'droiture d'esprit' (p.83). These virtuous protestations conceal, without Madame Arnoux or Frédéric being aware of the fact, feelings and impulses over which she does not have complete control and which have already manifested themselves on two occasions. On the first of these, her visit to Frédéric's apartment to thank him for the help he has given her husband, she performs the task of begging further favours 'avec effort', suggesting a degree of embarrassment at having to follow her husband's ill-judged instructions that they should trade on Frédéric's attachment to her, but there are hints – the almost provocative way she twirls the rose Frédéric has offered her, for instance – that she does not find her new role totally uncongenial. On the second, Frédéric's unexpected visit to Creil, although he has clearly announced his arrival ('Il appela trés haut'), she appears to him in the half-clad state associated with Rosanette and with her hair emblematically half-down. It is, of course, possible that Madame Arnoux has simply failed to hear Frédéric but her exclamation and rapid exit when he enters do not entirely dispel the suspicion created by her subsequent blushing when he compliments her on her earlier appearance that what happens is not altogether accidental. However, at this stage, any impulse to give way to a growing attraction to Frédéric is rapidly undercut by the virtuous determination to remain not so much 'insensible' as 'sourde quand il le faut' (p.201).

Like Emma in her relationship with Léon in Part II of *Madame Bovary*, Madame Arnoux is only dimly aware of what is happening to her and it is not until Deslauriers's announcement of Frédéric's marriage to Louise that she comes to the realisation that she loves Frédéric. On this occasion, the first time that the reader is given direct access to her inner life, she proves to be remarkably similar to Frédéric in her readiness to experience love as a great limitless void ('Il lui semblait descendre dans quelque chose de profond, qui n'en finissait plus', p.249) and subsequently she is shown sharing the same extravagant aspirations ('Et ils s'imaginaient une vie exclusivement amoureuse, assez féconde pour remplir les plus vastes solitudes, excédant toutes les joies . . . ', p.272). It is as difficult for her to realise her dreams as it is for Frédéric, however; birds of a feather, they are both affected by the image of the ideal mother-figure. For Madame Arnoux Frédéric's reverential attitude is mandatory, confirming her ecstatic sense of herself as a kind of Madonna; it is noticeable how, even before she realises she loves him, Madame Arnoux expects unquestioning loyalty from him and is deeply shocked at the thought that he might be attracted to another woman. With an overpowering, almost religious, sense of her own purity, the sexual element in her love for Frédéric is problematic; it is only when she is caught unawares (p.269) that she responds directly, the rest of the time the same 'pudeur' as hampers Frédéric leading her to feel ashamed of her sexual responses ('"Oui . . . ! je fais mal! j'ai l'air d'une coquette"', p.274). Madame Arnoux can neither sustain nor throw off the maternal ideal; on the one hand, a variety of factors, growing dissatisfaction with her husband, deepening affection for Frédéric, a hypersensitivity caused by the repression of sexual desire, combine to make her agree 'avec une bravoure de décision' to the meeting in the rue Tronchet, a meeting whose tacit purpose is the consummation of their love. On the other hand, the illness of her child brings home to her the inescapability of her maternal responsibilities and leads to a resuscitation of the maternal drive when she offers up the sacrifice of her passion for the sake of her son (p.282). The constraints imposed by the maternal ideal, symbolized by the dog which in her dream tugs at her dress (p.280), have an inexorable effect, preventing her from following her natural inclination, trapping her in the prison of motherhood.

Madame Arnoux's trials and frustrations do not end with the illness of her child; in Part III, though she sees little of Frédéric, the same factors in an intensified form lead her to surrender to passion again (p.360), only to be deprived once again of the opportunity of fulfilment, this time by the interruption of Rosanette, claiming her rights. The manic laughter of Madame Arnoux ('un rire aigu, déchirant', p.361), echoing her earlier response to Deslauriers's declaration of love ('un rira aigu, desespérant, atroce', p.248), suggests an uncontrollable anguish at the way her desires are frustrated by a malign 'fatalité' which conspires to make the wrong people turn up at the wrong time, as well as hinting at a suppressed mental instability brought about by her unsatisfactory lot. In the final meeting she experiences her last and most decisive disappointment. Released now from her maternal responsibilities, just as Frédéric is released from his obligations towards Rosanette, Madame Arnoux is in a state of unequivocal receptivity, which Frédéric chooses to ignore, offering her instead adoration for the woman she no longer is, which she touchingly accepts 'avec ravissement'. Frédéric's renunciation both delights and dismays her; it is evidence of the purity of his devotion yet deprives them both of an experience which she, at least, believes would have been rewarding, if only as a long-delayed compensation for all her suffering. While Frédéric is content for her to bestow upon him no more than a maternal blessing, Madame Arnoux's last gesture, the savage cutting of the lock of white hair, indicates her bitterness and resentment not just as the way she has been overtaken by time but also at the way she has been forced – by cultural pressures, by her own inclinations, by Frédéric – into a role which imposes severe restrictions upon her activity and development.

In comparison to Madame Arnoux, the reader is given very little direct access to the inner life of Rosanette but he is told enough about her background and behaviour to form a picture of a woman who, like Madame Arnoux, is not altogether at home in the role accorded to her. If Madame Arnoux illustrates the drawbacks of the maternal ideal, Rosanette shows that the lot of the *lorette*, carrying as it does a very different set of obligations, is no more congenial. While Madame Arnoux is frustrated ultimately by Frédéric's excessive seriousness, Rosanette is frustrated by his frivolousness, his inability to see in her anything other than the woman of easy virtue. As with Madame Arnoux, the psychological interest of Rosanette consists in her manifestation of traits which, while not undermining, are not altogether consistent with the stereotyped expectations Frédéric has of her, suggesting that she is more than the feather-brained, inconsequential, flighty creature he imagines her to be. While not wishing to idealise Rosanette as possessing a heart of gold, it is possible to detect in her an intensity of feeling which belies her habitual superficiality.

Although Rosanette is expert in the art of sexual provocation and although she stares at Frédéric much longer than duty calls for, an element of desperation is apparent in the frantic pleasure-seeking which she organises with mock-military imperiousness and the account of her background reveals just how reluctant she had been too embark upon her career as a woman of easy virtue. The mobility of Rosanette's responses and the inconsistency of her attitudes makes her difficult to understand ('Il était impossible de la connaître', p.150) but can be interpreted as evidence of a conflict between her true nature and the role she is forced to play. Fecklessness, frivolity, mendacity, infidelity, a mercantile attitude to her own sexual attractions can all be seen as professional deformations which do not necessarily reflect her true needs and desires. There are several signs that Rosanette is not inured to the role of the *lorette*; from the bitterness of casual remarks such as ' "ça ne coûte rien" ' (p.135) and ' "Oh! moi, on m'aime toujours! ... Reste à savoir de quelle manière" ' (p.260), her genuine embarrassment at the liberties taken by Frédéric (p.149), the readiness with which she responds to his impractical suggestion that she should give up Oudry (p.153) to the strength of her resentment against 'les femmes honnêtes' and the determination and sentimentality with which she attempts to devote herself to Frédéric and her child, there is abundant evidence to suggest that Frédéric's remark to Madame Arnoux in (' "Vous n'avez personne qui réponde à vos besoins de dévouement" ') applies equally well to her. Deliberately, if unconsciously, Rosanette protests against the role she is forced to adopt by playing it badly; her carefully timed absences, her playing of one man off against another, the humiliating way she keeps Frédéric in reserve, represent an attempt to gain some kind of revenge against the sex which fails to take her seriously, while her bursts of disinterestedness are a reaction against the cupidity she is supposed to manifest. But the conflict between real desires and the exigencies of her role produces behaviour which appears to Frédéric inconsistent, even incoherent; on the one hand she flaunts her sexuality and advertises her availability, on the other she resists his advances; at one moment she makes open invitations to him, at the next wantonly betrays or humiliates him, suggesting that her attitude to him is as contradictory as Madame Arnoux's, since in her case, too, he activates but fails to recognise the real person beneath the stereotype.

It is above all in Part III that a new depth to Rosanette's character is revealed; removed from the environment which has corrupted her, she manifests a sentimentality and sensitivity beneath her sensuality and ignorance, a truthfulness about her past which contrasts with her earlier mendacity, while the intensity of her joy in motherhood, her frantic attempts to extract the most from her trips to the countryside, including the childish collecting of dung to take back to Paris, her desire to be faithful to Frédéric ('elle se jura intérieurement de ne plus appartenir à d'autres', p.373), her domestic and social ambitions (p.393), all show her belieing the role to which Frédéric and society insist so unreasonably on confining her: 'Elle mentait à son rôle enfin, car elle devenait sérieuse . . .' (p.393). Although for Rosanette, as for Madame Arnoux, Frédéric is more sensitive than other men ('La pauvre Maréchale n'en avait jamais connu de meilleure', p.333), she too is the victim of his inability to see beyond the stereotypes of his age.

While Frédéric is uncertain about the precise nature of Rosanette's feelings, he is left in no doubt about those of Louise Roque, on account of the forthright, direct, totally sincere manner in which she demonstrates her affection on more than one occasion. The harsh conditions of Louise's upbringing, neglected by her mother, humoured by Catherine, ostracised by respectable society, develop in her a headstrong unconventionality (' "Est-ce bête, les convenances!" ', p.250) which leads her to dispense with the reserve and passivity traditionally expected of a woman and display in their various encounters an unabashed sensuality. The quality of Louise's love can be explained largely in terms of its being rooted in an infatuation of childhood:

> Toute petite, elle s'était prise d'un de ses amours d'enfant qui ont à la fois la pureté d'une religion et la violence d'un besoin. Il avait été son camarade, son frère, son maître, avait amusé son esprit, fait battre son cœur et versé involontairement au fond d'elle-même une ivresse latente et continue. (p.251)

But, for all the frank intensity of her passion and the courage she shows in the pursuit of her desires, Louise's love lacks the reticence which is held to characterise more profound feelings ('Les affections profondes ressemblent aux femmes honnêtes; elles ont peur d'être découvertes', p.172). While Frédéric finds himself held back by complex inhibitions, Louise approaches the object of her adoration with the frenzied violence of a lioness pouncing on her prey and, while he appears remarkably undemanding in his worship of Madame Arnoux, she imagines that her passion confers automatic rights over Frédéric. Seen at her best in the provincial setting which so frustrates her, Louise blunders in Paris, when she makes her most decisive bid to secure Frédéric's affection, failing, in spite of her undoubted intelligence, to appreciate the alternative attractions that surround her. But for Louise Frédéric represents the one and only possibility of fulfilment, ensuring – as her repeated reproaches and tears emphasise – that she is not the least deceived of all the woman he fails.

Madame Dambreuse is the least sympathetic, most unfeeling of the main female characters. She gives herself to Frédéric, 'par ennui' (p.375) and, desiring 'un grand amour', attempts to rule over him with a rod of iron, showering him with gifts and mementoes 'pour qu'il n'eût pas une action indépendante de son souvenir' (p.375), fiercely interrogating him when she suspects him of infidelity and insisting 'par esprit de domination' (p.391) that he accompany her to church. In numerous ways Madame Dambreuse reveals herself to be less attractive than her gilded image and her graceful, polite, considerate social persona conceals a ruthlessly egoistic, relentlessly domineering, haughtily indifferent nature. The delicate charm, controlled coquettishness and practised badinage which characterise her early treatment of Frédéric give way to less desirable traits, the crude outbursts and increasingly astringent manner, a possessiveness that threatens to take over his whole existence and the venomous persiflage of the auction scene. With the unthinking arrogance of the *grande dame*, Madame Dambreuse tends to take Frédéric's subservience too much for granted, allowing the sheer violence of her hatred for her husband and Cécile to be witnessed by him and too readily assuming that he will want to marry her after the loss of her fortune. Madame Dambreuse's distress on learning of Frédéric's attempts at rescuing Madame Arnoux is genuine enough but the vindictive way in which she retaliates – attacking Madame Arnoux rather than Frédéric – proves to be her downfall. Ironically, this most calculating of women miscalculates just how far she can go in asserting her authority over Frédéric. In the case of Madame Dambreuse our understanding does not lead to sympathy. We may know and see how she has suffered, in the past, over her husband's introduction of his illegitimate daughter into their household and Martinon's abandonment and appreciate why she is so fearful of losing Frédéric but her struggle for her emotional dues – when she is not more preoccupied with her financial rights – leads to a cynically calculating, coldly domineering type of behaviour which is difficult to excuse.

On the whole, however, the reactions of the female characters are made to seem more mature, less divided, less wayward than those of the male characters. Each is able to add something missing in Frédéric's response to them, Madame Arnoux finally revealing herself to be less sexually inhibited, Rosanette less emotionally uncommitted, Louise less lacking in the courage of her convictions, while even Madame Dambreuse is faithful to Frédéric once he becomes her lover, whereas he continues to see Rosanette. *L'Éducation sentimentale*, like *Madame Bovary*, displays a good deal of insight into the unsatisfactory predicament of women under the patriarchal system and its account of female attitudes is broadly more sympathetic, less critical, than its presentation of male attitudes, which are shown to be governed by a number of highly restrictive stereotypes. Broadly speaking, it seems that Flaubert achieves a degree of detachment from the sexual stereotypes of his age. A recent study sees inscribed in Flaubert's works all the prejudices of patriarchal society but this is to underestimate the persistence of the urge in Flaubert to query all the assumptions that make up the conventional view of life.[30] Doubtless, in his life, Flaubert was often as blinkered as the next man but this does not prevent his moving, in his novels, towards an almost total rejection of accepted views about sexual difference, which goes a long way towards explaining the vitality and complexity of both his male and female characters.

Relations between the sexes are at the heart of the psychological element in the novel and to a large extent the impact the novel makes as a psychological study depends upon its presentation of love, in particular Frédéric's love for Madame Arnoux. Some critics locate much of the uncertainty of the novel in this sphere:

> The novel does not simply portray a banal personality but shows a marked lack of interest in what we might expect to be the most important questions: what is the precise quality and value of Frédéric's love for Madame Arnoux? for Rosanette? for Mme Dambreuse?[31]

Although, as the preceding account has tried to show, *L'Éducation sentimentale* seeks to establish the precise quality of Frédéric's responses to various women, it does leave open the whole question of the value to be attached to his responses. In particular, his love for Madame Arnoux has provoked widely different critical reactions. For some it is the most obvious example of the 'bêtise' that characterises the behaviour of a whole generation.[32] For others it is the aspect of his experience which redeems an otherwise base and undistinguished existence.[33] This uncertainty need not necessarily have a detrimental effect on the psychological dimension. On the contrary, if all that is ambiguous about the search for the ideal through the senses is to be brought out, it is necessary that a psychological context be established, so that the repercussions and implications of adoration can be examined. And although Madame Arnoux as an object of desire exists almost entirely in the mode of absence,[34] if the fact that she is first and foremost an image for Frédéric is to emerge clearly, her reality as a harassed, middle-class woman, increasingly dissatisfied with her lot needs to be adumbrated. If the character of love is to be revealed as problematic, the characters in love need to bear a semblance of reality.

VII

Friendship

Although Frédéric's main preoccupation is with the opposite sex, he maintains a close if intermittent relationship with Deslauriers, is a frequent companion of Arnoux and keeps up a looser contact with a wide range of acquaintances. *L'Éducation sentimentale* is, therefore, concerned not simply with the complex psychology of relations between the sexes but also with the shifting pattern of intimacy and estrangement, allegiance and treachery, which characterises relations between friends. Just as his 'sentimental' nature makes Frédéric more considerate in his relations with women, so it also makes him a generous and affectionate friend, though in this sphere too he is not above reproach. Flaubert suggests that there is a kind of rivalry between love and friendship; although, on the whole, friendship takes second place in Frédéric's life, the last chapter shows it outlasting love, the bonds which bind him to Deslauriers proving more durable than those that have attached him to Madame Arnoux. At the same time the distinction between love and friendship is broken down. An element of 'camaraderie' is present in his relationship with Rosanette, while the pattern of his relationship with Deslauriers echoes the opposition between male and female roles, Frédéric, submissive, concerned with domestic matters and physical appearances, acting as the feminine partner, and Deslauriers, dominant, outgoing, less preoccupied with décor and appearance, acting as the masculine partner. Although Frédéric has always exerted 'un charme presque féminin' upon Deslauriers, and although there are frequent physical displays of affection between them, it seems inappropriate to talk of Frédéric's bisexuality;[1] in spite of the blurring of the distinction, love is shown to owe its pre-eminence over friendship largely to the way it provides an outlet for sexual as well as emotional energy and if friendship is shown outlasting love, it is partly because by this time Frédéric is a spent force.

Flaubert was intensely interested in the rationale of friendship and the plans for his last novel speculated at length about the complex play of similarity and difference upon which it rests. On the one hand, in spite of their differences, Bouvard and Pécuchet resemble each other; 'Contraste et pourtant ils se ressemblaient'.[2] On the other hand, it is the differences between them which seem most important, differences which allow them to complement each other: 'Ils s'emboîtaient; – se complétaient. Les dissemblances faisaient une harmonie.'[3] Although it is difficult, as is recognised in the final version, to 'expliquer les sympathies', an important insight into the mysterious alchemy of friendship is provided by the comment, 'chacun en écoutant l'autre retrouvait des parties de lui-même oubliées.'[4] If the two men find solace in each other's company, it is because each awakens in the other something dormant in himself, suggesting that the attraction of opposites is rooted in the need to escape the limitations of the self one has become as a result of a process of suppression. The sense of lack which this process of suppression gives rise to can be overcome by means of the vicarious contact that friendship can afford with the missing or suppressed elements. The appeal of friendship is that it puts one in touch with one's shadow, with one's lost other self. Certainly, the friendship between Frédéric and Deslauriers is rooted in the principle of complementarity, each supplying what is missing in the other. In almost every respect they are opposed; as a result of a background as harsh as Frédéric's has been comfortable, Deslauriers is active, forceful, rational, irascible, while Frédéric is passive, flabby, sentimental, gentle; and, corresponding to their opposed dispositions, each has a different objective, power or love. These multiple differences give rise to disagreements and antagonism but also, as a result of the way each intermittently admires and emulates the other, draw them together.[5]

With the principle of complementarity in mind, *L'Éducation sentimentale* charts the origins, intermittencies and final triumph of friendship. Frédéric and Deslauriers are attached by bonds which are established at an early stage, when both are still at school, and the pattern of their relationship is based upon the original dominance of an older boy over a younger. They are first brought together, in spite of the 'mille différences de caractère et d'origine' (p.13) which separate them, by Deslauriers's bold, violent, self-assertive attack upon a servant who has insulted him, which fills Frédéric with misplaced admiration. From the outset, Frédéric looks up to Deslauriers, offering him a 'dévouement' to which his harsh background makes him unaccustomed and which he repays with a flattering 'affection', coming as it does from 'un grand'. A strong emotional intimacy is rapidly established, strengthened by the constant sharing of interests and projects, the participation in escapades like the visit to the brothel and the opposition to their association from school and Frédéric's mother.[6] When the two friends are reunited after a long separation, the differences in outlook have intensified, Deslauriers's surly resentment at the limitations imposed on his pursuit of power by his straitened financial circumstances contrasting with Frédéric's ready renunciation of the quest for perfect helpmeet (' "Quand à chercher celle qu'il me faudrait, j'y renonce!" ', p.17). Yet, although they have diametrically opposed aims and temperaments, they continue to be drawn together; Frédéric is easily affected by his friend's mood and 'ébranlé' by the confidence Deslauriers shows in his ability to achieve a Rastignac-like success, while Deslauriers, financially, is dependent upon Frédéric, having to ask him for money for a meal, a request to which Frédéric responds with extreme generosity. In spite of this, the strong physical bond which unites them, marked by frequent embraces, cannot conceal the fact that Frédéric, 'retenu par une pudeur', has not seen fit to tell Deslauriers about Madame Arnoux (p.15).

In the main body of the novel the friendship between Frédéric and Deslauriers is constantly threatened by their attachment to opposing ideals. Throughout Part I, however, the attainment of these ideals still seems sufficiently remote for the amount of friction to be considerably restricted. Once Deslauriers is installed with Frédéric in Paris, their relationship passes through a period of emotional and intellectual harmony, evoked in almost lyrical terms. Frédéric's 'grande passion' always takes precedence over his allegiance to Deslauriers, however, and leads, directly or indirectly to their various disagreements. The coincidental timing of Deslauriers's arrival in Paris and Frédéric's first opportunity of meeting Madame Arnoux again allows love to be shown eclipsing friendship, though not without a measure of trepidation on Frédéric's part ('Frédéric ... se mit à trembler comme une femme adultère sous le regard de son époux', p.43). Subsequently, Deslauriers greets Frédéric's endless and inconsequential talk of his meetings with Madame Arnoux with yawns and blank incomprehension ('Il ne comprenait rien à cet amour, qu'il regardait comme une dernière faiblesse d'adolescence', p.56). His own unenthusiastic evaluation of Madame

Arnoux ('"Pas mal"', p.60) and his annoying habit of repeating
Arnoux's name at every opportunity precipitate a quarrel which ends in
the half-apologetic, half-accusatory '"Oh! pardon ... on respectera
désormais les nerfs de Mademoiselle!"' (p.60). The heavy expenses
incurred by Frédéric in sustaining his devotion to Madame Arnoux
provoke recrimination (p.54) and dissension but Deslauriers's financial
dependency upon Frédéric prevents his speaking his mind over the
extravagant purchase of the sunshade (p.79). But it is, above all, the
pattern of dominance which is disrupted by Frédéric's enervating attachment to Madame Arnoux: 'Il aurait voulu le conduire absolument, le voir
se développer d'après l'idéal de leur jeunesse; et sa fainéantise le
révoltait, comme une désobéissance et comme une trahison' (p.59).

The friendship between Frédéric and Deslauriers undergoes a marked
deterioration in Part II as each character becomes more engrossed in the
pursuit of his chosen ideal. Frédéric's wealth puts Deslauriers's long-
cherished dream of running a paper within his reach: "Deslauriers
touchait à son vieux rêve, une rédaction en chef, c'est-à-dire au bonheur
inexprimable de diriger les autres' (p.179–80). His relationship with
Frédéric revolves principally around his attempts at obtaining the
necessary financial support for his enterprise, beginning with the
reminder of schoolboy promises ('"on constituera une phalange, on
imitera *les Treize* de Balzac!"', p.155) and ending in violent indignation
at what he considers to be Frédéric's treachery: 'Il s'estimait volé,
comme s'il avait subi un grand dommage. Son amitié pour Frédéric était
morte, et il en éprouvait de la joie' (p.186). Frédéric's reluctance to
comply with his friend's request is rooted in resentment at his presump-
tuousness: 'Frédéric n'aima point cette manière de s'associer tout de suite
à sa fortune', p.112) and his greater commitment to the Arnoux who
require exactly the same sum of money from him, but there are still
moments when he is fired by Deslauriers's enterprising approach to life:
'Frédéric, en l'écoutant, éprouvait une sensation de rajeunissement,
comme un homme qui, après un long séjour dans une chambre, est
transporté au grand air' (p.180). If such responses do not produce any
practical results, Deslauriers's harsh, demeaning attitude to his mistress,
Clémence Daviou, combined with the totally dismissive '"Est-ce que tu
peux causer avec une femme, toi?"' (p.181) is largely to blame.

The rift created by Frédéric's 'betrayal' does not take long to heal,
such is the need – intellectual in Frédéric's case, emotional in Des-

lauriers's – each has of the other. There are still lasting causes of friction,
however; Deslauriers continues to find the persistence of Frédéric's love
for Madame Arnoux irritating (p.246), and he continues to try to recover
a lost dominance over Frédéric by making him commit actions such as the
purchase of Pellerin's painting of Rosanette that displease him and
steering him away from enterprises such as the secretaryship of Monsieur
Dambreuse's company which might prove successful (p.267). Just when
the discrepancy between them has increased, however, a kind of crossing
over[7] takes place when Deslauriers sets off to seduce Madame Arnoux,
'se substituant à Frédéric et s'imaginant presque être lui, par une
singulière évolution intellectuelle où il y avait à la fois de la vengeance et
de la sympathie, de l'imitation et de l'audace' (p.246). Strange though it
is, Deslauriers's behaviour is the logical culmination of the 'mille
différences de caractère et d'origine' which separate him from Frédéric.
Only someone so enterprising and embittered would embark upon such a
foolhardy and revengeful course of action, while the admiration which
leads him to emulate Frédéric is rooted in his possession of diametrically
opposed qualities. In a way which is psychologically plausible, Deslauriers seeks to be like Frédéric precisely because he is so different from
himself. Ironically, the substitution that takes place, treacherous as it is,
serves Frédéric's interest, since it leads to Madame Arnoux realising she
loves him; the injection of Deslauriers's determination into the relationship ensures its progress.

The pattern of betrayal in Part II becomes more marked in Part III.
Envious of his friend's good fortune, Deslauriers acts in a way which is
damaging to his electoral and marital prospects, as well as using his legal
expertise against the Arnoux. With friends like Deslauriers, Frédéric has
no need of enemies. It is not, however, solely out of revenge that
Deslauriers follows on after Frédéric – his imitation of Frédéric with
Louise Roque (p.401) stems also from his desire to be like him, a desire
which this time meets with success. The final reconciliation, which takes
place in spite of Deslauriers's multiple acts of betrayal, suggests that
friendship does not depend upon the treatment one gives or receives but
upon deeply-rooted emotional needs. Frédéric can pardon Deslauriers
for much the same reason that Deslauriers betrays him – he is different
from himself. In their final resurrection of the past, Frédéric and
Deslauriers are at and as one, like Bouvard and Pécuchet, who 'dans la
joie de la copie' become 'le même homme'.[8] The ideals which had

separated them having been abandoned, Frédéric and Deslauriers finally achieve the harmony and understanding to which their opposite natures have always predisposed them.

Both Frédéric and Deslauriers feel the need for a kind of supplement to their main friendship and in both cases choose a person who resembles themselves in outlook and temperament and who lacks the shortcomings of their main friend. Frédéric's friendship with Dussardier is based upon likeness and likemindedness. Dussardier, it is said, 'avait *le génie du cœur*' (p.73); it is possible to see in him 'an extension of the naive sensibility of Frédéric'.[9] Not only does Dussardier display the same idealism in his cherishing of the ideal Republic as Frédéric shows in his worship of Madame Arnoux, he also shares Frédéric's wish to devote all his energies to a single woman ('"Je voudrais aimer la même, toujours"', p.57) and, like Frédéric, finds himself forced to compromise his ideal. Dussardier also shares with Frédéric an instinctive generosity and propensity for self-sacrifice. There is a strong similarity between Frédéric's sexual inhibitions and Dussardier's social inhibitions ('il éprouvait une sorte de honte en se voyant haussé au rang social d'étudiant', p.31), both characters being inclined to underestimate their own worth on account of the strength of their admiration for an ideal above themselves. Lastly, both show a degree of consideration and softness towards women and are genuinely shocked at the sheer vindictiveness they encounter in their mistresses.[10]

Unsullied by treachery, envy or malice, the friendship between Frédéric and Dussardier is characterised by mutual concern and generosity. Frédéric twice goes to Dussardier's aid, once when he is about to be arrested, once when he has been wounded in the June Days. When he inherits, he offers to lend him money, and later acts as his mentor, passing on his books to him. Dussardier is the only guest at Frédéric's celebration party to show unqualified delight ('"Vous êtes donc riche, maintenant! Ah! tant mieux, tant mieux!"' p.138), seeks to avoid bloodshed when he acts as Frédéric's second (p.230), and, when Frédéric experiences passing financial problems, makes the generous offer of his life savings, an offer which is accepted, unlike Frédéric's at the beginning of Part II. Though each character is moved by the other's treatment of him, their friendship lacks the closeness of that which exists between Frédéric and Deslauriers. In spite of the warmth of feeling between them, Frédéric finds that there is something missing in his relationship with Dussardier: 'Sa solitude intellectuelle était profonde, et la compagnie de Dussardier insuffisante.' (p.241) The way in which Dussardier is dispensed with, once Frédéric's friendship with Deslauriers is resumed, is the only blot on an otherwise consistently warm-hearted relationship. Decency and dependence do not go together; Frédéric and Dussardier are able to treat each other so well partly because they can admire their own virtues reflected back at them, but also because they are not bound together by the powerful needs which characterise the relationship between Frédéric and Deslauriers and which lead them at times to act in ways detrimental to each other's interests.[11]

The equivalent of Dussardier as far as Deslauriers is concerned is Sénécal, who, likewise, bears a certain resemblance to him. Both are hard-headed, logical, authoritarian, their lives as a result being defective in personal feeling, and both become increasingly embittered and envious of the wealthy as the book progresses, though Deslauriers's political opinions are considerably less disinterested and less dogmatic.[12] On various occasions Deslauriers helps Sénécal out, persuading Frédéric to obtain a post for him (p.147), passing on his old clothes (p.400) and making him his secretary (p.374). His admiration for Sénécal is, however, variable, increasing with his frustration at his own lack of progress or disappointment with Frédéric, but decreasing when he objects to his doctrinaire Socialism or the company he keeps ('Leur séparation n'avait eu rien de pénible. Sénécal, dans les derniers temps, recevait des hommes en blouse, tous patriotes, tous travailleurs, tous braves gens, mais dont la compagnie était fastidieuse à l'avocat,' p.137). Deslauriers is basically too self-seeking, Sénécal too unemotional for their friendship to develop the same generosity and warmth as exists between Frédéric and Dussardier.

Whereas Deslauriers feels a measure of respect for Dussardier's qualities (' "Tu es honnête, toi! Quand je serai riche, je t'instituerai mon régisseur." ', p.86), Frédéric takes an instant dislike to Sénécal: 'Ce garçon déplut à Frédéric. Son front était rehaussé par la coupe de ses cheveux taillés en brosse. Quelque chose de dur et de froid perçait dans ses yeux gris' (p.51). This hostility is fuelled by his resentment at Sénécal's association with Deslauriers, though this is not as close as he thinks. Frédéric's wealth and elegance are antipathetic to Sénécal, who is a most ungracious and unappreciative guest at his party, striking matches on his hangings and criticising 'la futilité de son intérieur' (p.143). The suppressed antagonism between the two characters rises to the surface at Creil, where Frédéric takes exception to the harshness of his treatment of the workers ('"Ah! pour un démocrate, vous êtes bien dur!"', p.199) and at the Club de l'Intelligence, where Sénécal opposes Frédéric's canditature (p.310).

Even more striking than the contrast between Frédéric and Sénécal is the opposition between Dussardier and Sénécal. Although they share a high degree of political commitment, there is a considerable difference, as has been seen, between their views and outlook,[13] Dussardier supporting the Republic because for him it is synonymous with freedom and universal happiness, Sénécal because he seeks a more rational, egalitarian organisation of society. The two characters also differ in their personal lives, Dussardier being far more open-hearted, affectionate and generous in his support of friends, where Sénécal is cold, dispassionate, lacking in concern for individuals. When Sénécal is arrested, Dussardier immediately rallies round and tries to work out a way of freeing him (p.234), whereas Sénécal, when it comes to enforcing the rule of authority, does not baulk at taking his companion's life. In his naive and idealistic search for the ideal Republic, Dussardier, it could be said, manifests 'trop de sentiment', while, Sénécal, in his uncompromising and hard-headed determination to organise society along more rational lines, is guilty of 'trop de logique'. But whereas there is some accommodation between Frédéric and Deslauriers, who are the main examples of these diametrically opposed extremes, the naked opposition between Sénécal and Dussardier finally culminates in the destruction of the one by the other.

Frédéric's relationships with a wide range of minor characters lack the closeness of his friendships with Deslauriers and Dussardier. They are tolerated because of their connection with Madame Arnoux or put up with because they belong to a fixed circle of friends. Frédéric sees them in instrumental terms: Pellerin is used as part of an elaborate ploy ('l'inexactitude habituelle de l'artiste faciliterait les tête-à-tête', p.150), just as Sénécal is strategically placed in a post with Arnoux, Hussonnet provides a link with Arnoux and Regimbart purveys essential information about his whereabouts. While often being interested in them for ulterior reasons, Frédéric does not behave in a way detrimental to the interests of his various acquaintances, whereas they often do, though in response to his lack of support. Pellerin's exhibition of his painting of Rosanette is designed to coerce Frédéric into making a purchase, while Hussonnet's article in *Le Flambard* is an act of revenge against Frédéric for failing to provide promised financial backing for his newspaper. At other times rivalry leads to enmity. Martinon's conspicuous success both in his legal career and with women provokes strong feelings of jealousy in Frédéric while Cisy, who in his foppish ways, pretensions to elegance and timorous attitude to women, bears a resemblance to Frédéric, having at first relied upon Frédéric to initiate him into the iniquities of metropolitan life, finally 'steals' Rosanette from him as a wager and thereby sets in motion the comical train of events which culminates in the grotesque antics of the duel. In all, an unedifying catalogue of indifference, mean-mindness, petty revenge, envy, rivalry and malice is presented. This type of casual friendship is clearly not a sphere in which there is much scope for Frédéric's more generous impulses.

Frédéric's friendship with Arnoux belongs to a category of its own and generates an extraordinary range of responses from naive admiration to intense exasperation, from obscure attachment to sudden loathing. Frédéric's changes of attitude are the result of the ambiguity of Arnoux's position as a necessary adjunct to his wife, whose charm lies essentially – at first at least – in the fact that she is not unmarried, and an obstacle to fulfilment. He is also a surrogate father, filling a gap left by the premature death in a duel of Frédéric's biological father. Lastly, the fact that Frédéric meets Arnoux before his wife and feels 'un certain respect' for him suggests that he also appeals in his own right as an experienced, outgoing, enterprising and energetic man of the world. Nor is the friendship one-sided; Arnoux is drawn to Frédéric as a sympathetic companion, brother-in-crime and easily manipulated boost to his morale. Flaubert presents, in the long-standing association between the two men, a complex amalgam of ambiguous loyalty and surreptitious treachery, of physical attraction and equally strong physical repulsion, of genuine admiration and repeated exasperation.

Although Frédéric falls in love with Madame Arnoux, it is with her husband that he spends most of his time in the opening stages of the book. Ironically, since he is attached to everything that is in any way connected with Madame Arnoux, he is also drawn to Arnoux, who is never allowed to become the stock tyrannical husband. Initially, it is the differences between the two men which are the most striking, Arnoux, the mature Parisian, active, brash, dishonest, contrasting with Frédéric, the green provincial, passive, retiring, full of scruples. The former's easy familiarity and entertaining ways on the boat make a strong impression on Frédéric, who seizes on every opportunity of meeting the owner of *L'Art industriel*, looking up to him 'à la fois comme millionnaire, comme dilettante, comme homme d'action' (p.39). An innocent abroad, Frédéric finds it difficult to come to terms with Arnoux's infidelities or his underhand business practices, some of Madame Arnoux's shining moral rectitude seeming to brush off on to her unscrupulous and self-indulgent husband. At this stage he does everything in his power to keep them together and it is difficult to say where his devotion to Madame Arnoux ends and his attachment to her husband begins, so much so that Arnoux is 'attendri par tant d'affection' (p.65) and adopts him as a dinner-companion during his wife's absence, in spite of the annoyance he on one occasion feels when Frédéric interupts his love-making (pp.63–4).

Frédéric's relationship with Arnoux in Part II is changed by his more enterprising attitude to Madame Arnoux and the appearance of Rosanette. While in Part I, Frédéric had relished the security of a harmonious union, in Part II he tries to drive a wedge between Arnoux and his wife, a project which fills him with a feeling of uneasiness whenever it looks like succeeding. Thus, when the scheming over the cashmere shawl finally results in the intended quarrel, 'Il se sentait coupable et avait peur' (p.166). As well as participating parasitically in Arnoux's married life, Frédéric also accompanies him on his stolen visits to Rosanette, once again following, as it were, in his father's footsteps. Significantly, in the symbolic dream at the end of Chapter i Frédéric visualises himself teamed up with Arnoux; there is, he senses, room for two, in this new sphere, since Rosanette does not 'belong' to Arnoux in the same way as his wife does. Frédéric begins, therefore, to play a particularly complicated double game, following in Arnoux's wake, fluctuating between his wife and mistress, drawn into ambiguous complicity with both women and seeking to prise now one, now the other, from his protector's grasp. Once again, Arnoux is the beneficiary of support – financial and moral – which is really intended for his wife. Ironically, Frédéric becomes the saviour of the couple he seeks to separate and any feelings of guilt he has had on account of the way he has undermined the stability of their ménage give way to intense exasperation at the content-ment in Arnoux which he has helped to produce: 'Au lieu de la rupture qu'il attendait, voilà que l'autre, au contraire, se mettait à la chérir complètement, depuis le bout des cheveux jusqu'au fond de l'âme. La vulgarité de cet homme exaspérait Frédéric. Tout lui appartenait, donc, à celui-là! . . . D'ailleurs, l'honnêteté d'Arnoux offrant des garanties pour son argent l'humiliait; il aurait voulu l'étrangler' (p.186). Try as he might, however, to muster real hatred for the chief impediment preventing the fulfilment of his passion, Frédéric finds that he 'éprouvait un certain entraînement pour sa personne' (p.173), and although he fights the duel primarily in order to defend Madame Arnoux's reputation, it is also partly for Arnoux's sake (p.223), so deeply ingrained is his attachment to him.

As far as Arnoux is concerned Frédéric provides a sympathetic ear when he wishes to pour out his various troubles and a useful cover for his infidelities. Arnoux also plays in a calculating manner upon his affection for his wife, spelling out the exact implications of any failure to provide financial aid (p.182). The reader may also suspect that his appreciative account of his wife's physical charms is deliberately designed to aggravate Frédéric. In spite of all this, Arnoux's reaction on learning of the duel points to an almost paternal pride in Frédéric's prowess and a genuine appreciation of what he takes to be his devotion: ' "Comme vous êtes bon! Ah! cher enfant!" Il le contemplait et versait des larmes, tout en ricanant de bonheur' (p.231). Based partly on misunderstanding and double-dealing, the friendship between Frédéric and Arnoux is sealed by an ineradicable emotional attachment, reminiscent of that between father and son.

In Part III, like almost everything else, Frédéric's relationship with Arnoux undergoes a marked decline. Now that Rosanette is his mistress, roles are reversed in a way which is flattering to Arnoux's vanity: 'Les relations de Frédéric et de la Maréchale ne l'avaient point attristé; car cette découverte l'autorisa (dans sa conscience) à supprimer la pension qu'il lui refaisait depuis le départ du prince, . . . Alors M. Arnoux se considéra comme l'amant de cœur, – ce qui le rehaussait dans son estime, et le rajeunit' (p.316). Frédéric, on the other hand, is less happy. Although his patience has been sorely tried in the past, he has never harboured feelings of real hostility towards Arnoux. Now, however, as a result of his disappointment at having lost Madame Arnoux and distress at having to share Rosanette with her husband, he is strongly tempted to engineer the 'accidental' shooting of Arnoux (p.319). But Frédéric can no more take Arnoux's life than he can seduce Madame Arnoux; none the less the oedipal temptation to which he nearly succumbs casts a dark shadow over his relationship with Arnoux. Aggression gives way to compliance, however, as Frédéric fears that his homicidal impulses will be apparent to Arnoux and finally the two men are once again joined in brotherly union ('quand ils remontèrent la rue Vivienne, leurs épaulettes se touchaient fraternellement', p.320). As it turns out, this is the last encounter of any significance between them; Arnoux disappears from Frédéric's life once Madame Arnoux's star has begun to sink, upsetting the balance of the life of the older man ('L'absence prolongée de Frédéric troublait ses habitudes', p.357) and leaving Frédéric, when he witnesses his friend's decline, with a lingering sadness ('Frédéric, devant cette décadence, fut pris de tristesse', p.396) In spite of the 'ressemblances profondes' (p.173) which exist between them and account for the way they perform a kind of comic double act for much of the time, Frédéric and Arnoux are not drawn together by 'la fatalité de leur nature', but rather brought into a shifting, suspect and often sordid alliance by their sharing of common erotic objectives.

L'Éducation sentimentale devotes considerably less space to the exploration of friendship than to love and yet we are presented at the end of the novel with the spectacle of Frédéric and Deslauriers locked in a relationship which has outlasted love and belittling love from within the apparent security of this relationship. The moment in *Bouvard et Pécuchet* when the two ex-clerks renounce the company of women does not seem far off:

> C'était le désir d'en avoir qui avait suspendu leur amitié. Un remords les prit.
> – Plus de femmes, n'est-ce pas. Vivons sans elles!
> Et ils s'embrassèrent avec attendrissement.[14]

It can hardly be said, however, that the ending marks the apotheosis of friendship. There is something peremptory about the account of the reunion which prevents the reader taking it seriously and the explanation of the basis upon which friendship rests points to a hidden contradiction: while inner needs may create a mutual dependency, Frédéric and Deslauriers have not actually spent much time together in the course of the novel. The logic underlying this contradiction might be explained as follows: the differences in nature which provide the basis upon which a close attachment rests ('la fatalité de leur nature') begin to be undermined as a result of the influence each character exerts upon the other; however, to the extent that each begins to resemble the other, he not only begins to threaten his interests (Deslauriers as a rival in love, Frédéric as a potential wielder of power and influence), he also ceases to embody the appeal of a diametrically opposed nature. The image of enduring friendship evoked at the end is, therefore, deeply problematic, if not bogus. Flaubert does not allow the reader to entertain illusions about friendship any more than about love. In both cases Flaubert insists that the reality is more complicated than earlier writers, Balzac in particular, have allowed.

VIII

History and Psychology

Although *Madame Bovary* is set in a definite period of French history, references to events that took place at the time are rare and there is little attempt at recreating an atmosphere specific to a particular period.[1] *Salammbô*, which in certain respects resembles a conventional historical novel, while conveying a good deal of information about ancient Carthage and following the historical account of the war between Carthagians and mercenaries contained in Polybius's *Histoire*, is dealing with an era unfamiliar to Flaubert's readers and thus more easily manipulated to meet the exigencies of the fictional narrative.[2] *L'Éducation sentimentale*, in contrast, gives a detailed account of the recent historical past and posed problems which were new to Flaubert:

> J'ai bien du mal à emboîter mes personnages dans les événements politiques de 1848. J'ai peur que les fonds ne dévorent les premiers plans; c'est là le défaut du genre historique. Les personnages de l'histoire sont plus intéressants que ceux de la fiction, surtout quand ceux-là ont des passions modérées; on s'intéresse moins à Frédéric qu'à Lamartine. Et puis, quoi choisir parmi les faits réels?[3]

There is a real danger, Flaubert appreciated, that the colourful historical background – particularly the events of 1848 – will eclipse the lacklustre figures in the fictional foreground, allowing 'the frame to overpower the picture'.[4] Flaubert finds various ways of overcoming this danger, the most important being the intensification of the emotional life of Frédéric Moreau at the various turning-points of history when he risks being oveshadowed. But Flaubert is concerned to do more than simply damp down the interest of the historical element in the novel; there would be little point in setting the novel in the period 1840–51 if he were going to turn his back on the various changes and upheavals that took place during it.

'Montrer que le sentimentalisme . . . suit la politique et en reproduit les

phases'[5]; this well-known statement of intention from the *Carnet 19*
reflects Flaubert's most subtle and ingenious solution to the problem of
integrating history into his novel. Rather than functioning simply as a
backdrop for the fictional developments in the foreground of the novel,
the historical element was to be linked with the fictional element by a
series of developing parallels in a complex pattern synchronising history
and psychology. The investigation of the plans for the novel reveals
Flaubert putting most emphasis upon the psychological element, grafting
on historical material after the main outline of Frédéric's development
has been worked out. Thus, although there is less room for manoeuvre as
far as the historical element is concerned, on account of the events having
taken place in a specific order, it is none the less more a question of
adjusting the historical events to the psychological changes than of
making Frédéric's development 'follow' the course of politics. When one
considers the various restrictions imposed upon Flaubert – on the one
hand, a psychological evolution already laid down, on the other a set of
historical events which had already occurred, it is remarkable that he was
able to achieve so full and intricate a synchronisation of history and
psychology.

Since Jacques Proust's seminal analysis of the 'correspondances poétiques' between Frédéric's private life and the political events taking place
in the public arena, there have been several discussions of the parallelism
engineered by Flaubert.[6] It is generally accepted that the main parallel is
between Frédéric's love life and the progression towards and final demise
of the Second Republic. There are, however, differences of opinion over
certain elements within this broad parallelism; is it merely Frédéric's
relationship with Madame Arnoux which is made to correspond to
political developments or should his relationship with other women be
included? Should the parallel be with what is actually shown taking place
or also with what is known to have taken place in the historical sphere? Is
there a single character in the political sphere whose development
parallels Frédéric's in the private sphere or should all the politically
committed characters be brought into the pattern of synchronisation?
Clearly the most convincing account will be the one which integrates the
most elements, Frédéric's relationship with Rosanette and Madame
Dambreuse as well as his relationship with Madame Arnoux, the June
Days which, even if not directly portrayed, the reader knows to have
taken place, the attitudes of both Sénécal and Dussardier as well as that

of Deslauriers, conscious and unconscious processes, superficial and hidden reactions. It may well be that if certain truths or insights are repressed in one area they will reappear in another; once established the parallelism between the public and private spheres allows for displacement of material from one sphere to another, history and psychology each becoming an extension of the other.

A clear demarcation exists between two areas or spheres of activity in *L'Éducation sentimentale*: the emotional development of Frédéric Moreau, on the one hand, and the political evolution of France from the bourgeois monarchy of Louis-Philippe, to the Second Republic, leading finally to the Second Empire, on the other. The most striking similarity between the two spheres is the widespread fixation upon the ideal. What Flaubert referred to in a conversation with the Goncourt brothers as 'l'adoration religieuse de la femme'[7] has as its counterpart 'l'adoration de l'humanité pour elle-même et par elle-même'[8] Flaubert establishes a network of parallels between the two spheres as Frédéric, on the one hand, and political activists, on the other, embark upon a problematic quest for the ideal woman or the ideal Republic. As has been seen, Flaubert took a dim view of the poeticisation of woman, linking it to the influence of religion.[9] Likewise he was highly sceptical about the efficacy of 'la race stérile et sèche (inactive dans le bien comme dans l'idéal) des humanitaires, républicains'[10], in general, but was particularly scornful towards Utopian Socialism: 'O Socialistes! C'est là votre ulcère: l'idéal vous manque et cette matière, que vous poursuivez, vous échappe des mains'.[11] Socialism, Flaubert repeatedly claimed, was steeped in the values of primitive Christianity.[12] Bringing the worship of woman and the worship of the people together, he attributes the sorry state of his country to the dual influence of religion and Socialism: 'Le néo-catholicisme d'une part et le socialisme de l'autre ont abêti la France. Tout se meurt entre l'Immaculée-Conception et les gamelles ouvrières.'[13] The main criticism to be levelled against the idealistic and Utopian reformism of the modern era is that it either ignores or fails to take account of what Flaubert referred to as 'l'évolution fatale des choses'[14] or 'l'organisation essentielle de l'historie',[15] that is to say a higher necessity rooted in the basic antagonism between haves and have-nots.[16]

After his first encounter with Madame Arnoux, Frédéric basks contentedly in the expectation of future fulfilment: 'et bercé par le mouvement de la voiture, les paupières à demi closes, le regard dans les nuages, il s'abandonnait à une joie rêveuse et infinie' (p.10). Deslauriers, likewise, has high hopes for the future: ' "Patience! un nouveau 89 se prépare!" ' (p.16). Very little happens, however, to bring the dream of either character any closer. For a whole year Frédéric sees nothing of Madame Arnoux and Deslauriers is unable for financial reasons to be in Paris. Although Frédéric is subsequently invited to dinners at the Arnoux' his relationship with Madame Arnoux remains on a very formal footing, while in the political sphere, apart from the street disturbances of I iv, there is little action. The attitude of Frédéric's friends is one of hostility to the existing régime: 'Tous sympathisaient. D'abord, leur haine du Gouvernement avait la hauteur d'un dogme indiscutable' (p.57); in contrast, in the private sphere, Frédéric does not harbour feelings of antagonism either to Arnoux or his wife. At this early stage the illusory faith later invested in the ideal Republic has not crystalised, just as the hostile component in Frédéric's response to Madame Arnoux has not yet surfaced.

While in Part I, Frédéric's aims in relation to Madame Arnoux remained ill-defined, in Part II it is not long before he entertains more precise hopes of making both Rosanette and Madame Arnoux his mistress, just as Deslauriers now takes a 'prochaine révolution' for granted (p.113). But, in fact, in both spheres, in spite of the progress made, there are setbacks and rebuffs, followed by pardons and concessions. Frédéric's crude advances at Creil meet with firm rejection while Sénécal's equally premature 'tentative suprême pour établir la République' (p.233) leads to his arrest and imprisonment, followed by his release in the last chapter, just as Madame Arnoux's treatment of Frédéric softens into acceptance of his love. Finally, at the end of Part II the moment is ripe both for revolution and for Frédéric's love for Madame Arnoux to be consummated.

Although the main parallel between erotic and revolutionary aspirations emerges clearly, the relationship between the two spheres has increased in complexity on account of Frédéric's involvement with Rosanette as well as Madame Arnoux, and the diversification of political outlook and activity amongst Frédéric's friends. The progress of Frédéric's relationship with Rosanette, as has been seen, follows the progress of his relationship with Madame Arnoux and it is finally Rosanette who becomes his mistress in the apartment in the rue Tronchet. To what extent, therefore, is it Frédéric's involvement with

Rosanette which duplicates what is happening on the political front? Whereas in Part I there was near unanimity amongst Frédéric's friends with respect to the government in power, in Part II, Sénécal becomes a Socialist and makes the most concerted bid to establish a Republic, Deslauriers remains sceptical about political ideologies of various kinds but about Socialism in particular and, less disinterested, longs for a 'un grand bouleversement' principally because 'il comptait bien faire son trou, avoir sa place' (p.137), while Dussardier remains emotionally committed to the republican ideal because 'elle signifiait, croyait-il, affranchissement et bonheur universel' (p.233), but does nothing actively to bring about a revolution. Arguably these different outlooks correspond to different strands in Frédéric's increasingly complex attitude to women, Sénécal's combination of disinterestedness and determination to his own mixture of self-denial and more resolute action, Deslauriers self-seeking and desire for power to an overtly exploitative desire for mastery over Rosanette and Dussardier's naive faith in the liberating effect of a Republic to his fixation on the idealised image of Madame Arnoux.

Although varying considerably in political outlook, Frédéric's friends continue to share a hatred of the government in power, culminating in a common exasperation: 'tous ayant contre le Pouvoir, la même exaspération' (p.263). But within this broad hatred there are differences in intensity. Dussardier's is the strongest: 'Tout le mal sur la terre, il l'attribuait naïvement au pouvoir, et il le haïssait d'une haine essentielle, qui lui tenait le cœur et raffinait sa sensibilité' (p.233). Frédéric himself, though never as politically committed, can for personal reasons, bay with the wolves: 'Frédéric se soulageait en déblatérant contre le Pouvoir' (p.274). This hatred of the government is accompanied, in the case of Deslauriers, by the desire for 'la destruction complète de l'ordre actuel' (p.14), 'un bouleversement universel' (p.274), a revolution which will remove the despised régime of Louis-Philippe and usher in a new era. The counterpart of these feelings in the private life of Frédéric is not immediately apparent but he does experience both hatred and growing exasperation in the face of the resistance he encounters from both women (p.201, p.212, p.273). More pertinently perhaps, Frédéric resents Arnoux's enjoyment of both his wife and his mistress, the two women he himself desires: 'La vulgarité de cet homme exaspérait Frédéric. Tout lui appartenait donc, à celui-là' (p.185). In sexual terms,

Arnoux belongs to the category of 'ceux qui ont' while Frédéric belongs to the category of 'ceux qui tâchent d'avoir' (p.178); much as he is drawn to Arnoux, Frédéric cannot hope to be immune to the equivalent of the resentment felt by the poor towards the rich which Flaubert believed to be inevitable.

The outcome of the feelings of adoration and hatred that have built up in both spheres throughout the 1840s is rich in ambiguity, an ambiguity sustained by the image of the ripe pear, which is used in Deslauriers's message to Frédéric informing him of the imminent revolution ('la *poire* est mûre', p.277). Louis-Philippe was frequently caricatured as a pear and Deslauriers is suggesting that he is, as it were, ripe for the picking. His message also conveys the idea of the moment being ripe for revolution and invites Frédéric to view revolutionary action as an opportunity not to be missed. The image used also has resonances in the private sphere. Already in *Madame Bovary* Flaubert has used a similar image making a suggestive distinction between a fruit being picked and a fruit falling unaided to the ground in order to evoke different kinds of emotional and sexual release.[17] It might be thought that Madame Arnoux has reached a kind of personal fruition ('elle touchait au mois d'août des femmes ...', p.273) and in a different sense is ripe for the picking; the notion of the moment being ripe for the consummation of the relationship was also present from the very early stage.[18] Ripe fruit can be picked or, alternatively, as in *Madame Bovary*, it can fall to the ground. The negative associations of falling are also ambiguously present; Madame Arnoux is on the point of losing her virtue or becoming a 'fallen' woman, just as the king is about to lose his throne and become a 'fallen' monarch. The disjunction between the two spheres when it comes to the fulfilling of the prophecy is once again ambiguous; on one level, it might seem that Madame Arnoux's failure to attend the rendezvous is both a loss and a gain, since, though depriving both her and Frédéric of possible fulfilment, it spares her an indignity similar to the one that befalls the king. More problematically, on a deeper level, inasmuch as Rosanette functions as an extension of Madame Arnoux, the idealised image worshipped by Frédéric is not spared indignity and what happens in the historical sphere reflects rather than contrasts with an upheaval taking place in Frédéric.

Madame Arnoux's failure to attend the rendezvous constitutes a turning-point in the narrative, leading Frédéric to switch his attention to

Rosanette, a development which he himself jokingly compares to what is happening in the political sphere ('"Je suis la mode, je me réforme"', p.289). The gaiety of Frédéric's mood corresponds to the atmosphere in Paris; 'A la nouvelle d'un changement de ministère, Paris avait changé. Tout le monde était en joie' (p.284). In both spheres, however, something more powerful and more painful is about to break out; the shooting of the demonstrators in the Boulevard des Capucines, which constitutes a turning-point in history, leading to the February Revolution, is likened to the 'craquement d'une immense pièce de soie que l'on déchire' (p.284) and is paralleled by Frédéric's sobbing after he has taken the decisive step and substituted Rosanette for Madame Arnoux. A whole era in Frédéric's life has come to an end just as a whole era of history has been completed. Frédéric's explanation of his reaction ('"C'est excès de bonheur ... Il y avait trop longtemps que je te désirais"', p.285) is bitterly ironical; it is Madame Arnoux whom he had really desired and Rosanette falls short of his ideal, just as what will actually be achieved in the political sphere will fall short of the long desired ideal Republic. But is is perhaps the disparity between the inordinate time spent dreaming of the ideal and the sudden rapidity of the release when it finally occurs in both spheres which generates a powerful sensation of painful loss. The huge piece of silk being ripped carries overtones of Frédéric's whole, carefully constructed, 'système', entailing the focusing of his energies on the idealised figure of Madame Arnoux, being wantonly destroyed. In this way history is made to provide an objective correlative for a psychological state.

In Part III the parallelism between the two spheres again intensifies. Frédéric having failed (for so long) to make either Madame Arnoux or Rosanette his mistress, suddenly finds himself loved by several women simultaneously and obliged, in particular, to sustain two relationships – with Rosanette and Madame Dambreuse – while in the political sphere a series of crucial changes takes place, particularly in the first chapter. So rich and complex is the material in both spheres, that it is not immediately apparent what are the significant correlations. If one puts all the emphasis on Madame Arnoux, the parallelism between the two spheres fades and Duquette's linking of Frédéric's disappointment of Madame Arnoux's failure to attend the rendezvous with the sack of the Tuileries and the Insurrection ignores both the differences between these events themselves and the distance – in time and textual space – which separates them from Frédéric's reaction at the end of Part II.[19] Throughout the first chapter of Part III it is Rosanette who is Frédéric's principal preoccupation, though clearly she does not exist in complete independence from Madame Arnoux. The most striking parallel, therefore, is between the development of Frédéric's attitude to Rosanette and the course of revolutionary and counter-revolutionary politics.

The account of the events of February 1848 puts most emphasis on the wanton destruction and mindless pillaging of the Parisian mob as it goes on the rampage. The figure of the prostitute, posing as the statue of Liberty, is a particularly vivid image of a kind of profanation that is taking place in the public sphere: 'Dans l'antichambre, debout sur un tas de vêtements, se tenait une fille publique, en statue de la Liberté, – immobile, les yeux grands ouverts, effrayante (p.294). Hussonnet's mocking comment, ' "Quel mythe! ... Voilà le peuple souverain!" ' (p.293), though characteristically cynical, none the less serves to undermine over-optimistic assumptions about the benefits to be derived from giving power to the people and, in particular, Dussardier's naive faith expressed in ' "tout va bien! le peuple triomphe! les ouvriers et les bourgeois s'embrassent" ' (p.295). Doubts about the desirability of entrusting power and influence to the people persist, as the entry of the masses into politics is marked by the spouting of all kinds of nonsense in the political clubs and culminates finally in the election of a virtual dictator, lending support to Deslauriers's earlier objection: 'en quoi la souveraineté du peuple serait-elle plus sacrée que le droit divin' (p.179).

It is, perhaps, no accident that the woman who now dominates Frédéric's attention is 'une fille du peuple' and that she should finally have become his mistress with the same startling rapidity as the Second Republic had been proclaimed. Ironically, Rosanette herself speaks disparagingly of the Republic, assimilating it to a woman of her own status (' "elle se fait entretenir, ta République! Eh bien, amuse-toi avec elle!" ', p.312). Frédéric's mood of euphoria and light-hearted gaiety in the early part of his relationship with Rosanette echoes the 'gaité de carnaval' (p.297) which prevails in Paris immediately after the February Revolution, just as his feelings of disappointment when confronted by her 'avalanches de sottises' (p.312) and 'langage populacier' correspond to his dismay over the 'nuages de sottise' (p.304) and populist absurdities encountered in the 'Club de l'Intelligence'. In both spheres there is a powerful opposition between the ideal and reality. The reality of the people on the rampage and political life under the provisional government of the Second Republic is vastly different from the idealized expectations of the political activists in the book, although Dussardier is slow to recognise this, just as the reality of the woman Frédéric actually succeeds in making his mistress is vastly different from the idealised image of saintly purity which he has longed for. There is also a sense in which the opposition between the ideal and reality crumbles. In both spheres February 1848 represents a moment of realisation, when the ideal is about to be attained. As well as reality falling short of the ideal, the ideal seems, as it were, to collapse into reality. At one level Rosanette is an extension of Madame Arnoux and Frédéric comes into scandalous contact with the ideal through its opposite, just as in the political sphere the dream of giving power to the people is turned into a frightening reality.

From an early stage Flaubert envisaged the episode in the guardroom where Frédéric has visions of Arnoux being shot, accidentally or otherwise, finally making it coincide with the beginning of the June Days. The link between these two episodes is not immediately apparent but what seems to be taking place in both spheres is a struggle to remove a figure of paternal authority which is seen as blocking certain aspirations. Frédéric's antagonism towards Arnoux is rooted both in his continuing relationship with Rosanette ('Ce partage blessait Frédéric', p.317) and in the awareness that he represents the principal obstacle standing in the way of a life of bliss with Madame Arnoux. Previously he had felt irritated, even exasperated by Arnoux but now he experiences murderous urges of frightening intensity (pp.318–9), which are interrupted by Arnoux's sudden awakening and followed by the resumption of the almost brotherly relationship of comrades in pleasure-seeking (p.329). The equivalent drama which is played out in the political sphere is not resolved so amicably. Soon after the February Revolution a reactionary movement manifests itself, as members of the bourgeoisie fear for their property and their lives. Collectively, the French nation suffers from the absence of any clear figure of authority: 'La France, ne sentant plus de maître, se mit à crier d'effarement, comme un aveugle sans bâton, comme un marmot qui a perdu sa bonne' (p.299). The closure of the National Workshops is interpreted as a reactionary move, an attempt at destroying the Republic and a betrayal of all the promises made after February. The Parisian workers experience a frustration and resentment similar to Frédéric's but, unlike him, take drastic action, setting up barricades and engaging in the titanic struggle indirectly evoked in the description of the oak-trees of the Fontainebleau forest (p.326). The outcome of the June Days is that the principle of authority is established and the revolutionary aspirations of Republicans and Socialists decisively squashed. The brutal repression which follows the June Days allows the paternal principle to be asserted. Le père Roque, less hesitant than Frédéric, does ensure that his rifle goes off, killing the 'jeune homme' who had had the temerity to ask for bread (p.338). The collapse of Frédéric's opposition to the father-figure, Arnoux, is balanced by the collapse of the Parisian proletariat's opposition to 'le père politique'.

Ironically, during the June Days, Frédéric's relationship with Rosanette is going through an idyllic phase in Fontainebleau, creating a strong contrapuntal effect. The lyrical illusions and pantheist ecstasy of the Fontainebleau episode have been compared to the political idyll of the spring which has the same insubstantial, frothy quality. There is, however, a considerable interval separating the two, departing from the pattern of close synchronisation which Flaubert establishes elsewhere. One alternative possibility is that, in a ripple effect, psychology is being displaced into history, the June Days corresponding to something taking place in Frédéric. What this could be is far from clear, since not only is something within him being 'repressed', but also the June Days are being 'suppressed' in the sense that there is no direct representation of them. On a conscious level Frédéric may be experiencing a brief period of harmony with 'une fille du peuple', just as earlier in the political sphere, as Dussardier notes, ' "les ouvriers et les bourgeois s'embrassent" ', but at an unconscious level, the aborted oedipal drama of the guardroom is being continued, for Rosanette is not only a mistress whom Frédéric is stealing from Arnoux, she is also an extension of Madame Arnoux, so that it is also the 'mother' whom Frédéric is seeking to wrest from the 'father', provoking at an unconscious level a violent upheaval similar to the one experienced by the Parisian workers in June. A further possibility is that history provides the opportunity for acting out a more extreme, hypothetical version of what takes place in the psychological sphere. The profanation of the royal palace corresponds to what would have happened had Madame Arnoux attended the rendezvous in the rue Tronchet; the bloody fighting during the June Days evokes what would have happened if Frédéric had not resisted the oedipal temptation of the guardroom and the savage repression of the 'terrasse du bord de l'eau' expresses the inevitable outcome of that struggle had it not dissolved into a false fraternalism. In this way history extends psychology, either by suggesting what may be taking place at an unconscious level or by exploring psychological possibilities which the narrative line adopted by Flaubert precludes.

In what remains of *L'Éducation sentimentale* the historical element ceases to loom so large but it is none the less possible to detect significant parallels between what is happening in the two spheres. Apart from one brief episode Frédéric sees nothing of Madame Arnoux, though he claims later that her image was always alive within him (p.423). When Frédéric learns that Arnoux is forced to leave France on account of his financial position, he makes a desperate attempt to come to his aid and subsequently quarrels with both Rosanette and Madame Dambreuse largely because of what he considers to be their hostile treatment of Madame Arnoux (p.412, p.415). The auction, at which both his mistresses are present, marks the point at which Frédéric's ideal disintegrates: 'et le partage de ces reliques, où il retrouvait confusément les formes de ses membres, lui semblait une atrocité, comme s'il avait vu des corbeaux déchiquetant son cadavre' (p.414). At the same time there is a kind of internal disintegration: 'C'était comme des parties de son cœur qui s'en allaient avec ces choses'. Madame Dambreuse's wilful brutality in insisting on purchasing the precious casket that belongs to Madame Arnoux leads to a final pointless act of sacrifice on Frédéric's part: 'Il était fier d'avoir vengé Madame Arnoux en lui sacrifiant une fortune' (p.416). It is not difficult to see in these developments the equivalent of the fading of hopes for an ideal Republic, entertained, in particular, by Dussardier. In June Dussardier had not known on which side of the barricades to fight and finally comes to feel he has made a mistake: 'Peut-être qu'il aurait dû se mettre de l'autre bord, avec les blouses; car enfin on leur avait promis un tas de choses qu'on n'avait pas tenues. Leurs vainqueurs détestaient la République; et puis, on s'était montré bien dur pour eux!' (p.339). From this point he becomes progressively disillusioned as he sees the various reactionary measures being taken, finally exclaiming ' "ils tuent notre République" ' (p.399), a cry of despair which anticipates Frédéric's anguish at the auction, just as his final sacrifice – in his case of his life, not just a fortune – accompanied by the vain cry ' "Vive la République" ' (p.419) corresponds to Frédéric's less strenuous effort to make a final gesture on behalf of a vanishing ideal.

In spite of the lingering influence that the ideal continues to exercise on the lives of Frédéric and Dussardier, the course of events from June onwards in both spheres on the whole reflects a retreat from the high hopes that had preceded the February Revolution. In his relationship with Rosanette, Frédéric experiences a mixture of sensual pleasure and exasperation as her shortcomings become apparent; Rosanette's pregnancy affords him little satisfaction and when the child is born he feels little affection for it, just as its death does not really affect him. Although the political developments of the time are not portrayed in any detail, there seems to be a significant parallel with the growing disillusionment with 'le peuple' in the political sphere, reflected in comments such as 'le peuple est mineur' (p.372). The prolonged pregnancy of Rosanette corresponds, it might be thought, to the delayed development of the official constitution of the Second Republic and it is significant that the death of the child coincides with the effective end of the Second Republic.

Frédéric's relationship with Madame Dambreuse, on the other hand, corresponds to the growing authoritarianism in politics. Frédéric desires Madame Dambreuse, out of a mixture of admiration for her social graces and social opportunism, and is content to allow her to dominate him: 'Par esprit de domination, elle voulait que Frédéric l'accompagnât le dimanche à l'église. Il obéit et porta le livre' (p.391). The autocratic, imperious element in her treatment of Frédéric culminates appropriately in the auction scene. Madame Dambreuse is seeking to dictate the terms on which their relationship will be conducted and is symbolically attempting to excise his residual attachment to the ideal of Madame Arnoux. In the political sphere there is a corresponding tendency to seek to 'relever le principe d'autorité' (p.392) and a demand for 'un bras de fer' (p.346). Sénécal, more than any other character, exemplifies the belief in Authority ('Sénécal se déclara pour l'Autorité', p.376) and it is not surprising that he should aid and abet Louis-Napoléon's *coup d'état* which is designed to establish definitively the principle of authority. Frédéric, of course, never goes this far in the private sphere, but he is sufficiently ambitious and hard-headed by this stage to make the necessary concessions and compromises to retain the interest of Madame Dambreuse. As Alison Fairlie puts it, 'his personal life reflects in detail the process through which post-insurrectionary activities have moved by way of chaos and compromise to the disillusioned desire to draw personal profit from immediate opportunity.'[20] But underlying the behaviour of 'tous ces gens qui avaient voté la Constitution s'évertuant à la démolir' (p.365), which so shocks Frédéric but which is perhaps not so different from his own lack of principle, is a latent desire for the arrival of 'un maître', a single individual sufficiently powerful to enforce a totally rational organisation of society by suppressing what are seen as the anarchic claims of the masses.

The parallelism that is established between politics and private life constitutes a major instrument of psychological exploration. What happens in the historical sphere does not simply reflect what is happening to Frédéric according to the explicit account of his development, but rather seems to point to something negative, less attractive, which is taking place at a deeper level of his psyche. Marx makes a distinction between the 'beautiful' revolution of February and the 'ugly' revolution of June; in Flaubert's scheme there is little that is 'beautiful' about what happens in February, while the 'ugliness' of the June Days themselves is obscured by the superficial 'beauty' of Frédéric's brief idyll in Fontaine-bleau. In both cases, however, there is a sense that what is shown or known to be happening in the historical sphere corresponds to what is taking place at an unconscious level in Frédéric, but which is at variance with what he is reported to be experiencing at a conscious level. The drama of profanation, the violent oedipal struggle, the re-assertion of paternal authority, which are only lightly alluded to in the ostensible account of Frédéric's development, all have striking counterparts in the February Revolution, the June Days and the events leading up to the *coup d'état*. Once the pattern of parallels between the two spheres is established, it acts as a powerful stimulant to the reader's imagination. In the expectation that the synchronisation between the two spheres will persist throughout the novel, the reader considers connections of all kinds, postulating unconscious processes and hidden responses which correspond to historical developments where there is no obvious parallel with conscious experience. Once again gaps do not necessarily subvert meaning; rather, they lead to an extension of the novel's psychological range. It has been recently suggested that as a result of the desire to make his novel so much more comprehensive with respect to history, Flaubert reduces the amount of psychology and attacks what had previously been the very foundation of fiction – character.[21] The preceding analysis has tried to show that the contrary is true; rather than psychology being impoverished and character shrinking, the running parallel between the two spheres has the effect of making psychology expand beyond its traditional limits as the reader is forced to adduce some of the more obscure transactions taking place in the foul rag-and-bone shop of the heart in order to find a fitting equivalent of the horrors of history, with the result that Frédéric Moreau, at least, ends up as a character apparently endowed with various layers, conscious and unconscious, making him a remarkably complicated mediocrity.

Conclusion

'S'il n'y avait pas de difficultés, où serait l'amusement?'[1] *L'Éducation sentimentale* presents the fascinating spectacle of a novelist at the height of his powers rising to the challenge of doing what is difficult, if not impossible, in the novel.[2] Almost every aspect of the work, as Du Camp pointed out to Flaubert, seems designed to increase the size of the task: 'Tu as fait une sorte de tour de force en écrivant un livre pareil sur un sujet qui n'en est pas un, sans intrigue aucune et sans caractère pour tes personnages.'[3] Flaubert's *Correspondance* reveals that he was fully aware of the many features which risked making the novel unreadable, from its flabby hero and extended plot to its constant deferral of meaning, repetitiousness and lack of strong pyramid structure.[4] It would seem that he derived a hidden pleasure from living dangerously, from courting disaster, from eroding the basis upon which the novel had hitherto rested. It needs to be stressed, however, that the appeal of these multiple self-imposed difficulties lay partly in the fact they could be overcome and the danger of the novel becoming completely unreadable averted. As important as the elements which push the novel to the brink of destruction are the balancing or compensatory resources which pull it back from the brink. It is this tension between the demolition of the novel and a vigorous rescue operation which constitutes the real 'modernity' of Flaubert's work. As Barthes has insisted, if the defining feature of works of modernity is that they contain both a conventional and a subversive edge, in Flaubert 'jamais les deux bords de la faille n'ont été plus nets et plus ténus.'[5] For the reader not to be deprived of that rapturous sense of uncertainty celebrated by Barthes, the rift that opens up in the Flaubertian text between anarchy and order, incoherence and coherence, new and old must be fully recognised.

   This study has attempted to show that, in spite of the indisputable novelty of many of the devices employed in *L'Éducation sentimentale*, the novel is not totally lacking in coherence and that the various techniques which create the impression that psychology and character are being dispensed with coexist with techniques which produce the opposite effect. The emphasis has fallen on those elements which provide the basis for a meaningful understanding of Frédéric and those who surround him; it would be unfortunate, however, if the attempt to recuperate the novel as one which can be made to yield an intelligible account of the development of a recognisable character were to have the effect of obscuring the profound originality of the work or minimising the undoubtedly disturbing effect it produces, particularly on a first reading. To present *L'Éducation sentimentale* as a totally conventional work, operating compliantly within the constraints of the traditional novel and offering no challenge to the reader's expectations as far as character and psychology are concerned would not be doing Flaubert a service, any more than seeing it as consistently and unrelievedly subverting character and psychology would. Flaubert's grappling with the novel form was conducted on a homeric scale[6] and the end product of all his efforts possesses a complexity and contradictory quality which invalidate the presentation of the work either as an essentially traditional novel or as a *nouveau roman* before its time.

The originality of Flaubert's approach becomes immediately apparent when *L'Éducation sentimentale* is compared with other nineteenth-century novels which explore similar themes. The central theme of failure in itself is familiar; the novelty of Flaubert's work lies in the far from straightforward way in which the nature and causes of failure are presented. While the conclusion of Balzac's *Un Début dans la vie* offers a clear account of the various mistakes made by Oscar Husson and the lessons he learns from these mistakes, Frédéric and Deslauriers flounder in their attempt to reach a clear understanding of where they went wrong.[7] In *La Joie de vivre*, in which the theme of *L'Éducation sentimentale* is consciously reworked by Zola,[8] the narrator leaves the reader in no doubt about the reasons for Lazare's failure to realise his various schemes.[9] While Flaubert may have believed that a similar personal inadequacy was the main factor at work in Frédéric's failure to fulfil his dream of becoming an artist,[10] explicit analysis is confined to the earliest plans for the novel and the question of why he fails left disconcertingly open. In contrast with both Balzac and Zola, Flaubert does not make the narrator display a solid grasp of the theme of failure, which constantly threatens to replicate itself at all levels.

In a similar fashion the theme of disintegration is treated in such a way as to make it seem as if the novel itself is coming apart. In *Illusions perdues* an insistent narrative voice charts the various stages in the inevitable decline of the ambitious 'homme de poësie' when confronted by the irresistible attractions of a corrupt society in which commercial considerations prevail, ensuring that a firm thematic grip is retained on the gradual collapse of Lucien. In *La Joie de vivre*, too, Zola's exploration of 'l'émiettement moral',[11] akin in certain respects to that depicted by Flaubert, never carries the novel towards the same problematic brink, partly because Lazare's point of view is not adopted in the same way as Frédéric's is and partly because a powerful corrective to his jaundiced outlook is embodied in the luminous figure of Pauline. *La Joie de vivre* does not convey the same strong impression of disintegration and fragmentation as *L'Éducation sentimentale* and other characters are more clearly defined. On the other hand, Zola is perhaps less successful in giving an in-depth portrayal of 'le *moi* moderne, actuel'[12] than Flaubert, and Lazare's inner life lies at a remove from the reader when compared with Frédéric's.

Intimately connected with the exploration of the themes of failure and disintegration in *L'Éducation sentimentale* is Flaubert's depiction of what he believed to be a characteristically modern form of love; Frédéric's relationship with Madame Arnoux ends in failure and collapse and has a destructive effect on the rest of his life. The type of love which lies at the heart of the novel had already been explored, though once again without the same far-reaching side-effects, in Balzac's *Le Lys dans la vallée*, which depicts a similar adoration of an idealised figure and was itself conceived as a reworking of Sainte-Beuve's *Volupté*.[13] Flaubert's treatment differs in a number of important respects from Balzac's, all of which tend to make *L'Éducation sentimentale* a more problematic work. Although Félix de Vandenesse, like Frédéric, refers to his 'vie manquée', he is not shown as being so drastically affected or incapacitated by his love for Madame de Mortsauf, pursuing a successful political career in the long periods he is separated from her in Paris; secondly, in spite of the strong sexual element in his response to Henriette, the opposition between two different kinds of love, one spiritual, one physical, remains free from the kind of contamination and interferences which problematize the opposition between sacred and profane love in *L'Éducation sentimentale*; thirdly, although *Le Lys dans la vallée* is written in the first person, the attitude towards idealising love, while not unambiguous, is less equivocal than that found in *L'Éducation sentimentale*. The use of a first-person narrator in theory makes any direct evaluation impossible but an at times critical authorial voice on occasion displaces that of Félix and the letters from Henriette and Natalie help to correct 'les abusives croyances de l'amour platonique'.[14] In comparison to this articulation of clearly differing views, *L'Éducation sentimentale* appears to leave the whole question of the value to be attached to Frédéric's love for Madame Arnoux in abeyance. Perhaps the most important difference of all is the figure of the woman that emerges: it is not simply a question of Flaubert's substituting for Balzac's 'châtelaine' a harassed, middle-class and ultimately less 'virtuous' heroine and thereby increasing the gap between idealised image and reality;[15] what is particularly striking is how indistinct Madame Arnoux is and how uncertain our knowledge of her seems to be in contrast to Madame de Mortsauf, who is perceived with greater clarity by Félix, engages in more sustained discussions with him and is made to convey her secret in a long letter.

The presentation of the love of Frédéric for Madame Arnoux is complicated by the oedipal configuration which is adumbrated in the novel. A strong fixation on the image of the mother is clearly presented in *Le Lys dans la vallée* and Félix de Vandenesse's devotion to Madame de Mortsauf has a similarly ambiguous quality. However, Félix's relationship with her husband, never close, lacks the complex mixture of admiration and antagonism which Frédéric feels for Arnoux. Although more developed than in Balzac's novel, the oedipal tensions that are presented in *L'Éducation sentimentale* are a good deal less prominent than those that can be perceived in a later novel like Maupassant's *Pierre et Jean*. If in *L'Éducation sentimentale* Frédéric's love for Madame Arnoux resembles that of a son for a mother, Pierre's love for his mother resembles that of a man for a woman, leading to an intensification and highlighting of the oedipal element; in his jealous obsession with his mother's adultery, which in an oblique reference to Flaubert's novel takes place in an apartment in the rue Tronchet, Pierre behaves more like a jealous husband than a deceived son and he is displaced as the object of his mother's affection, not only by his father and Maréchal, but also by his brother, which produces a more sustained and sharpened version of the feeling of rivalry and antagonism experienced by Frédéric.[16] In *Pierre et Jean* the oedipal situation functions a good deal less equivocally as the 'sens profond et caché des événements'[17] and Pierre is much more obviously the victim of unconscious forces than Frédéric.[18]

When compared with other nineteenth-century novels, it is not so much the thematic material itself as the manner of its presentation which makes *L'Éducation sentimentale* stand out as profoundly different. Whereas novels written both before and after appear as relatively stable structures, capable of supporting clear thematic conclusions and housing recognisable characters, *L'Éducation sentimentale* is a work in which everything seems to have been destabilised, creating the impression of a thematic emptiness, where the reader expects to find fullness of meaning, and a certain hollowness in the characters, where the expectation is of a richly individuated personalities. Although from the vantage point of the twentieth century we might regard the novel's characters as less lacking in substance than Du Camp when he referred to their being 'sans caractère', it is not difficult to see why in 1869 they should have appeared so unusual. *L'Éducation sentimentale* departs from previous norms when it comes to the amount, organisation and nature of the information that can be used for the construction of character. With the exception of Frédéric, the account of the behaviour of virtually all the characters is felt to be incomplete or fragmentary. The main focus of the novel falls upon Frédéric Moreau in a way that generally excludes keeping the reader abreast of what happens to other characters once they fall outside the orbit of his experience. Although the narrator will on occasion refer to past experiences of characters when they reappear, this is usually not sufficient to dispel the prevailing impression of incompleteness which stems from the marked shortage of information provided about their various actions over the long period of time covered by the novel. But it is not merely a question of the amount of information provided being insufficient to allow the reader to form a clear view of character; the actual dissemination of information along the syntagmatic axis is such that the reader is often required to possess considerable powers of recall to piece together material which is widely dispersed. The gaps between one action and another or between action and motivation may often be so great as to make it difficult to connect the two; rather than reinforcing each other to produce a sense of the characteristic or habitual, actions which are not linked may simply convey an impression of gratuitousness. The greatest problem, however, is posed by the aura of uncertainty with which much of the action is tinged. Reflected through the distorting lens of Frédéric's muddled awareness, the actions of other characters shimmer unreally before the reader's eyes. Even when the point of view is the narrator's and not Frédéric's, it can often seem that we are being offered not an authoritative account of events but, as Prendergast has argued, a kind of ironic debunking of the novelistic codes and conventions through which such events are customarily viewed, an ironic debunking which alarmingly produces a self-inflicted wound when turned against the narrator's own discourse.[19] When Frédéric's mind is used to relay not action but interpretation the tentative quality of the information provided increases; the behaviour of other characters is bathed in a semi-permanent mist of uncertainty and indistinctness. There are, of course, exceptions to this characteristic procedure; direct access is at times provided to the minds of other characters and, although he occupies a crumbling stronghold, the narrator's voice intermittently displays a residual authority which makes it difficult to settle on the notion of point of view as a way of composing the text and reducing one's expectations of clarity and coherence, as far as other characters are concerned, accordingly.

In spite of the wilful obscurantism which appears to characterise the presentation of their behaviour along the syntagmatic axis, the characters of *L'Éducation sentimentale* are not as shadowy as some of the characters of *Les Faux-Monnayeurs*, for instance, or as shifting as the figures of the father and daughter in Nathalie Sarraute's *Portrait d'un inconnu*, for example. This can be explained in part by the suggestions which are generated through different types of paradigmatic relation. While clearly much less rich than those found in *Madame Bovary*, the symbolic networks of *L'Éducation sentimentale* are a source of hints and possibilities which compensate for the dearth of information presented syntagmatically. It is often the case that several characters are implicated in a single symbolic motif. Although a given detail may be focalised, it can have a significance that goes beyond Frédéric's limited point of view. The descriptions of the Renaissance chest, for instance, point to changes taking place in Frédéric's 'subjective' perception of Madame Arnoux, some at an unconscious level, but they also correspond to more 'objective' changes in the position of Madame Arnoux herself. Differential relations between characters are also carefully organised. Sexual and political attitudes frequently emerge more clearly as a result of the systematic contrast with those of other characters. The significance of characters is determined in part by the relations of similarity and difference that exist with other characters with respect to a whole range of types of behaviour. We may not be told a great deal about the reactions of the various characters to major political upheavals but the hesitations and uncertainty of a Dussardier in June 1848 make an instructive contrast with both the hard-line approach of Sénécal and Frédéric's lack of commitment. As far as the last type of paradigmatic relationship is concerned, the long time-scheme in theory allows a large number of adjustments of the vertically arranged paradigm of traits to be made. At times this may consist in complex modifications which involve the crossing-over or exchange of traits between two characters who are generally opposed, as when Deslauriers briefly takes on some of the characteristics of Frédéric or Madame Arnoux of Rosanette. Such developments are potentially subversive but may in fact produce a richer, more complex view of character.

Much of what has been said so far does not apply to Frédéric who clearly is a much more fully developed character than the rest. Although, in some respects, the information relating to him is defective – we are told virtually nothing, for instance, about his physical appearance – we are in receipt of a good deal more information than is the case for all the other characters. It is his point of view which is predominantly adopted and his reactions which are summarised or analysed, often in considerable detail, and which form the 'backbone' of the novel. Frédéric is also at the centre of most of the symbolic motifs and benefits more than any other character from the systematic use of differential relations as a means of bringing out what is peculiar to various individuals. The disparity between the attentiveness of the account of his various experiences and his apparent nullity or mediocrity provokes the well-known Jamesian query 'Why, why him?'[20] It has recently been argued that in certain respects Frédéric should be regarded as an exemplary character on account of the way his consciousness operates in a privileged mode that can be defined in terms of the Sartrean notion of derealisation.[21] Whether such an approach is sufficient to allay persistent doubts about the generally derivative nature of his perceptions, his frequently flabby or shabby behaviour and comical inability to understand what is going on around him is debatable. Rather than regarding Frédéric's 'tendency to hallucinate', his 'total self-investment in an unknown image', his 'autistic poses' and 'stupid states' in a positive light as signs of a 'radical passivity' which is valorised by virtue of the fact that it gives him access to the aesthetic realm, as defined by Sartre,[22] they might be viewed negatively as symptoms of a profound psychic disability which consists in the way he restricts himself – damagingly and debilitatingly – to a limited repertoire of responses as a result of a deep-seated dependence upon an idealised image. It can be agreed that the pattern of Frédéric's behaviour is that of the 'neurotic' but it is far from certain that Flaubert presents this condition as being in any way desirable.

The frequently unorthodox nature and organisation of the narrative discourse of *L'Éducation sentimentale* can be expected to give rise to characters which, when detached from the narrative discourse in which they originate, are either defective or different from characters of a more traditional kind. It will be remembered that, as an aspect of the fictional world, character can be defined as 'a tree-like, hierarchical structure in which elements are arranged in categories of increasing integrative power'.[23] The paucity of information available in the case of certain characters means that such a tree-like structure remains imperfectly developed; the number of actions at the lowest level of this structure, the level at which 'character' meshes with story, may be insufficient to allow the reader to formulate a clear idea of habitual attitudes or thought-processes and there may not be much attempt to define rather than illustrate such attitudes and thought-processes either; with insufficient material being arranged at this level, it becomes difficult to fill the next level with a collection of traits, and at the top of the tree-like structure no clear character type may emerge, the more so since direct definitions of character are avoided. It would, however, be wrong to suggest that no kind of hierarchical arrangement is arrived at. It has already been suggested that the frequent dearth of information of a direct kind is compensated for by the use of more oblique methods of presentation. It is also often the case that characters are constructed in opposition to the stereotype with which they are associated. Although material at various levels may point in Madame Arnoux's case to the stereotype of *la femme vertueuse*, which Frédéric adheres to, there are a number of indications which encourage, if not an alternative view of Madame Arnoux, at least the notion of a conflict between the mandatory responses of her adopted role and actual needs which makes it impossible to accept the stereotype of *la femme vertueuse* as an adequate category of maximum integrative power into which to place her. Likewise, other female characters in the novel act in ways which suggest needs and attitudes corresponding to traits which contradict the simplistic overall view that Frédéric has of them, and the reader may well come to identify as most significant precisely that element which gives the lie to a kind of reductive process of character-construction on Frédéric's part. Flaubert is interested in undoing stereotyped views of what different kinds of women are like, not necessarily as a prelude to a dismantling of 'character' as a hierarchical structure, but with a view to refining the terms in which a global view of character is elaborated. In the place of character as a readily identifiable paradigm of homogeneous traits, he substitutes a more flexible 'package' which is capable of accommodating contradictions. When he goes to visit Madame Arnoux, Deslauriers is seeking to take the place of Frédéric and in so doing briefly takes on some of his traits; the overall image of hard-headed 'ambitieux' with little interest in women is modified in order to include a susceptibility to the influence of Frédéric and the goals with which he is associated. Compared to more traditional characters, the characters of *L'Éducation sentimentale* often appear opaque and lacking in consistency yet it is precisely these features which render them viable in the eyes of a modern reader.

In Frédéric's case, there is, as has been seen, no shortage of information and the various levels of the tree-like structure seem relatively well-stocked. The character type at the top of this structure is customarily perceived as that of the 'fruit sec' and the traits which are integrated into it those of 'spinelessness', 'flabbiness' and 'passivity', which in turn grow out of sets of habitual responses such as the preference for meetings with Madame Arnoux over other forms of contact, a readiness to serve both Madame Arnoux and her husband, a reluctance to make a decisive bid or to take positive action to achieve various objectives, all of which habitual responses are amply illustrated at the lowest level by a series of specific pieces of behaviour. While it does allow the character to be constituted in this way, *L'Éducation sentimentale* also supports an alternative and more sophisticated approach based upon the postulate of the unconscious. At the highest level it is possible to adduce not so much a social category ('fruit sec') or traditional psychological category ('tempérament mou') as the Flaubertian concept of a 'système', whose most salient characteristic in Frédéric's case is dependency upon the psychic constellation connected with the mother, a trait which is associated with various habitual responses, such as the overvaluation of Madame Arnoux and the undervaluation of Rosanette, both of which are exhibited in numerous thoughts and actions at the lowest level. It is of course at the highest level that this way of constituting Frédéric's character most obviously breaks new ground. The notion of the 'système', neither judgemental nor reductive, involves thinking of character in dynamic but unified terms as an integrated set of strategies, dictated in the main by the unconscious, by means of which the self seeks to negotiate its passage through the world.

It is, clearly, possible to sustain the argument that Flaubert is seeking to do away with character and psychology only if both character and psychology are defined in the traditional way. As has been seen, in numerous ways *L'Éducation sentimentale* marks a radical departure from the norms and conventions of the traditional novel and anyone expecting to find a straightforward account of the experiences of a range of well-defined characters is destined to be disappointed. The surface texture of Flaubert's novel has a distinctly problematic and at times anarchic quality which repeatedly creates the impression that meaning of all kinds is draining out of the novel. The reader may well feel inclined to take the text at face value as a perverse and negative exercise in opacity for its own sake. However, so persistent is the demand for intelligibility and so strong the notion that there is always something hidden behind any narrative, that the reader seeks to penetrate beneath the novel's refractory surface, to read between the lines, to find some way of making the work yield a hidden meaning. Such efforts are not altogether frustrated. Psychology, for Flaubert, is located beneath the surface and is all the more important for not being explicit; one of the unspoken injunctions that could be extended to the reader of *L'Éducation sentimentale* might well be 'Tu devineras la psychologie sous les faits'.[24] The considerable trouble to which Flaubert went during the planning of the novel to work out a detailed sequence of appropriate reactions for both Frédéric and those around him allows the basis for the novel's hidden psychology to be laid and is more than just a temporary phase through which Flaubert must pass before reaching maturity as a novelist. The coherence which is missing at the level of 'discours' may be posited at the level of 'histoire' on the basis of a processing of a number of cues pointing to a psychic dependency upon an idealised image at an unconscious level; adopting this approach, the unconscious becomes that which 'allows us to re-establish a coherent sequence, an intelligible relation'.[25] In sifting through the text for information which will allow an understanding of Frédéric's behaviour to be reached, the reader may find that the narrator discloses considerably less than he would like to hear; on the other hand, the implied author offers a more sophisticated brand of suggestion with the result that the novel ends up communicating a good deal more than it says. The account of the experience of Frédéric and his generation is not as lacking in either substance or direction as might at first appear to be the case; beneath the frequently opaque and problematic surface of *L'Éducation sentimentale* a rich psychological seam seems to lie hidden, and embedded in it are characters which, if not instantly recognisable, are not totally unknowable.

Notes

References to *L'Éducation sentimentale* (hereafter *L'ÉS*), given in brackets in the text, are to P. M. Wetherill's edition of the novel (Garnier, 1984). References to the correspondence are to the Conard edition, *Correspondance* (hereafter *Corr.*) 9 vols, 1926–33 and *Correspondance Supplément* (hereafter *Corr. Supp.*) 4 vols, 1954. Full bibliographical details of works referred to in the notes can be found in the appropriate section of the Select Bibliography, which is divided into the following parts: I Works of Flaubert; II Critical Studies of *L'Éducation sentimentale*; III General Critical Studies of Flaubert and Studies of Other Works of Flaubert; IV General Studies of the Novel and Critical Theory; V Other works (Novels, Criticism, General Reference).

Introduction

1. See Raitt ('État présent des études sur Flaubert', p.23): 'Flaubert occupe une place charnière dans l'histoire du roman. Héritier d'une tradition romantique et balzacienne qu'il récusait à moitié, prétendu chef d'une école réaliste qu'il exécrait, patron d'un mouvement naturaliste qu'il encourageait sans tout à fait l'approuver, il est aux origines de presque tous les développements de l'art romanesque au vingtième siècle.'
2. This phrase was used by Genette in a talk given at the 'Colloque Flaubert' organised by the Société d'histoire littéraire de la France and held in Paris on 28 and 29 November 1980. See also his 'Présentation' in *Travail de Flaubert*.
3. Genette, 'Silences de Flaubert', p.243.
4. Culler, *Flaubert: the uses of uncertainty*, p.109.
5. *Le Plaisir du texte*, p.18: 'la narrativité est déconstruite et l'histoire reste cependant lisible.'
6. Ibid., p.15: 'La culture ni sa destruction ne sont érotiques: c'est la faille de l'une à l'autre qui le devient.' See also Prendergast's discussion of the way the Flaubertian text 'operates a simultaneous dialectic of simulation and subversion, in which paradoxically the force of the latter depends crucially on the efficacy of the former' (*The Order of Mimesis: Balzac, Stendhal, Nerval, Flaubert*, p.203).
7. 'La Décomposition des personnages dans *L'ÉS*', p.167.
8. 'Le Défaut de ligne droite', p.87.

Notes for pages 2–6

9. *Clefs pour 'L'ÉS'*, p.7.
10. See Raitt, 'La Décomposition des personnages dans *L'ÉS*', p.166.
11. 'Flaubert: Writing and Negativity', p.211.
12. Cogny, *'L'ÉS' de Flaubert: Le Monde en creux*, p.169. See, however, Culler (*Flaubert*, p.135): 'Flaubert creates characters. We can discuss the personalities of Emma and Charles, of Frédéric and Deslauriers and though the psychological material in the later works does become remarkably thin, we are still very far from the empty voice of Beckett's *Comment c'est*, or the shifting and confused figures of Sollers' *Le Parc, Drame* and *Nombres*.'
13. Bem, *Clefs pour 'L'ÉS'*, p.13.
14. Culler, *Flaubert*, p.147.
15. 'Flaubert: Writing and Negativity', p.211.
16. See Brombert's claim (*The Novels of Flaubert*, p.172) that the consciousness of Frédéric is 'largely opaque as an object'.
17. 'Le réalisme subjectif dans *L'ÉS*', p.307.
18. The distinction between 'qui parle' and 'qui voit' will be discussed in Chapter IV.
19. *Flaubert*, pp.115–22.
20. 'Flaubert et la matière', p.206.
21. Raitt, '*L'ÉS* et la pyramide', p.139.
22. Gleize, 'Le défaut de ligne droite', p.76.
23. Bem, *Clefs pour 'L'ÉS'*, p.95.
24. Brombert, *The Novels of Flaubert*, p.164
25. See Raitt ('La Décomposition des personnages dans *L'ÉS*' p.166): 'Flaubert s'est bien gardé de fournir des explications plausibles pour toutes les actions de ses personnages ou de les préparer de longue main. Au contraire, très souvent il les fait agir d'une façon imprévisible au point de paraître presque gratuite.'
26. See Gleize ('Le Défaut de ligne droite', p.80): 'Une autre forme d'écart ajoute encore au morcellement du récit: celui qui sépare la notation d'un fait de son explication ou de sa motivation: il est toute une série de faits qui apparaissent inexplicables aux yeux du héros et leur explication pour le lecteur est différée jusqu'au moment où elle est fournie au héros lui-même'. See also Raitt ('La Décomposition des personnages dans *L'ÉS*', p.167): '[Le] refus de montrer l'enchaînement de la cause à l'effet est typique de la présentation lacunaire de la psychologie dans *L'Éducation sentimentale*.'
27. See Raitt (Introduction to *L'ÉS*, i.59): 'Cette impression de mystère et de secret caractérisent toute une série d'événements et de personnages dans le roman.'
28. *The Novels of Flaubert*, p.184.
29. 'Le Défaut de ligne droite', p.87.
30. 'The Theme of disintegration in *L'ÉS*', p.163.
31. *L'ÉS* et la pyramide', p.138.
32. Digeon, *Flaubert*, p.171.

Notes for pages 6–11

33. See Raitt ('*L'ÉS* et la pyramide', p.141): 'tous les facteurs d'unification que nous venons de passer en revue sont soit des éléments thématiques, soit des techniques de microstructure.'
34. See Prendergast, 'Flaubert and the Cretan Liar paradox'.
35. Ibid, p.265. See also Prendergast, *The Order of Mimesis*, pp.180–211.
36. The disclaimer was made when, on the occasion of his seventieth birthday, he was greeted as 'the discoverer of the unconscious' and is recalled in Trilling's 'Freud and Literature', p.95.
37. See Barthes ('Introduction à l'analyse structurale des récits', p.19): 'narrateur et personnages sont essentiellement des "êtres de papier"'.
38. *S/Z*, p.101.
39. For a fuller discussion of the legitimacy of attributing unconscious motives to fictional characters see Kaplan and Kloss, *The Unspoken Motive*, p.4 and Le Galliot (*Psychanalyse et langages littéraires*, p.96): 'Quant à cet argument de la critique littéraire traditionnelle selon lequel le personnage de roman, étant une créature de pure fiction, ne peut être conçu comme doté d'un inconscient, on peut rétorquer qu'à prendre les choses au pied de la lettre, ce personnage n'a pas de "conscient" non plus. Dans ces conditions, il est aussi légitime (ou aussi peu) d'attribuer des motivations inconscientes à sa conduite réalisée que de s'en tenir aux motivations conscientes, comme le fait la critique traditionnelle.'
40. *The Novels of Flaubert*, p.184.
41. Quoted in Ricardou, *Problèmes du nouveau roman*, p.77.
42. See Barthes, *S/Z*, p.74.
43. See Culler, *Structuralist Poetics*, p.230. See also Knight (*Flaubert's Characters*, p.5): 'Character and discourse are accomplices, and to study the construction and characteristics of the former hardly involves assuming that they are "real people".' I am fully in agreement with Knight when she claims that Flaubert works within the convention of character as a major totalizing force in fiction but would not wish to see his characters as exemplary in the way she does.
44. Weinsheimer, 'Theory of Character: *Emma*', p.195.
45. *Story and Discourse: narrative structure in fiction and film*.
46. *Narrative Fiction: contemporary poetics*.
47. *Story and Discourse*, p.119.
48. *Narrative Fiction*, p.33.
49. Wetherill, *Flaubert: La Dimension du texte*, p.3.
50. See Chatman, p.111.
51. James, *Selected Literary Criticism*, p.58.
52. *Problèmes de linguistique générale*, pp.239–44.
53. See Todorov ('Les Catégories du récit littéraire', p.126): 'L'œuvre littéraire a deux aspects: elle est en même temps une histoire et un discours. Elle est histoire dans ce sens qu'elle évoque une certaine réalité, des événements qui se seraient passés, Mais l'œuvre est en même temps discours: il existe

Notes for pages 11–19

un narrateur qui relate l'historie, et il y a en face de lui un lecteur qui la perçoit.'

54. *Nouveau discours du récit*, p.13.
55. Hrushovski's views, at present elaborated only in Hebrew, are summarised in Rimmon-Kennan, p.37.
56. *S/Z*, p.58.
57. For further discussion of direct definition and indirect presentation of character see Rimmon-Kenan, pp.60–7.
58. See *S/Z*, p.74: 'Le nom propre fonctionne comme champ d'aimantation des sèmes; renvoyant virtuellement à un corps, il entraîne la configuration sémique dans un temps évolutif.'
59. *S/Z*, p.101.
60. Ibid., p.197.
61. Ibid., p.74.
62. See Lichtenstein, quoted in Holland, *5 Readers Reading*, p.57.
63. See Garvey, 'Characterization in Narrative', p.75.
64. See Barthes, 'Introduction à l'analyse structurale des récits', pp.8–11 and *S/Z*, pp.25–7.
65. See Hamon, 'Pour un statut sémiologique du personnage', p.69. For a more recent discussion by the same author see *Le Personnel du roman*.
66. See Chatman, pp.126–7.
67. Ibid. See also Lotman *The Structure of the Artistic Text*, p.255: 'The hero's behaviour is always unpredictable, first, because his character is constructed, not as a previously known possibility, but as a paradigm, a set of possibilities unified on the level of conceptual structure and *variational* on the level of the text. Second, the text unfolds along the syntagmatic axis, and although in the general paradigmatics of character the succeeding episode is just as natural as the one which is being realised at the present moment, the reader nonetheless has not yet mastered the whole paradigmatic image of the language.'
68. *L'Ere du soupçon*, p.112.
69. See *Corr. Supp.* ii.65: 'je veux représenter un état psychologique – vrai selon moi – et non encore décrit.'
70. See Barthes, *S/Z*, p.101.
71. *Corr.* v.331.
72. For a very different view of the relation between 'character' and 'psychology' see Hamon, *Le Personnel du roman*, p.13.

I Analysis, Synthesis and Hidden Psychology

1. See '*Bovary* . . . sera sous ce rapport, la somme de ma science psychologique et n'aura une valeur originale que par ce côté' (*Corr.* ii:457) and 'L'enchaînement des sentiments me donne un mal de chien, et tout dépend de là dans ce roman' (*Corr.* iii.53).

Notes for pages 19–21

2. See 'Ce qui m'inquiète le plus, c'est le fonds, je veux dire la partie psychologique' (*Corr.* iv.175).
3. See 'Je veux représenter un état psychologique – vrai selon moi – et non encore décrit' (*Corr. Supp.* ii.65) and 'Bien que mon sujet soit purement d'analyse, j'aborde quelquefois les événements de l'époque' (*Corr.* v.327).
4. See Hill, 'Flaubert and the Rhetoric of Stupidity'.
5. See criticism of novels sent to him for comment: 'Je veux dire que les événements *ne dérivent plus* du caractère des personnages ou que ces mêmes caractères ne les produisent pas' (*Corr.* v.277) and 'on ne croit pas à l'histoire, parce que les événements ne dérivent pas fatalement des caractères . . . la raison du vœu n'est pas motivée . . . la mort de celle-ci (la veuve) ne me paraît pas la conséquence naturelle de sa passion . . . .' (*Corr.* v.179).
6. See criticism of the incoherence of the characters in Louise Colet's 'L'Institutrice' ('Je n'y comprends rien. Ils sont parfois très cyniques et d'autres fois très vertueux, sans que ce soit fondu', *Corr.* ii.287) and the comment made about *Salammbô*: 'si les caractères ne sont pas suivis . . . je suis dans le faux' (*Corr.* v.67).
7. See 'Ce qui est atroce de difficulté c'est l'enchaînement des idées et qu'elles dérivent bien naturellement les unes des autres' (*Corr.* ii.448).
8. See criticism made of a novel sent for comment: 'La lâcheté du comte est concevable en ce sens qu'elle est bien amenée; mais l'atrocité d'Hélène . . . aurait dû être préparée, dans les parties précédentes, par des motifs, des faits plus explicites' (*Corr.* v.296).
9. See 'Il n'y a point dans mon livre une description isolée, gratuite; toutes *servent* à mes personnages et ont une influence lointaine ou immédiate sur l'action' (*Corr.* v.60).
10. Green, *Salammbô and the Historical Novel*, p.30: 'Even with the plans for the novel complete, the psychological element continued to give trouble' and 'Ce qui m'embête à trouver dans mon roman, c'est l'élément psychologique, à savoir la façon de sentir' (*Corr.* iv.200).
11. *Corr.* vi.2. See also *Corr. Supp.* ii.65: 'Mon but est complexe.'
12. 'A me voir d'aspect, on croirait que je dois faire de l'épique, du drame, de la brutalité des faits et je ne me plais au contraire que dans les sujets d'analyse, d'anatomie, si je peux dire' (quoted Colling, *Gustave Flaubert*, p.164).
13. *Corr.* ii.344.
14. *Corr.* iv.349: 'C'est une chose étrange, comme je suis attiré par les sciences médicales . . . J'ai envie de disséquer . . . Si j'étais plus jeune, de dix ans, je m'y mettrais.'
15. See *Corr.* i.39; i.201; i.262; iii.373. But see Sartre (*L'Idiot de la famille*, i.489): 'il médite sur son cas mais ne se dissèque pas'.
16. *Corr.* ii.457.
17. Sartre, *L'Idiot de la famille*, i.499: 'il s'acharne à substituer les schèmes paternels à sa compréhension spontanée du vécu jusqu'à ce qu'il ait tout rapporté au modèle, c'est-à-dire à l'atomisme analytique.'

Notes for pages 21–22

18. Ibid., p.460: 'C'est le regard du père, sublimé, généralisé, que Flaubert tentera plus tard de s'approprier sous le nom de "coup d'œil médical".'
19. Ibid., p.493: 'L'analyse, personnifée et sacralisée, devient pour toujours son surmoi.'
20. Ibid., p.498.
21. Ibid., p.488.
22. Ibid., p.489: 'L'intellectualisme analytique est en lui, comme une plaie, comme une connaissance complète et, en réalité, parfaitement vide de la vie, comme une malédiction, comme la rationalisation de son pessimisme et de sa misanthropie' and p.493: 'L'analyse s'introduit en lui comme sa condamnation . . .'.
23. Ibid., p.488.
24. Ibid., p.499: 'Gustave ne sera jamais que le regardé; sa vérité reste au niveau de ce qui est disséqué, elle n'atteindra jamais au niveau de l'acte analytique.'
25. Ibid., ii.1130: 'les sentiments d'Emma ne sont jamais analysés' and ii.1131: 'Gustave, Dieu soit loué, n'a jamais su "faire un plan".'
26. Ibid., i.488.
27. See *Corr.* i.277: 'Celui qui vit maintenant et qui est moi ne fait que contempler l'autre, qui est mort. J'ai eu deux existences bien distinctes; des événements extérieurs ont été le symbole de la fin de la première et de la naissance de la seconde.'
28. *L'Avenir de la science*, p.803: 'Sans doute les patientes investigations de l'observateur, les chiffres qu'accumule l'astronomie, les longues énumerations du naturaliste ne sont guère propres à réveiller le sentiment du beau; le beau n'est pas dans l'analyse, mais le beau idéal, celui qui ne repose pas sur les fictions de la fantaisie humaine, est caché dans les résultats de l'analyse. Disséquer le corps humain, c'est détruire sa beauté; et, pourtant, par cette dissection, la science arrive à y reconnaître une beauté d'ordre bien supérieur et que la vue superficielle n'aurait pas soupçonnée.'
29. *Corr.* i.27 (Written 24 June 1837).
30. *L'Idiot de la famille*, i.475.
31. See *La Muse du département. La Comédie humaine*, iv.67: 'une de ces longues et monotones tragédies conjugales qui demeureraient éternellement inconnues, si l'avide scalpel du Dix-Neuvième siècle n'allait pas, conduit par la nécessité de trouver du nouveau, fouiller les coins les plus obscurs du cœur . . .'.
32. See Prendergast, *Balzac: fiction and melodrama*, pp.112–28.
33. Neefs, *'Madame Bovary' de Flaubert*, p.16.
34. *Corr.* iv.347; iv.399; vi.33 and iii.154; iii.368.
35. Debray-Genette, 'Flaubert: Science et écriture', p.44.
36. *Corr.* viii.135: 'Il n'y a de vrai que les "rapports", c'est-à-dire la façon dont nous percevons les objets' and viii.370: 'Il n'y a pas de Vrai! Il n'y a que des manières de voir.'
37. Debray-Genette, 'Flaubert: Science et écriture', p.45.

Notes for pages 22–27

38. *Corr*. v.347.
39. *Souvenirs*, p.105.
40. *Œuvres complètes*, i.421.
41. *L'Idiot de la famille*, i.488: 'A quinze ans, il donne mission à l'écrivain de restituer comme totalité syncrétique le cosmos que le savant pulvérise, non point après l'analyse et comme recomposition mais avant.'
42. *Carnet* 2, p.261.
43. *Œuvres complètes*, i.351.
44. Ibid.
45. See the views of Poulet and Richard and my discussion of them in 'Determinism in the first *ÉS*'. For a more recent discussion see Unwin, 'Flaubert and Pantheism'.
46. *Œuvres complètes*, i.327.
47. For more recent discussion of the dog episode see Unwin, 'The Significance of the Encounter with the Dog in Flaubert's first *'ÉS'*.
48. *Œuvres complètes*, i.370.
49. *Corr*. iii.128.
50. See *Œuvres complètes*, i.351: 'La nature se prêtait à ce concert et le monde entier lui apparut reproduisant l'infini et reflétant la face de Dieu.'
51. *Œuvres complètes*, i.446.
52. Ibid.
53. *Corr*. ii.61.
54. See *Corr*. iii.61–2: 'L'auteur, dans son œuvre, doit être comme Dieu dans l'univers, présent partout, et visible nulle part.'
55. *Corr*. vi.103.
56. G. Genette, *Figures III*, p.209. For a full discussion of the implications of the terms used by Flaubert to designate the narrator see Gothot-Mersch, 'Sur le Narrateur chez Flaubert', pp.344–6.
57. See, for instance, Pascal, *The Dual Voice: free indirect speech and its functioning in the nineteenth-century European novel*, p.98: 'Flaubertian objectivity . . . meant an imaginative self-submergence in the object, participation in the imagined character's experience.'
58. For a stimulating discussion of the implications of the analogy between author and Spinozist God see Unwin, 'Flaubert and Pantheism'.
59. 'Le Roman' (Preface to *Pierre et Jean*), pp.41–2.
60. See the description of his method in 'Gustave Flaubert', p.85: 'Au lieu d'étaler la psychologie des personnages en des dissertations explicatives, il le faisait simplement apparaître par leurs actes. Les dedans étaient ainsi dévoilés par les dehors, sans aucune argumentation psychologique.' For a recent discussion of Maupassant's essay, 'Le Roman', see Woollen, '"Roland furieux" and "le roman d'analyse pure"' and Lethbridge, 'Maupassant, Scylla and Charybdis'.
61. Likewise, Maupassant in practice departs from the simplified model proposed in the preface which reads, he admits, like 'la critique du genre d'étude

Notes 225

Notes for pages 27–32

psychologique que j'ai entrepris dans *Pierre et Jean*' ('Le Roman', p.35). For a stimulating discussion of the 'caractère hybride' of *Pierre et Jean* see Lethbridge, *Maupassant: Pierre et Jean*.
62. 'Le Roman', p.42.
63. Ibid.
64. See Kermode, *The Genesis of Secrecy* for a discussion of this equation in relation to the Gospels.
65. *Corr.* iii.53.
66. *Corr.* iv.3.
67. The same phenomenon in a different context is described by Freud, *Three Essays on the Theory of Sexuality*, p.69: 'The progressive concealment of the body which goes along with civilization keeps sexual curiosity awake. This curiosity seeks to complete the sexual object by revealing its hidden parts.'
68. *Corr.* vi.434.
69. 'Le Roman', p.42.
70. See James, *Selected Literary Criticism*, p.94.
71. *Aspects of the Novel*, p.145: 'it is the function of the novelist to reveal the hidden life at its source.'

II The Planning of *L'Éducation sentimentale*

1. Cf. *Corr.* iv.272: 'La *Bovary* m'a dégouté pour longtemps des mœurs bourgeoises. Je vais, pendant quelques années peut-être, vivre dans un sujet splendide et loin du monde moderne dont j'ai plein le dos.'
2. *Corr.* v.58. Advised by Bouilhet not to 'se noyer dans trop d'analyses psychologiques' (Bart, 'Louis Bouilhet – accoucheur de Flaubert', p.210), Flaubert makes the narrator adopt an ingenuous view of psychological matters which creates an impression of simplicity of characterisation. Such an impression is, however, undermined by the complex symbolic effects generated by objects such as the sacred veil. See Neefs ('Le parcours du zaïmph', p.232): 'les signes narratifs et diégétiques, tous les indices s'accumulent pour formuler une opposition qui dépasse infiniment l'explication psychologique donnée dans l'explicite du texte'.
3. *Corr.* iv.318.
4. *Corr.* v.331.
5. *Journal*, v.84.
6. *Corr.* v.141.
7. Cf. Raitt's 'Introduction' to *L'ÉS*, i.19–20. In his recent edition of the novel, Wetherill (p.xviii) rejects 1862 as the year of conception, suggesting instead that Flaubert did not begin work on what was to become *L'Éducation sentimentale* until early 1863.
8. 'Introduction', i.26 'Les plans sommaires du *Carnet 19* ont dû être énormément développés avant le début de la composition proprement dite.'
9. Durry, *Flaubert et ses projets inédits*, pp.99–101.

Notes for pages 32–34

10. Ibid., p.135.
11. Ibid., p.137, f.35. All subsequent references will be followed by the folio number. For the significance of the various brackets used see Note 53.
12. 'Ton idée . . . de faire passer la femme mariée par tous les degrés serait fort bonne, si un nommé Flaubert n'avait déjà fait un chef-d'œuvre, qui s'appelle *Madame Bovary* . . . c'est au fond retomber dans la même étude' (quoted in Bart, 'Bouilhet – accoucheur de Flaubert', p.195). Wetherill ('Préface' to *L'ÉS*, p.xlvi) suggests that the change of emphasis from the woman to the man is accompanied by the transfer of the name Moreau.
13. See f.35: 'adultere mêlé de remords et de [peur] ‹terreurs›'.
14. Cf. the contrast outlined in the following comment, made in all probability at the time the first *scénario* was drafted (i.e. on the reverse side of the previous page): 'A mesure que le jeune homme se perfectionne et se *durcit* dans la société des Lorettes M Moreau de plus en plus vertueuse, devient plus jalouse' (f.34 verso).
15. Cf. 'elle ne vient au rendez-vous que deux ou trois fois. – Mais agitée, en larmes – mauvais coup – deception pr l'amant qui est deja très fort' (f.34 verso).
16. Cf. Raitt, 'Introduction', i.9.
17. Cf. the direct reference to personal experience 'Me Sch. – Mr Sch.moi' (f.35). Wetherill rightly asserts that there is no question of Flaubert wishing to recount his 'grand amour' in this novel ('Préface', p.xxiv).
18. Cf. *Corr*. iv.59: 'Une réaction terrible se fait dans la conscience de ce qu'on appelle l'Amour. Cela a commencé avec des rugissements d'ironie (Byron, etc.), et le siècle tout entier . . . dissèque sur sa table la petite fleur du sentiment qui sentait si bon . . . jadis!'
19. Cf. in particular *Par les champs et par les grèves. Œuvres complètes*, i.517: 'C'était un petit coin embaumé, mystérieux, doux, à l'écart dans l'église, retraite cachée, ornée avec amour, toute propice aux exhalaisons du désir mystique et aux longs épanchements des oraisons éplorées. Comprimée par le climat, amortie par la misère, l'homme reporte ici toute la sensualité de son cœur, il la dépose aux pieds de Marie, sous le regard de la femme céleste et il y satisfait, en l'excitant, cette inextinguible soif de jouir et d'aimer.'
20. *Corr*. ii.400.
21. *Corr*. iv.356. See also the reference to 'ce pauvre siècle à scrofules et à pâmoisons . . . qui se complaît sur les genoux féminins, comme un enfant malade' (*Corr*. iv. 304).
22. Cf. '*Le culte de la mère* sera une des choses qui fera pouffer de rire les générations futures. Ainsi que notre respect pour l'*amour*' (*Corr*. iv.304).
23. Cf. 'Ce brave organe génital est le fond des tendresses humaines . . . Jamais aucune femme n'a aimé un eunuque . . . Oui, tout dépend de là, quelqu' humiliés que nous en soyons' (*Corr*. iii.24).
24. See Goncourt, *Journal*, vi. 173.

Notes for pages 34–38

25. *Corr.* v.274.
26. *Corr.* v.271.
27. Cf. 'Je suis repu [de la femme] comme doivent l'être ceux qu'on a trop aimés. C'est peut-être moi qui ai trop aimé. C'est la masturbation qui en est cause, masturbation morale, j'entends. Tout est parti de moi, tout y est rentré. Je suis devenu impuissant pour ces effluves magnifiques que j'ai trop senties bouillonner pour les voir jamais se déverser' (*Correspondance*, ed. Bruneau, Pléiade, i.235). At the time he was working on the plans for *L'ÉS* Flaubert told the Goncourt brothers that 'les civilisés sont masturbateurs' and that 'l'homme n'a pas besoin d'une émission séminale, mais d'une émission nerveuse' (*Journal*, vi.173).
28. See Chapter V, p.134.
29. *Carnet 15*, p.444.
30. See Cottin, 'Le "vieux manuscrit" de *L'ÉS*', p.101: 'A la mort de Mme Franklin-Grout, en 1931, le manuscrit fut mis en vente et acheté par Sacha Guitry pour sa collection où il demeura à peu près inaccessible.'
31. N. A. F. 17611. See the 'Notice' to the collection: 'Au fur et à mesure du dépouillement ont été relevés tous les feuillets (de dimensions diverses) qui n'appartiennent pas à une rédaction narrative, à savoir: plans, scénarios, notes documentaires et autres, afin de constituer un volume à part.' Where a folio has been used both for a plan and a rough draft, it has been bound with the rough drafts. A certain number of *scénarios* are, therefore, interspersed amongst the *brouillons*.
32. Folios 65–104 measure, for the most part, 310 mm. x 200 mm. Folios 1–64 measure 345 mm. x 215 mm.
33. The distinction between different types of *scénario* used here is that proposed by Gothot-Mersch (*La Genèse de 'Madame Bovary'*, p.120 and p.164). For a discussion of Bouilhet's role see Bart, 'Louis Bouilhet – accoucheur de Flaubert'. References to the work he was doing on the plans in 1864 can be found in Flaubert's letters. See, in particular, *Corr.* v.141: 'J'ai hier travaillé toute la journée avec Monseigneur au plan de mon livre'.
34. See Wetherill; Préface', p.xli: 'Si une partie de la documentation et les scénarios généraux sont préparés d'avance (c'est-à-dire avant septembre 1864), Flaubert rédige chaque épisode à partir de scénarios et d'une documentation entreprise *au fur et à mesure*.'
35. See, in particular *Corr.* v.212 and *Corr. Supp.* ii.116 and 164.
36. *Corr.* v.141.
37. See Wetherill, 'Appendice II' to *L'ÉS*, p.610: 'Flaubert y (i.e. in the *scénarios*) cherche avant tout à préciser et à renforcer l'articulation et l'enchaînement des faits.'
38. See Wetherill,' "C'est là ce que nous avons eu de meilleur" ', Herschberg-Pierrot, 'Le Travail des stéréotypes dans les brouillons de la "prise des Tuileries" ' and Cajueiro-Roggero, 'Dîner chez les Dambreuse; "La réaction commençante" '.

Notes for pages 38–39

39. See, however, Bruneau, 'L'avant-dernier chapitre de *L'ÉS*' and my own brief account, 'The Plans for *L'Éducation sentimentale*'. Wetherill's recent edition of the novel marks a major step forward with its discussion of Flaubert's 'méthode de composition' (pp.xxxix–lx), brief description of the corpus of *scénarios* (pp.609–14) and transcription of a wide-ranging selection of complete *scénarios* (pp.615–47) and short excerpts from the *scénarios* and *brouillons* in the notes (pp.431–507). Wetherill does not, however, seek to identify the *scénarios* which correspond to the various stages in the development of the novel or attempt, as this study does, to determine the sequence in which the *scénarios* were written and the precise relationship between those written before the composition of the novel began and those written after.

40. See my 'The Plans for *L'ÉS*' for a tentative discussion of the possible sequences. A number of modifications to this early analysis are necessary and the following sequences now seem more plausible but, given the fact that many *scénarios* are missing, cannot be advanced with complete certainty. First series (folio followed by Flaubert's pagination): 65(1), 66(2), 67(3), 69(4), 74(5), –, –, 76(8), 77(8), 78(9) and 81(9), 89(10), 85(11), –, –, 92(14), 94(15), 96(16), –, –, –, –; Second series: –, –, –,70(4), 73(5), –, –, –, 80(9) and 79(9), 84(10) and 83(10), 86(11) and 87(11), –, –, –, –, 95(16), 101(17), –, –, –; Third series: –, –, –, 68(4), 72(5), 75(6), –, –, 82(9), –, –, –, 90(13), –, –, 91(16), –, 93(18), 100(19), 97(20), 103(21), 104(22). Part of a possible fourth series can be found in *scénarios* interspersed amongst the *brouillons*: N.A F. 17603, f.83(9), f.215(9), f.230(11); 17608, f.83(18), f.128(19).

41. The complete absence of plans for certain chapters (e.g. II i and II vi) suggests that some plans have been lost; on the other hand the existence of only one set of plans for the last three chapters of the novel may result from their being carried forward.

42. N.A F. 17611, f.65 contains the following marginal addition: 'd'abord un peu de brouillard – à l'avant Arnoux – puis Fr. revient et apperçoit Me qui se tenait dans la chambr jusque-là'.

43. See N.A.F. 17611, ff.69, 70 and 68.

44. See N.A.F. 17611, f.75.

45. See N.A.F. 17611, ff.74 and 72.

46. Two résumés (N.A.F. 176n, ff.105, 108) also specify five chapters. Originally Chapter iii covered both Frédéric's first year in Paris and the second year up to Deslauriers's arrival and Chapter iv began with their 'vie à deux' (N.A.F. 17611, ff.69, 70 and 68).

47. See N.A.F. 17611, f.106.

48. See N.A.F. 17611, ff.78 and 81. In N.A.F. 17611, f.84 the visit to the races occupies its present position.

49. A résumé (N.A.F. 17611, f.106) stipulates nine chapters, which are reduced to seven in another résumé (N.A.F. 17611, f.105). In the *scénarios* Flaubert reaches Chapter viii but the last chapter of Part II is missing. The sequence of

Notes for pages 39–57

chapters in the second series (see note 40) is from i to vii, which is reduced in the third series to i to vi. Chapter divisions do not necessarily correspond to the present divisions.

50. See the résumés (N.A.F. 17611, ff.106 and 105) and the *scénarios* (N.A.F. 17611, ff.96, 99 and 101).

51. See N.A.F. 17611, ff.103 and 104.

52. Ten chapters are envisaged in a résumé (N.A.F. 17611, f.106) while in the third series of *scénarios* (see note 40) seven chapters are finally reached.

53. N.A.F. 17611, f.105. All future references to plans from this volume will be given immediately after the passage quoted. Unless otherwise indicated, it is the recto which is referred to. Passages which have been crossed out are enclosed in square brackets: [...]. Passages which have been added are enclosed in pointed brackets: ‹...›. Material added or omitted by me is enclosed in double brackets: ((...)). Flaubert's punctuation, use of accents, abbreviations and spelling are all retained. In some cases material transcribed here also appears in Wetherill's edition of the novel.

54. See the reference to his 'rêves romantiques' and 'Frederic s'abandonne à ses rêveries' in f.65.

55. See ff.109, 109 verso, 111, 111 verso, 115 and 116.

56. See ff.143 and 144 which contain instructions such as 'montrer les deboires de Desl, leur progression, et comment à mesure que l'on avance vers 1848, il tourne au Senecal', 'motiver mieux le renvoi de Senecal' and queries such as 'le relier à la Vatnas? (quelle sera l'infamie finale que l'on va lui proposer?)', 'il faut que chez Mr D Fr. subisse une avanie effective. Le Ministre ne fera rien pr. un homme qui a de telles opinions politiques?' and 'Faut-il montrer là, la jalousie de Me Dambr [pour] ‹contre› Me Arn?'. It is perhaps worth noting (in the light of comments that have been made about II ii (see p.87)) that Flaubert insisted in a marginal addition (f.77) that 'les dejeuners doivent decouler des faits'.

57. *Corr.* v.158.

58. *Corr.*v.92.

59. See my 'The Plans for *L'ÉS*'. Once again the early suggestions made need modifying and the following part plans appear to form sequences: Part I: ff.1, 4, 8 and 7; 2, 5, 9 and 6; Part II: ff.20, 27, 37 and 40; 18, 30, 35 and 41; Part III: 46, 55 and 63; 155, 59 and 156; 45, 59 and 64. Chapter plans are as follows: I i: –; I ii: –; I iii: –; I iv; –; I v: 12, 10, 11 and 3; I vi: 13, 14, 15, 15 verso, 16 and 16 verso; II i and II ii: 19 and 28; 17 and 29; II ii: 22, 21 and 26; 23, 25 and 24; II iii: 33, 36 and 34; II iv: 39; II v and II vi: 42; II vi: 43; (There is evidence that 23, 25, 36, 39 and 42 were all worked on in sequence and they might therefore be classified as part plans); III i: 47, 44 and 48; III ii: 52, 50, 49, 51 and 51 verso; III iii: 54 and 53; III iv: 60, 58 and 57; III v: 61 and 62; III vi: – III vii: –.

60. In f.4 Desroches is corrected to Laroque; in ff.7, 40 and 46 (first series part plans) Laroque is corrected to Roque; in later part plans Roque is used

Notes for pages 57–70

from the outset.

61. *Corr.* v.212.
62. *Corr. Supp.* ii.164.
63. See Wetherill, Préface', p.liii for a stimulating discussion of this possibility.
64. There are still two dinners in f.4 (first series part plan) but in f.5 the first is crossed out and in f.9 'chante' is added to the second dinner, suggesting that the two are going to be fused.
65. This episode, despite having been crossed out in a *scénario d'ensemble* (f.72), is retained in the part plans (ff.7 and 6) but suppressed in a chapter plan (f.3). Even before this Flaubert had already felt the need for greater concision: 'La partie de canot et la chasse aux grisettes en un seul mouvement une seule scène' (f.120).
66. Ff.7 and 6 retain the reference; f.3 introduces the references to L'Alhambra for the first time.
67. See ff.1, 4, 8 and 7; 2, 5, 9 and 6.
68. See ff. 11, 12 and 10; 13, 14 and 15.
69. See ff.27 and 30 ('dispute violente'); 37 and 35 ('visite à la fabrique').
70. See ff. 20 and 18. This placing is suggested in a marginal addition in a *scénario d'ensemble* (f.77): 'à etaler dans le courant du chapitre quand il est bien avec les 2 dames et tout fier de cela'.
71. Only two visits are envisaged in the part plans. The visit to Madame Dambreuse is added in the chapter plans (ff.19, 17, 22, 21, 23).
72. See ff.37 and 35.
73. See ff.40 and 41 (part plans) and 42 (chapter plan).
74. A reduction from seven chapters to six takes place in the first series of part plans (ff. 20, 27, 37 and 40).
75. In f.27 (first series part plan) Chapter iii begins with Frédéric's disappointment on discovering Delmar has become Rosanette's lover but in f.35 (second series part plan) it begins at the present point ('Des lors Frederic ne quitte plus les Arnoux').
76. See f.55.
77. See f.63.
78. The reduction takes place in the first series of part plans (ff.46, 55, 63): ii is suppressed; iv becomes iii; v and vi remain; vii is suppressed; ix becomes vii.
79. See f.46.
80. See ff.46 and 55.
81. Flaubert uses either capital letters or roman numerals to distinguish the *esquisses* from the *brouillons*. The identification of all the *esquisses* still remains to be done.
82. References to the *esquisses*, following the quotation, give first the volume number, then the folio number. Unless otherwise specified it is the recto which is referred to.
83. See Debray-Genette, 'La Technique romanesque de Flaubert dans "Un Cœur simple"', p.95: 'là ou l'on perçoit dans le texte final évidemment du

Notes for pages 71–76

sens, travail de l'implicite, synthèse et raccourci, on trouve dans les manuscrits de l'explicite, de l'analytique d'une part; d'autre part de remarquables
développements libres, censurés ensuite sans pitié'. See also Wetherill
('Préface', p.viii): 'Flaubert développe les dimensions de l'opacité du texte
en instaurant un point de vue, une focalisation, une voix narrative, qui ne
livrent pas tout ou qui ne sont pas vraiment fiables.'
84. See Wetherill ('Préface', p.liii): 'Les procédés de suppression déterminent
quasiment tous les aspects de l'évolution des brouillons.'

III Plot-Structure

1. See Introduction, note 5.
2. See discussion of these terms in the introduction, pp.10–11.
3. *The Pursuit of Signs*, pp.169–70.
4. *Narrative Fiction; contemporary poetics*, p.6.
5. See Culler, *The Pursuit of Signs*.
6. Rimmon-Kenan, p.44.
7. The conventional nature of this frame has been stressed by narratologists
(see Rimmon-Kenan, pp. 16–17).
8. See Sternberg, *Expositional Modes and Temporal Ordering in Fiction*.
9. See Genette, *Figures III*, pp.145–9.
10. *Narrative Fiction*, p.17.
11. *Poétique*, p.74.
12. See Gleize ('Le Défaut de ligne droite', p.80): 'le récit introduit des blancs
que l'écriture comble parfois par le jeu des notations psychologiques; . . . Ce
type de notation vise à donner l'impression d'une continuité dans l'espace
référentiel psychologique: L'amour de Frédéric'.
13. See Robbe-Grillet, *Pour un Nouveau Roman*, p.37.
14. See Introduction, note 6.
15. See *Chroniques*, p.219: [Flaubert] sait donner avec maîtrise l'impression du
Temps.'
16. 'The Chronology of *L'ÉS*', p.87.
17. In *Clefs pour 'L'ÉS'*, p.25, Bem argues that the Nogent interlude 'symbolise
à un moment diachroniquement situé une structure globale prévalente.' See
also Wetherill, 'Préface', p.lxiii.
18. For full details see Bem, 'Sur des hiatus temporels dans *L'ÉS*'.
19. See Buck, p.88: 'Flaubert does not acknowledge the existence of the year
preceding September 1844.'
20. Cf. Imprimerie Nationale edition of the novel, i.333; 'toutes les allusions à
l'actualité qui émaillent ces pages où Flaubert raconte la vie de Frédéric
après son retour à Paris nous mettent dans les premiers mois de 1847.'
21. 'The Chronology of *L'ÉS*', p.88.
22. *Clefs our'L'ÉS'*, p.19.
23. Cf. the suggestion made by Raitt (Imprimerie Nationale edition, i.334): 'Il y

Notes for pages 76–85

a eu . . . inadvertance dans la transcription d'un seul chiffre, un 5 pour un 6; si on rétablit le 6, tout rentre dans l'ordre.'

24. See Gothot-Mersch ('Aspects de la temporalité dans les romans de Flaubert', p.47): 'Ni avant, ni pendant, ni après la rédaction, Flaubert ne se préoccupe de doter ses romans d'un cadre temporel cohérent.'
25. Buck, p.91.
26. See Bem ('Sur les hiatus temporels'); 'la chronologie des romans de Flaubert a souvent intrigué ses lecteurs par ses précisions sélectives et ses imprécisions calculées.' See also Brombert (*The Novels of Flaubert*, p.179): 'the narration oscillates between extreme precision of dates . . . and a trancelike vagueness . . .'.
27. Duquette has pointed out that seven chapters begin with clear indications of time. Phrases such as 'deux mois plus tard', 'les jours suivants' occur frequently (*Flaubert ou l'architecture du vide*, p.99).
28. See Brombert (*The Novels of Flaubert*, p.180): 'Unquestionably, the very subjectivity of the point of view . . . slows down the rhythm of the novel. Time and subjectivity are intimately related.'
29. With few exceptions time passes *in* rather than *between* chapters.
30. See Sagnes, 'Tentations balzaciennes dans le manuscrit de *L'ÉS*'. See also Wetherill, 'Préface', p.liv.
31. See Danahy, 'Narrative Timing and the Structures of *L'ÉS*', p.32.
32. See Genette, *Figures III*, pp.145–9.
33. *Approximations*, p.173. See also Gleize, p.81: 'Le récit s'emploie . . . à disjoindre bien plus qu'à lier, à souligner les disjonctions bien plus qu'à les effacer et proclame son indépendance à l'égard de la (chrono) logique de l'histoire.'
34. See Barthes (*Le Plaisir du texte*, p.18): 'Une asyndète généraliseée saisit toute l'énonciation, en sorte que ce discours très lisible est en sous main l'un des plus fous que l'on puisse imaginer.'
35. See Wetherill ('Flaubert et la cohésion du texte', p.437): 'L'étude des manuscrits . . . montre que Flaubert opère délibérément des suppressions tendant à couper l'enchaînement.'
36. See Wetherill, 'Le Style des thèmes. Le Dernier manuscrit de *L'ÉS*'.
37. *'L'ÉS' de 1869 et la poétique de l'œuvre autonome*, p.160: 'Si nous sommes plongés dans cette séquence morcelée d'événements, nous essayerons, en revanche, par un réflexe de lecteur involontaire, d'en comprendre l'enchaînement logique.'
38. Ibid., p.72: 'La disparition de la causalité extérieure et la consolidation de la cohérence intérieure s'avèrent être deux aspects complémentaires de l'œuvre autonome.'
39. See Introduction, p.5.
40. The same process is at work in Henry James's *What Maisie Knew*.
41. See Brombert, *The Novels of Flaubert*, p.185. See also Friedrich, *Die Klassiker des französishen Romans*, pp.137 ff.

Notes for pages 85–97

42. See Gleize, p.80.
43. Ibid.
44. See, for instance, p.239 and p.345.
45. The implication is that Frédéric has not 'betrayed' his love. For Bem (*Clefs pour 'L'ÉS'*, p.95), however, the episode remains totally obscure: 'Au troisième degré, la réticence ressortit à la voix du Narrateur, qui pratique un récit extraordinairement condensé, sec, elliptique auquel le lecteur ne comprend goutte.'
46. 'Le Défaut de ligne droite', p.79. See, however, Chapter II, Note 56.
47. 'Structure et sens de *L'ÉS*', p.71.
48. See Culler, *Structuralist Poetics*, p.209.
49. Moser, p.27.
50. See Knight, *A Theory of the Classical Novel*, pp.27–8.
51. Culler, *Flaubert*, p.156.
52. The narrator of *Un Début dans la vie* leaves the reader in no doubt about the educative process that has been recorded: 'L'aventure du voyage à Presles avait donné de la discrétion à Oscar, la soirée de Florentine avait raffermi sa probité, les duretés de la carrière militaire lui avaient appris la hiérarchie sociale et l'obéissance au sort. Devenu sage et capable, il fut heureux . . .' (*La Comédie humaine*, i.751).
53. *Flaubert*, p.147.
54. 'Le Défaut de ligne droite', p.82.
55. Ibid., p.84.
56. See Chapter II, p.68.
57. See Chapter II, p.68.
58. See Raitt, *L'ÉS* et la pyramide', p.139.
59. See Berthier, 'La Seine, Le Nil et le voyage du rien', p.10.
60. Ibid.: '[le] dernier chapitre . . . invalide et disqualifie tout ce qui l'a précédé . . . Madame Arnoux se trouve donc entraînée dans la dépréciation générale.'
61. See p.18.
62. Torgovnik, *Closure in the Novel*, p.115.

IV Narrative Techniques

1. See Jenkins, 'Flaubert', p.52.
2. For a discussion of this conflict see my '"Flaubert, le premier des non-figuratifs du roman moderne"?'
3. For a discussion of the idea of 'pure' narration see Hamburger, *The Logic of Literature*, pp.139–40. The case for there always being a narrator is clearly stated by Genette (*Nouveau Discours du récit*, p.68): 'Dans le récit le plus sobre, quelqu'un me parle, me raconte une histoire, m'invite à l'entendre comme il la raconte, et cette invite – confiance ou pression – constitue une indéniable attitude de narration, et donc de narrateur.'

Notes for pages 97–108

4. Benveniste, *Problèmes de linguistique générale*, pp.239–44.
5. See Mitterand ('Discours de la politique et politique du discours dans un dragment de *L'ÉS*', p.134): 'Le virtuel devient actuel, patent, manifeste, dans les segments d'analyse.'
6. For a recent discussion of some of these different criteria see Rimmon-Kenan, *Narrative Fiction*, pp.94–103.
7. See Reinhart, 'Reported Consciousness and Point of View', p.64.
8. See Sternberg, *Expositional Modes and Temporal Ordering in Fiction*, p.282.
9. *Narrative Fiction*, p.87.
10. Chatman, *Story and Discourse*, p.148.
11. *Narrative Fiction*, p.88.
12. For a spirited rejection of the notion of the implied author see Genette, *Nouveau Discours du récit*, pp.94–104.
13. *Corr.* v.396–7 and 347.
14. 'L'auteur, dans son œuvre, doit être comme Dieu dans l'univers, présent partout, et visible nulle part.' (*Corr.* iii.61–2). See also Chapter I, pp. 29–30.
15. The distinction between 'qui voit' and 'qui parle' is made in *Figures III*, p.203. For a more recent attempt to categorize different types of 'focalisation' see Vitoux, 'Le Jeu de la focalisation' and Genette, *Nouveau Discours du récit*, pp.48–52. For a discussion of Flaubert's use of point of view technique see Sherrington, *Three Novels by Flaubert*.
16. See Cohn (*Transparent Minds*, p.116): 'The narrator slides in and out of Frédéric's mind at will, adopting the protagonist's inner language at crucial moments, but always free to return to his objective narrative base, to describe minutely the protagonist's actions and surroundings etc.' Sherrington estimates that 'narrator' passages (i.e. passages where the narrator's viewpoint is given) represent about 11 per cent of the total book and that 70 per cent is narrated from Frédéric's point of view (*Three Novels by Flaubert*, pp.247 and 237).
17. See, for example, the passages beginning 'La contemplation de cette femme …' (p.67), 'et même son amour avait pris …' (p.97), 'La fréquentation de ces deux femmes …' (p.145), 'Bientôt ces mensonges …' (p.390).
18. See for example, 'Frédéric éprouvait un certain respect pour lui' (p.5).
19. See, for instance, 'Et il (Le père Roque) s'en alla, rebuté, sans doute, par l'accueil de Frédéric' (p.17) or 'Elle (Rosanette) le reçut aigrement, car elle lui en voulait de son abandon. Sa rancune s'évanouit sous des assurances de paix réitérées' (p.297). Such examples are, however, hard to find.
20. Raitt, 'Introduction' to *L'ÉS*, i.40.
21. Brombert, *The Novels of Flaubert*, p.163: 'The attenuating "no doubt" and "perhaps" seem to be introduced here as though to suggest the author's lack of solidarity with his own comments.' See also my *Psychological Determinism in 'Madame Bovary'*, pp.76–7.

Notes for pages 110–113

22. See Sherrington (*Three Novels by Flaubert* p.270) for a reading of this passage which suggests that Flaubert is criticising Frédéric's inability to come to terms with the basis of his experience.
23. See Chapter III, pp.84–6.
24. Brombert, *The Novels of Flaubert*, p.172.
25. For example: 'il se dit qu'avec une somme pareille . . .' (p.181), 'se disant qu'on peut ressaisir une occasion . . .' (p.273), 'il se dit qu'il n'avait besoin de personne' (p.236), 'Il se disait que, s'il l'eût secouru, Sénécal n'en serait pas là' (p.234). Similar examples with 'sentir' (p.208, p.238) and 's'imaginer' (pp.43, 46, 71, 85, 176, 282, 300, 347) can also be found.
26. See in particular: Banfield, 'Narrative Style and the Grammar of Direct and Indirect Speech'; Dillon and Kirchoff, 'Form and Function of Free Indirect Style'; McHale, 'Free Indirect Discourse: a survey of recent accounts', Pascal, *The Dual Voice: free indirect speech and its functioning in the nineteenth-century European novel*; Reinhart, 'Reported Consciousness and Point of View'; Ullman, *Style in the French Novel*.
27. Dillon and Kirchoff give the fullest account of the grammatical characteristics of *style indirect libre*.
28. This view has been advanced most forcefully by Banfield, 'Narrative Style' and defended against the attacks of Dillon and Kirchoff and others in 'The Formal Coherence of Represented Speech and Thought'. Banfield's argument is based on the One Expression/One Speaker principle (For every expression, there is a unique referent of I (the speaker) and a unique referent of you (the addressee)). From this principle Banfield deduces that 'In *style direct libre* expressive elements relate not to the suppressed speaker of the *inquit* clause but to a unique referent, the 'subject-of-consciousness.' (p.29)
29. The 'effaced narrator hypothesis' originates from Todorov ('Les catégories du récit littéraire', p.126) and posits that there is a narrator even where one does not explicitly appear. Such a narrator can be deemed to be 'present' in or to have left his mark on *style indirect libre*. See Pascal: 'The narrator is always effectively present in *style indirect libre*, even if only through the syntax of the passage . . .' (*The Dual Voice*, p.137) and '*style indirect libre* is never purely and simply the evocation of a character's thought and perception, but always bears, in its vocabulary, its intonation, its syntactical composition and other stylistic features . . . the mark of the narrator' (Ibid. p.43). The whole question might, however, become a good deal less contentious if the all-important distinction between angle of vision and narrative voice were recognised (cf. Genette, *Figures III*, p.203).
30. *The Dual Voice*, p.107.
31. Dillon and Kirchoff, p.438.
32. Genette, *Figures III*, p.194.
33. See McHale, pp.277–8. McHale discusses the many uses to which *style indirect libre* can be put, noting that it is naturally fitted to the representation of consciousness and acts as an ideal vehicle for rêverie, dreams, halluci-

Notes for pages 113–133

nations, moving in the direction of stream of consciousness. The potential psychological value of 'substitutionary perception' is indicated by the observation that 'by locating descriptive details within the perceptual apparatus of a character, the reader makes them serve no longer simply as residual signs of the "real", but as marks and measure of human consciousness.' (p.278).

34. *Flaubert: Madame Bovary*, p.20.
35. Pascal, p.98: '*Style indirect libre* mean an imaginative self-submergence in the object, participation in the imagined character's experience and communication of this imagined experience.'
36. For detailed discussion of the use of *style indirect libre* in *L'ÉS* see Bem, *Clefs pour 'L'ÉS'*, Poels, 'Le fonctionnement du style indirect libre dans *L'ÉS*', and Wagner, *Innenbereich Und Ausserung. Flaubertsche Formen indirekter Darstellung und Grandtypen des Erlebten Rede.*
37. 'Introduction à l'analyse structurale des récits', p.20, discussed by Genette, *Figures III*, p.210. For a discussion of the different ways of reporting consciousness see Reinhart who distinguishes between: 1. Quoted speech or consciousness; 2. Narrated speech or consciousness; 3. Indirectly reported speech or consciousness; 4. Summarised speech or consciousness; 5. Descriptions of a mental state; 6. Descriptions of mental activity.
38. See in particular the works of Bem, Gleize and Wetherill.
39. *Madame Bovary. Œuvres complètes*, i.684.
40. *Clefs pour 'L'ÉS'*, p.98.
41. Pascal, p.104.
42. *Corr*. iii.68. (quoted Wagner, p.196).
43. *Figures III*, p.213.

V Motive Forces

1. *Corr*. ii.344.
2. Culler (*Flaubert*, p.149): 'At the level at which these phrases are synonymous, or at least interchangeable, they are too vague to count as explanations.'
3. Ibid., p.149.
4. See N.A.F. 17611, f.64.
5. *Le Père Goriot. La Comédie humaine*, ii.937 (My italics).
6. *Corr*. iii.202–3 (My italics).
7. See Raitt, 'La Décomposition des personnages dans *L'ÉS*', p.165.
8. See Chapter III, pp.84–6.
9. *Œuvres complètes*, i.245.
10. *Corr*. i.214–15.
11. *Corr*. i.325: 'qu'y faire si c'est dans mon sang? Est-ce ma faute?'
12. *Corr*. vii.294. See also *Bouvard et Pécuchet. Œuvres complètes*, ii.274–5.
13. *Corr*. i.230. See also *Corr*. ii.364: 'mon organisation est un système ... Je suis un homme-plume' and *Corr*. i.267: 'Cela ... est dans mon système ...

cela devait être.' There are times, however, when Flaubert appears to adopt a less static view of the self: 'Je ne crois pas [qu'on éprouve jamais deux sensations identiques], puisque notre individu change à tous les moments de son existence' (*Corr.* v.270).

14. *Corr.* iv.423.
15. *Corr. Supp.* ii.161. See also *Corr.* v.160: 'Il y a autre chose dans l'Art que le milieu où il s'exerce et les antécédents physiologiques de l'ouvrier. Avec ce système-là, on explique la série, le groupe, mais jamais l'individualité, le fait spécial qui fait qu'on est *celui-là*. Cette méthode amène forcément à ne faire aucun cas du *talent*.'
16. *Corr.* v.240–1.
17. For a different view see Wetherill, 'Préface', p.lxxxi.
18. See Chapter IV, pp.106–7.
19. See for example, 'Frédéric souriait de plaisir malgré lui' p.130; 'malgré l'espèce de rancune qu'il lui portait ...', p.134; 'Malgré lui, il regardait la couche', p.168; 'Une sorte de pudeur, malgré son envie, l'empêchait ...', p.191; 'Et il se laissa tomber sur les genoux, malgré lui, s'affaissant sous un poids intérieur trop lourd', p.270.
20. Bruneau ('Le Rôle du hasard dans *L'ÉS*', p.100): 'Sous des apparences de déterminisme psychologique, *L'Éducation sentimentale* peut se définir comme le roman du hasard.'
21. See, however, Raitt, 'La Décomposition des personnages dans *L'ÉS*', p.165: 'Dans *L'Éducation sentimentale* c'est surtout le hasard qui domine le comportement des personnages.'
22. Oehler, 'L'Échec de 1848', p.59.
23. 'Structure et sens de *L'ÉS*', p.72: 'dans la philosophie sous-jacente à l'œuvre le hasard pur est une forme du déterminisme aussi bien que les grandes lois de la nature et de la société'.
24. 'il imaginait pour l'aborder, des complications du hasard, des périls extraordinaires dont il la sauverait', p.25; 'tant il souhaitait un hasard qui l'en débarrassât', p.393.
25. 'Pour savoir s'il irait chez Mme Arnoux il jeta trois fois dans l'air des pièces de monnaie. Toutes les fois le présage fut heureux. Donc la fatalité l'ordonnait', p.63.
26. 'Le hasard l'avait servi', p.19; 'Le hasard lui offrit un auxiliaire', p.147.
27. Arnoux tells his wife that the trouble over the cashmere shawl is 'une méprise, un hasard, une de ces choses inexplicables comme il en arrive', p.166; Frédéric tells Madame Arnoux that 'le hasard seul l'avait fait trouver avec cette femme', p.269.
28. See p.180 (Clémence Daviou); p.273 (Frédéric and Madame Arnoux); p.352 (Louise Roque).
29. See the long extract from *Antécédents de l'hégelianisme dans la philosophie française* by Don Deschamps which Flaubert copied into a notebook (*Carnet 15*, p.31): 'La liberté est un mot par lequel nous exprimons seulement ce qui

Notes for pages 142–150

nous paraît en nous le moins nécessité, ce que nous jugeons être le plus indépendant de l'action du dehors sur nous. Mais indépendamment de cette action qui a toujours lieu plus ou moins, il y a celle de nos parties sur nos parties, de nos fibres sur nos fibres et cette action, quelque déliée qu'elle puisse être, quelque cachée qu'elle soit à nos yeux, nous nécessite également que l'autre.' If this can be taken as reflecting Flaubert's own views on the different forms of determination to which human beings are exposed, his thinking is not far removed from that of Freud who declared: 'I believe in external (real) chance, it is true, but not in internal (psychical) accidental events.' (*The Psychopathology of Everyday Life*, p.320).
30. Culler, *Flaubert*, p.151.
31. *Corr.* v.348.
32. *Corr.* v.344.
33. Cento, *Il realismo documentario nel ÉS*, p.123.
34. *Corr.* ii.415.
35. *Corr.* v.349.
36. *Corr.* v.149: 'Je viens d'avaler Lamennais etc. Ce sont des hommes du Moyen Age, esprits enfoncés dans le passé.'
37. *Corr.* v.385.
38. *Corr.* v.149.
39. *Corr.* v.407.
40. *Corr.* iii.208.
41. *Corr. Supp.* iv.275: 'c'est parce que les socialistes sont encore dans la vieille théologie, qu'ils sont si bêtes et si funestes. *La Magie* croit encore aux transformations ... comme le *Socialisme*. Ni l'un ni l'autre ne tiennent compte du temps et de l'évolution fatale des choses.'
42. Cento, p.140: 'Le réformateur ne croit pas à l'organisation essentialle de l'histoire' (Ms VII 205).
43. *Corr.* v.412: 'la doctrine de la Grâce nous a si bien pénétrés que le sens de la Justice a disparu.'
44. Cento, pp.127–33.
45. Ibid., p.299 (Marginal Note).
46. Ibid., pp.298–9.
47. Ibid., p.131.
48. *Corr.* v.335.
49. Cento, p.119 and 153.
50. See p.233 for a description of the formative experience – the massacre in the rue Transnonain – on which his subsequent reactions are based.
51. See Chapter II, pp.33–4.
52. See p.15. and *Carnet 19*, f.25: 'violence que doit [etre] avoir un amour renforcé par des types litteraires admirés dans la jeunesse – il y a coincidence de l'ideal et du Reel'.
53. Bénichou, *Le Temps des prophètes*, p.566.
54. Oehler, p.60. See also my discussion of an 'underlying causality' in

Notes

239

Notes for pages 150–154

'Flaubert: *Sentimental Education*'.
55. Culler, *Flaubert*, pp.149 and 151.
56. Ibid., p.151.

VI Love

1. N.A.F. 17611, f.55.
2. *Corr.* v.331.
3. See Vial's 'Flaubert, émule et disciple émancipé de Balzac' and 'De *Volupté* à *L'ÉS*: Vie et avatars de thèmes romantiques'. Vial's main point is that 'Flaubert ne trace plus qu'une limite un peu indécise (between the two types of love for the virtuous woman and the woman of easy virtue or prostitute) et ménage des empiètements et des enclaves. Avec lui se substitue à la géographie morale, théorique et simpliste, de la génération précédente, un paysage d'âme plus nuancée, plus complexe.' (*Faits et significations*, p.100).
4. See in particular Freud, 'A Special Type of Object-Choice made by Men' and *Three Essays on the Theory of Sexuality*; Proust, *A la Recherche du temps perdu*; Barthes, *Fragments d'un discours amoureux*.
5. *Œuvres complètes*, i.237.
6. Ibid., i.242.
7. 'A Special Type of Object-Choice', p.236. In this essay Freud analyses a syndrome all the main components of which are apparent in the behaviour of Frédéric Moreau. See my 'Sacred and Profane in *L'ÉS*', pp.790–1 and the more recent discussion of Czyba in *La Femme dans les romans de Flaubert*, pp.227–56.
8. *Œuvres complètes*, i.233 and 236.
9. *Three Essays on the Theory of Sexuality*, p.145. See also Flaubert, *Novembre*. *Œuvres complètes*, i.270: 'Le type dont presque tous les hommes sont en quête n'est peut-être que le souvenir d'un amour conçu dans le ciel ou dès les premiers jours de la vie; nous sommes tous en quête de tout ce qui s'y rapporte, la seconde femme qui vous plaît ressemble presque toujours à la première.'
10. See Freud, 'A Special Type of Object-Choice', p.235.
11. See 'On the Universal Tendency to Debasement in the Sphere of Love', p.251: 'The sensual current that has remained active seeks only objects which do not recall the incestuous figures forbidden to it; if someone makes an impression that might lead to a high psychical estimation of her, this impression does not find an issue in any sensual excitation but in affection which has no erotic effect.'
12. See p.103: 'Mais, peu à peu, ses espérances et ses souvenirs, Nogent, la rue de Choiseul, Mme Arnoux, sa mère, tout se confondait.' A dizzying effect is produced by the constant changing of the order of past and future. Regression to infantile dependency on the mother becomes confused with progress-

Notes for pages 154–167

ion towards an idealised love-object, collapsing the distinction between the two.

13. See N.A.F. 17599, f.109 verso: 'Me Moreau le baisa au front'.
14. See p.92: 'lassé, énervé, vaincu enfin par la terrible force de la douceur, Frédéric se laissa conduire chez maître Prouharam.'
15. *Corr.* iv.304: 'le culte de la mère sera une des choses qui fera pouffer de rire les générations futures.'
16. p.16: 'il estimait par-dessus tout la passion: Werther, René, Franck, Lara, Lélia et d'autres plus médiocres l'enthousiasmaient presque également'; p.422: '"Je comprends les Werther que ne dégoûtent pas les tartines de Charlotte."'
17. *Fragments d'un discours amoureux*, p.39.
18. For a discussion of the symbolic significance of the recurrent rescue fantasy see Freud's 'A Special Type of Object-Choice', pp.239–40.
19. See Eliade, *The Sacred and the Profane*, p.63: 'The irruption of the sacred does not only project a fixed point into a formless fluidity of profane space, a centre into chaos; it also effects a break in places and makes possible ontological passage from one mode of being to another.'
20. Balzac, *Le Lys dans la vallée. La Comédie humaine*, viii.916.
21. A. Fairlie (p.282) has pointed out the similarity of this incident to the occasion in *Lucien Leuwen* where the hero takes leave of Madame de Chasteller but is roundly and perhaps ironically condemned by the author in a marginal note (Stendhal, *Romans et nouvelles*, i.1537). The same article contains the most detailed and perceptive analysis of the pattern of Frédéric's four 'inter-related, conflicting and overlapping desires' (pp.275–87) available.
22. Freud, 'On the Universal Tendency to Debasement in the Sphere of Love', p.252: 'As soon as the condition of debasement is fulfilled, sensuality can be freely expressed'.
23. *Le Deuxième sexe*, ii.341.
24. See 'Sylvie' by Nerval in *Œuvres*, i.272: 'Tour à tour bleue et rose comme l'astre trompeur d'Aldébaran, c'était Adrienne ou Sylvie, – c'étaient les deux moitiés d'un seul amour. 'L'une etait l'idéal sublime, l'autre la douce réalité.'
25. See Fairlie, p.275: 'Flaubert ... softened some sardonic parallels between bourgeoise and lorette which made an initial focus in the *scénarios* published by Mme Durry.'
26. Barthes, *S/Z*, p.72.
27. See Freud, 'A Special Type of Object-Choice', p.237: 'This very relation of the sharpest contrast between 'mother' and 'prostitute' will however encourage us to enquire into the history of the development of these two complexes and the unconscious relation between them, since we long ago discovered that what, in the conscious, is found split into a pair of opposites often occurs in the unconscious as a unity.' See also Czyba, p.242: 'Non seulement le "courant tendre" et le "courant sensuel", pour reprendre les expressions de

Notes for pages 167–184

Freud, ne fusionnent pas chez Frédéric. Qui plus est, il y a *dichotomie* entre ces deux courants qui *coexistent* chez lui. D'où la dualité complémentaire des deux figures féminines, la Madone et la Lorette'.

28. Sherrington, 'Louise Roque and *L'ÉS*', p.434: 'Louise is not a fourth possibility, but an all-inclusive symbol, a summary, in watered down form, of everything Frédéric is seeking ... In rejecting Louise, he is rejecting his true potential, in order to squander his meagre resources on grandiose schemes whose realisation is well beyond his capacity.'
29. *Corr.* iv.356.
30. Czyba, *La Femme dans les romans de Flaubert.*
31. Culler, *Structuralist Poetics*, pp.231–2.
32. See Wetherill, 'Préface', p.xxviii: 'Le grand amour ne serait à ce moment-là (if Madame Arnoux's sacrifice of her love is seen as the result of superstition) qu'un aspect, parmi d'autres, de la bêtise humaine que Flaubert place au centre de son roman.'
33. The idea that Frédéric's love for Madame Arnoux is a 'golden thread' in an otherwise undistinguished existence was first put forward by James. A more recent attempt to recuperate Frédéric's relationship as akin to what Sartre understands by the aesthetic attitude and entailing a total investment in an unknown image which makes him resemble an artist can be found in Knight's *Flaubert's Characters*. See Conclusion, pp.213–4.
34. See Prendergast, *The Order of Mimesis*, p.196 and Moussaron, 'Sur le récit flaubertien', p.190: 'S'agissant des personnages, aucun romancier du dix-neuvième siècle n'a sans doute suggéré comme Flaubert que le désir du sujet inscrit sa propre division dans un rapport de manque à l'objet, se soutenant du phantasme qui dédouble ou remplace le réalité environnante.'

VII Friendship

1. Sckommodau, 'Un mot-thème de *L'ÉS*', p.290: 'on pourrait parler à la rigueur de bisexualité en comprenant le couple des deux amis comme résultant d'une totalité "le moi et l'autre", et ce serait évidemment le rôle de Frédéric de représenter la composante féminine.'
2. *Carnet 19*, p.204 (quoted by Gothot-Mersch, '*Bouvard et Pecuchet*: Sur la genèse des personnages', p.150).
3. ms g 225[1], Folio 16 verso (quoted by Gothot-Mersch, 'Sur la genèse', p.152) Gothot-Mersch comments: 'L'affirmation est aisée, mais les difficultés commencent lorsqu'il s'agit de démontrer dans le détail que les bon-hommes se conviennent précisément parce qu'ils ne se ressemblent pas.'
4. *Bouvard et Pecuchet. Œuvres complètes*, ii.202 and 204.
5. See Jacques, '*L'ÉS*. Les bornes d'un texte', p.155: 'Moitié d'un être double en voie de constitution, chacun cherche dans l'autre le comblement du vide.'
6. See p.15: 'On surveilla leurs relations. Ils ne s'en aimèrent que davantage.'
7. See Proust, 'Sens et structure de *L'ÉS*', p.82: 'Ce qui donne au couple formé

Notes for pages 184–195

par les deux amis son caractère ambigu, donc attachant, c'est qu'à certains
moments de leur existence ils se "prêtent" pour ainsi dire leurs rêves.' See
also Fairlie's comments on the relationship between Frédéric and his "alter
ego" (pp.287–9).
8. See Rouen I (quoted Gothot-Mersch, 'Sur la genèse', p.151): "Leur différence intrinsèque doit s'apercevoir malgré leur union jusqu'à la fin ou ils
deviennent dans la joie de la copie et la communauté de la passion . . . un seul
être en partie double.' See also Jacques, p.161: 'L'histoire annoncée par le
titre est celle de deux êtres qui n'en forment finalement qu'un seul. Pris
isolément, aucun des deux n'a droit à l'autonomie.'
9. Fairlie, p.272.
10. 'Frédéric, en face d'elle, dans une bergère, réfléchissait, scandalisé' (p.379);
'Ces abîmes de noirceur effrayèrent Dussardier' (p.399).
11. See in particular p.267: 'Deslauriers aimait mieux Frédéric dans la médioc-
rité. De cette manière, il restait son égal et en communion plus intime avec
lui.'
12. See Fairlie, p.272: 'In the pattern of the whole, Sénécal gives a systematic
intensification of the logical, practical, mathematical principles of Deslauriers'.
13. See Chapter V, pp.143–4.
14. *Œuvres complètes*, ii.262.

VIII History and Psychology

1. Homais's reference to 'les inondés de Lyon' situates the action some time
after 1840 (Dumesnil, *'Madame Bovary' de Gustave Flaubert*, p.281), during
the same period as that in which *L'Éducation* is set.
2. See Green, *Flaubert and the Historical Novel*, p.52.
3. *Corr.* v.363.
4. See Scott's 'Must not let the background eclipse the principal figures – the
frame overpower the picture', *Journal*, pp.248–9 (18 Oct. 1826), quoted by
Green, p.9. For a discussion of the relationship of *L'ÉS* to the historical
novel see Crouzet, *'L'ÉS* et le "genre historique"'.
5. *Carnet 19*, p.187.
6. See articles by Oehler, Fairlie, Proust, Tétu and Duquette's, *Flaubert ou
l'architecture du vide*, pp.131–4.
7. *Journal*, vi.173.
8. *Corr.* iii.208.
9. See Chapter V, p.149.
10. *Corr.* iii.178.
11. *Corr.* iii.208.
12. *Corr.* v.385: 'Ce que je trouve de christianisme dans le socialisme est
énorme' and the six pages of notes entitled 'les socialistes sont catholiques'
referred to by Cento, p.138, note 1

Notes for pages 195–208

13. *Corr*. v.407.
14. *Corr. Supp*. iv.275.
15. MS VII, 209 quoted by Cento, p.140.
16. *Corr*. vi.287: 'je crois que les pauvres haïssent les riches et que les riches ont peur des pauvres.' See also Deslauriers's division of society into three groups, 'ceux qui ont, ceux qui n'ont plus, et ceux qui tâchent d'avoir' (p.179).
17. See *Madame Bovary. Œuvres complètes*, i.588: 'Si Charles l'avait voulu, cependant, s'il s'en fût douté, si son regard, une seule fois, fût venu à la rencontre de sa pensée, il lui semblait qu'une abondance subite se serait détachée de son cœur, comme tombe la récolte d'un espalier, quand on y porte la main' which is echoed by the sound of 'une pêche mûre qui tombait toute seule dans la nuit' (p.641), heard during the last meeting with Rodolphe.
18. *Carnet 19*, f.38 suite: 'Quant à l'empêchement de baiser, quand tout est mur pr cela . . .'.
19. Duquette, p.134: 'Mais dès lors, avec le rendez-vous manqué de la rue Tronchet et le sac des Tuileries, puis l'insurrection de Paris, c'est la fin des espoirs.'
20. A. Fairlie, p.268. For a critical view of the major parallelism in the novel see Danahy ('Narrative Timing and the Structure of *L'ÉS*', p.36): 'The neat parallel of Frédéric's sexual life and French political history is a gratuitous and too-perfect synchronization.'
21. Moussaron, 'Sur le récit flaubertien', p.177.

Conclusion

1. *Letters inédites à Tourgueneff*, p.118. The reference is to 'Hérodias' but could well have been made to *L'ÉS*.
2. See Genette, *Travail de Flaubert*, p.7: 'Flaubert . . . a vécu la littérature comme une sorte de difficulté permanente et de principe, et, plus précisément, à la fois comme une urgence et une impossibilité.'
3. *Les Lettres inédites à Gustave Flaubert*, p.313.
4. See *Corr*. v.331 and *Corr. Supp*. ii.211; *Corr*. v.158; *Corr. Supp*. ii.100 and 175–6; *Corr. Supp*. iii.287; *Autour de Flaubert*, ii.48. See also the frequent doubts about the conception of the novel expressed by Flaubert (*Corr*. v.228, 237, 417).
5. *Le Plaisir du texte*, p.18.
6. See the quotation on p.126.
7. See pp.129–31.
8. See the plan for the novel published in the Pléiade edition, p.1760: 'L'avortement de l'E.S. repris mais dans des faits plus serrés.'
9. See for instance *La Joie de vivre*, p.883: 'même il y avait chez elle de la pitié pour ce grand garçon, dont la volonté courte, le courage simplement

Notes for pages 208–217

nerveux, expliquaient les avortements'.
10. See *Carnet 19* in Durry, *Flaubert et ses projets inédits*, f.39: 'un defaut radical d'imagination un gout excessif – trop de sensualité – pas de suite dans les idées – trop de rêveries l'ont empêché d'être un artiste.'
11. See the sketch published in the Pléiade edition, p.1756.
12. Ibid., p.1747.
13. See Durry, p.156: 'Prendre garde au *Lys dans la Vallée*'; Balzac's declaration – 'je referai *Volupté*' – is quoted in the Introduction to the Garnier edition of the novel, p.xvii.
14. *Le Lys dans la vallée*, viii.850. See also Lachet, *Thématique et technique du 'Lys dans la vallée'*, pp.63–8.
15. See Vial, 'Flaubert, émule et disciple émancipé de Balzac'.
16. See Lethbridge, *Maupassant: Pierre et Jean*.
17. See 'Le Roman', p.38.
18. See Hainsworth, Introduction to *Pierre et Jean*, p.18: 'His conduct, far from being rational, is largely dictated by subconscious phenomena of a sexual nature' and Lethbridge (p.46): 'In the very process of trying to come to terms with the workings of the subconscious, Pierre's rational self is subverted by them'.
19. *The Order of Mimesis*, pp.180–95.
20. *Selected Literary Criticism*, p.200.
21. Knight, *Flaubert's Characters*, pp.85–93.
22. Ibid.
23. See Introduction, p.11.
24. See Chapter I, p.28.
25. See Laplanche and Leclaire, 'The Unconscious: a psychoanalytic study', p.125: 'The data of consciousness are defective, "lacunary"; the unconscious is what allows us to reestablish a coherent sequence "when we interpolate the unconscious acts we infer".'

Select Bibliography

Place of publication is Paris unless otherwise indicated.

I Works of Flaubert

(i) Manuscripts of *L'Éducation sentimentale*

Bibliothèque Historique de la Ville de Paris, *Carnet de Lecture 19*. Earliest Plans for *L'Éducation sentimentale* (First published by M. J. Durry, *Flaubert et ses projets inédits*).

Bibliothèque Nationale, Salle des Manuscrits, Nouvelles Acquisitions Françaises 17611. Main plans for *L'Éducation sentimentale* (Extracts published in P. M. Wetherill's edition).

Bibliothèque Municipale de Rouen, ms g 226$^{1-8}$. Documentation for *Bouvard et Pécuchet* which includes material first used for *L'Éducation sentimentale* (Partially published in *Œuvres complètes*, ed. M. Bardèche, vol.iii).

Bibliothèque Historique de la Ville de Paris, *Carnets de Lecture* 8, 12, 13 and 14. Documentation for *L'Éducation sentimentale* (Partially published in *Œuvres complètes*, ed. M. Bardèche, vol.viii).

Bibliothèque Nationale, Salle des Manuscrits, Nouvelles Acquisitions Françaises 17599–610. Rough drafts for *L'Éducation sentimentale* (Extracts published in P. M. Wetherill's edition).

Bibliothèque Historique de la Ville de Paris, Manuscrit autographe. Manuscript of *L'Éducation sentimentale* given by Flaubert to the copyist

(ii) Main Recent Editions of *L'Éducation sentimentale*

L'Éducation sentimentale, ed. M. Bardèche, *Œuvres complètes*, vol.iii (Club de l'honnête homme, 1971).
L'Éducation sentimentale, ed. Alan Raitt, 2 vols (Imprimerie Nationale, 1979).
L'Éducation sentimentale, ed. P. M. Wetherill (Garnier, 1984).
L'Éducation sentimentale, ed. C. Gothot-Mersch (Folio, 1985).

(iii) Other Works of Flaubert

Œuvres complètes, ed. B. Masson, 2 vols (Seuil, 1964).
Correspondance, 9 vols (Conard, 1926–33).

245

Correspondance. Supplément, 4 vols (Conard, 1954).
Correspondance, ed. J. Bruneau, 2 vols (Pléiade, 1973, 1980).
Lettres inédites à Tourgueneff (Monaco: Éditions du rocher, 1946).
Carnets de lecture. Œuvres complètes, ed. M. Bardèche, vol.iii (Club de l'honnête homme, 1973).
Souvenirs, Notes et Pensées intimes (Buchet-Chastel, 1965).

II Critical Studies of *L'Éducation sentimentale*

Bart, B., 'An Unsuspected adviser on Flaubert's *Éducation sentimentale*', *French Review*, 36 (1962) 37–43.
Bart, B., 'Louis Bouilhet – Accoucheur de Flaubert', *Symposium*, 17 (1963) 183–201.
Bem, J., 'Sur le sens d'un discours circulaire', *Littérature*, 15 (1974) 95–109.
Bem, J., 'Sur les hiatus temporels dans *L'Éducation sentimentale*', *Revue d'histoire littéraire de la France*, 80 (1980) 626–8.
Bem, J., *Clefs pour 'L'Éducation sentimentale'* (Tübingen: Gunter Narr, 1981).
Berthier, P., 'La Seine, le Nil et le voyage sur rien', in *Histoire et langage dans 'L'Éducation sentimentale'*, 3–16.
Brombert, V., 'Lieu d'idylle et lieu du bouleversement dans *L'Éducation sentimentale*', *Cahiers de l'Association Internationale des Études françaises*, 23 (1971) 271–84.
Brombert, V., '*L'Éducation sentimentale*: articulations et polyvalence' in *La Production du sens chez Flaubert*, 55–69.
Brombert, V., 'De *Novembre* à *L'Éducation sentimentale*: communication et voie publique', *Revue d'Histoire Littéraire de la France*, 81 (1981) 563–72.
Bruneau, J., 'Le Rôle du hasard dans *L'Éducation sentimentale*', *Europe*, 47 (1969) 101–7.
Bruneau, J., 'La Présence de Flaubert dans *L'Éducation sentimentale*', in *Langages de Flaubert*, 33–42.
Bruneau, J., '*L'Éducation sentimentale*, roman autobiographique?', in *Essais sur Flaubert*, ed. C. Carlut (Nizet, 1979) 313–30.
Bruneau, J., 'Sur l'avant-dernier chapitre de *L'Éducation sentimentale* (avec des documents inédits)', *Revue d'Histoire Littéraire de la France*, 83 (1983) 412–26.
Bruneau, J., 'L'avant-dernier chapitre de *L'Éducation sentimentale* d'après les scénarios de la Bibliothèque Nationale', *Nineteenth-Century French Studies*, 12 (1984) 322–8.
Buck, S., 'The Chronology of *L'Éducation sentimentale*', *Modern Language Notes*, 67 (1952) 86–92.
Cajueiro-Roggero, M. A., 'Dîner chez les Dambreuse: "La Réaction commençante"', in *Histoire et langage dans 'L'Éducation sentimentale'*, 63–76.
Carlut, C., Dubé, P. H. and Dugan, J. R., *A Concordance to Flaubert's 'L'Éducation sentimentale'*, 2 vols (New York and London: Garland Publishing Inc., 1978).
Castex, P. G., *Flaubert: L'Éducation sentimentale* (Société d'édition d'enseignement supérieur, 1980).

Cellier, L., *Etudes de structure* (Minard, 1964).

Cento, A., *Il realismo documentario nell 'Éducation sentimentale'* (Naples: Liguori, 1967).

Cogny, P., *'L'Éducation sentimentale' de Flaubert: Le Monde en creux*, (Larousse, 1975).

Cortland, P., *The Sentimental Adventure* (The Hague: Mouton, 1967).

Cottin, M., 'Le "vieux manuscrit" de *L'Éducation sentimentale*. Comment travaillait Flaubert', *Bulletin de la Bibliothèque Nationale* (1976) 99–108.

Crouzet, M., '*L'Éducation sentimentale* et le "genre historique"', in *Histoire et langage dans 'L'Éducation sentimentale'*, 77–110.

Crouzet, M., 'Passion et politique dans *L'Éducation sentimentale*', in *Flaubert, La Femme, La Ville*, 39–71.

Danahy, M., 'Narrative Timing and the Structure of *L'Éducation sentimentale*', *Romanic Review*, 66 (1975) 32–46.

Denommé, R. T., 'The Theme of Disintegration in *L'Éducation sentimentale*, *Romanic Review*, 20 (1973) 163–71.

Douchin, J. L., 'Rosanette et la ville corruptrice', in *Flaubert, La Femme, La Ville*, 139–42.

Dumesnil, R., *'L'Éducation sentimentale' de Gustave Flaubert* (Nizet, 1963).

Duquette, J. P., *Flaubert ou l'architecture du vide: Une Lecture de 'L'Éducation sentimentale'* (Montreal: Les Presses de l'Université de Montréal, 1972).

Fairlie, A., 'Some Patterns of Suggestion in *L'Éducation sentimentale*', *Australian Journal of French Studies*, 6 (1969) 266–93. Also in *Imagination and Language. Collected Essays on Constant, Baudelaire, Nerval and Flaubert*, ed. M. Bowie (Cambridge: Cambridge University Press, 1981) 379–407.

Fairlie, A., 'Aspects de l'art dans *L'Éducation sentimentale*', *Revue d'Histoire Littérature de la France*, 81 (1981) 597–608.

Falconer, G., 'Reading *L'Éducation sentimentale*: belief and disbelief', *Nineteenth-Century French Studies*, 12 (1984) 329–43.

Frey, H. J., 'La Périphrase narrative dans *L'Éducation sentimentale*', in *Gustave Flaubert, Les Actes de la journée Flaubert*, ed. J. Roudaut (Friburg: Friburg University Press, 1981) 73–80.

Gleize, J., 'Le Défaut de ligne droite', *Littérature*, 15 (1974) 75–87.

Goldmann, A., '*L'Éducation sentimentale* ou Les quatre femmes de Frédéric Moreau', in *Rêves d'amour perdus: Les Femmes dans le roman du dix-neuvième siècle* (Denoël/Gonthier, 1984) 57–75.

Herschberg-Pierrot, A., 'Le Travail des stéréotypes dans les brouillons de la "Prise des Tuileries"', in *Histoire et langage dans 'L'Éducation sentimentale'*, 43–61.

Histoire et langage dans 'L'Éducation sentimentale', articles by M. Agulhon *et al.* (Société d'édition d'enseignement supérieur, 1981).

Hollender, W., *Gustave Flaubert: L'Éducation sentimentale, Erziehung des Herzens* (Munich: Wilhelm Fink, 1983).

Jacques, G., '*L'Éducation sentimentale*: Les Bornes d'un texte', *Lettres Romanes*, 30 (1976) 52–66.

Levaillant, J., 'Flaubert et la matière', *Europe*, 47 (1969) 202–9.

Maranini, L., *Il '48 nella struttura della 'Éducation sentimentale' e altri studi francesi* (Pisa: Nistri-Lischi, 1963).

Masson, B., 'L'Eau et les rêves', *Europe*, 47 (1969) 82–100.

Miller, M. K., 'A Note on Structure and Theme in *L'Éducation sentimentale*', *Studies in Romanticism*, 10 (1971) 130–6.

Mitterand, H., 'Discours de la politique et politique du discours dans un fragment de *L'Éducation sentimentale*', in *La Production du sens chez Flaubert*, 125–41.

Moser, *'L'Éducation sentimentale' de 1869 et la poétique de l'œuvre autonome* (Minard, 1980).

Oehler, D., 'L'Echec de 1848', *L'Arc*, 79 (1980) 58–68.

Poels, F. T., 'Le fonctionnement du style indirect libre dans *L'Éducation sentimentale*', *Revue des sciences humaines*, 36 (1971) 365–72.

Proust, J., 'Structure et sens de *L'Éducation sentimentale*', *Revue des sciences humaines*, 32 (1967) 67–100.

Raimond, M., 'Le Réalisme subjectif dans *L'Éducation sentimentale*', *Cahiers de l'Association Internationale des Études françaises*, 23 (1971) 299–310.

Raimond, M., 'Le Corps féminin dans *L'Éducation sentimentale*', in *Flaubert, La Femme, La Ville*, 23–31.

Raitt, A. W., 'La Décomposition des personnages dans *L'Éducation sentimentale*', in *Flaubert: La Dimension du texte*, 157–74.

Raitt, A. W., '*L'Éducation sentimentale* et la pyramide', in *Histoire et langage dans 'L'Éducation sentimentale'*, 129–42.

Rey, P. L, *Flaubert: L'Éducation sentimentale* (Hatier, 1983).

Sagnes, G., 'Tentations balzaciennes dans le manuscrit de *L'Éducation sentimentale*', *L'Année balzacienne*, 1981, 53–64.

Sckommodau, H., 'Un Mot-thème de *L'Éducation sentimentale*: l'autre', *Cahiers de l'Association Internationale des Études françaises* (1971) 285–97.

Sherrington, R. J., 'L'Élaboration des plans de *L'Éducation sentimentale*', *Revue d'Histoire Littéraire de la France*, 70 (1970) 628–39.

Sherrington, R. J., 'Louise Roque and *L'Éducation sentimentale*', *French Studies*, 25 (1971) 427–36.

Slama, B., 'Une Lecture de *L'Éducation sentimentale*', *Littérature*, 15 (1974) 19–38.

Tétu, J. F., 'Desir et révolution dans *L'Éducation sentimentale*', *Littérature*, 15 (1974) 88–94.

Vial, A., 'Flaubert, émule et disciple émancipé de Balzac', in Vial, *Faits et significations* (Nizet, 1973) 55–107.

Vial, A., 'De *Volupté* à *L'Éducation sentimentale*. Vie et avatars de thèmes romantiques', in *Faits et significations*, 109–47.

Wetherill, P. M., 'Le Dernier stade de la composition de *L'Éducation sentimentale*', *Zeitschrift für Französische Sprache und Literatur*, 78 (1968) 229–52.

Wetherill, P. M., 'Le Style des thèmes. Étude sur le dernier manuscrit autographe de *L'Éducation sentimentale*', *Zeitschrift für französische Sprache und Literatur*, 81 (1971) 308–51 and 82 (1972) 1–52.

Wetherill, P. M., '"C'est là ce que nous avons eu de meilleur"', in *Flaubert à l'œuvre*, 37–68.

Wetherill, P. M., 'Paris dans *L'Éducation sentimentale*', in *Flaubert, La Femme, La Ville*, 123–35.

Williams, D. A., 'Flaubert: *Sentimental Education*', in *The Monster in the Mirror: studies in nineteenth-century realism*, ed. D. A. Williams, (Oxford: Clarendon Press for University of Hull, 1978) 75–101.

Williams, D. A., 'Sacred and Profane in *L'Éducation sentimentale*', *Modern Language Review*, 73 (1978) 786–98.

Williams, D. A., 'The Plans for *L'Éducation sentimentale*', *French Studies Bulletin* (1982) 8–10.

Yeschua, S., 'Les Dates dans *L'Éducation sentimentale* comme foyers de signification', in *La Production du sens chez Flaubert*, 297–311.

III General Critical Studies of Flaubert and Studies of Other Works of Flaubert

Brombert, V., *The Novels of Flaubert: a study of themes and techniques* (Princeton: Princeton University Press, 1966).

Brombert, V., 'Flaubert and the Temptation of the Subject', *Nineteenth-Century French Studies*, 12 (1984) 280–96.

Brombert, V., 'Flaubert and the Status of the Subject', in *Flaubert and Postmodernism*, 100–15.

Colling, A., *Gustave Flaubert* (Fayard, 1941).

Culler, J., *Flaubert: the uses of uncertainty* (London: Elek, 1974).

Czyba, L., *Mythes et idéologie de la femme dans les romans de Flaubert* (Lyon: Presses universitaires de Lyon, 1983).

Debray-Genette, R., 'Du Mode narratif dans les *Trois Contes*', *Littérature*, 2 (1971) 39–62.

Debray-Genette, R., 'Flaubert: Science et écriture', *Littérature*, 15 (1974) 41–51.

Debray-Genette, R., 'La Technique romanesque de Flaubert dans "Un Cœur simple"', in *Langages de Flaubert*, 95–108.

Debray-Genette, R., 'Présentation', in *Flaubert et après*, ed. B. Masson (Minard, 1984) 7–18.

Descharmes, R. and Dumesnil, R., *Autour de Flaubert*, 2 vols (Mercure de France, 1912).

Dethloff, U., *Das Romanwerk Gustave Flauberts* (Munich: Fink, 1976).

Digeon, C., *Flaubert* (Hatier, 1970).

Douchin, J. L., *Le Sentiment de l'absurde chez Gustave Flaubert*, (Minard, 1970).

Douchin, J. L., *Le Bourreau de lui-même. Essais sur l'itinéraire intellectuel de Gustave Flaubert*, (Minard, 1984).

Du Bos, C., 'Sur le Milieu intérieur chez Flaubert', in *Approximations*, (Fayard, 1965) 165–82.

Dumesnil, R., *'Madame Bovary' de Gustave Flaubert* (SFELT, 1946).

Durry, M. J., *Flaubert et ses projets inédits* (Nizet 1950).

Fairlie, A., *Flaubert: Madame Bovary* (London: Arnold, 1962).
Fairlie, A., 'La Quête de la femme à travers la ville dans quelques œuvres de Flaubert', in *Flaubert, La Femme, La Ville*, 77–88.
Flaubert à l'œuvre, ed. R. Debray-Genette (Flammarion, 1980).
Flaubert: La Dimension du texte, ed. P. W. Wetherill (Manchester: Manchester University Press, 1982).
Flaubert, La Femme, La Ville, articles by B. Masson *et al.* (Presses universitaires de France, 1983).
Flaubert and Postmodernism, ed. N. Shor and H. J. Majewski (London and Lincoln: University of Nebraska Press, 1984).
Genette, G., 'Silences de Flaubert', in *Figures II* (Seuil, 1966) 223–43.
Genette, G., 'Présentation', in *Travail de Flaubert* (Seuil, 1983) 7–9.
Genette, G., 'Demotivation in "Hérodias"', in *Flaubert and Postmodernism*, 192–201.
Gothot-Mersch, C., La Genèse de *'Madame Bovary'* (Corti, 1966).
Gothot-Mersch, C., 'Portraits et antithèses dans les récits de Flaubert' in *Essais sur Flaubert*, ed. C. Carlut (Nizet, 1979), 285–312.
Gothot-Mersch, C., *'Bouvard et Pécuchet*: Sur la Genèse des personnages' in *Flaubert à l'œuvre*, 137–67.
Gothot-Mersch, C., 'Aspects de la temporalité dans les romans de Flaubert', in *Flaubert: La Dimension du texte*, 6–55.
Gothot-Mersch, C., 'Sur le Narrateur chez Flaubert', *Nineteenth-Century French Studies*, 12 (1984) 344–65.
Green, A., *Flaubert and the Historical Novel: 'Salammbô' reassessed* (Cambridge: Cambridge University Press, 1982).
Hill, L., 'Flaubert and the Rhetoric of Stupidity', *Critical Inquiry*, 3 (1976) 333–44.
Jenkins, C., 'Flaubert' in *French Literature and its Background*, vol.5, *The Late Nineteenth Century*, ed. J. Cruickshank (Oxford: Oxford University Press, 1969) 51–66.
Knight, D., *Flaubert's Characters* (Cambridge: Cambridge University Press, 1985).
Langages de Flaubert, ed. M. Issacharoff (Minard, 1976).
Maupassant, G. de, 'Gustave Flaubert', in *Chroniques*, vol.iii (Union générale d'éditions, 1980) 77–124.
Moussaron, J. C., 'Sur le récit flaubertien', in *Flaubert et après*, ed. B. Masson (Minard, 1984) 173–92.
Neefs, J., *'Madame Bovary' de Flaubert* (Hachette, 1972).
Neefs, J., 'Le Parcours du zaïmph', in *La Production du sens chez Flaubert*, 227–41.
Porter, D., 'Flaubert and the Difficulty of Reading', *Nineteenth-Century French Studies*, 12 (1984) 366–78.
Prendergast, C., 'Flaubert; writing and negativity', *Novel*, 8 (1975) 197–213.
Prendergast, C., 'Flaubert: quotation, stupidity and the Cretan Liar Paradox', *French Studies*, 35 (1981) 261–77.

Production du sens chez Flaubert, La, ed. C. Gothot-Mersch (Union générale d'éditions, 1975).

Proust, M., 'A Propos du "style" de Flaubert', in *Chroniques* (Gallimard, 1927) 193–211.

Raitt, A. W., 'État présent des études sur Flaubert', *L'Information littéraire*, 34 (1982) 198–206 and 35 (1983) 18–25.

Sartre, J. P., *L'Idiot de la famille: Gustave Flaubert de 1821 à 1857*, 3 vols (Gallimard, 1971–2).

Sherrington, R. J., *Three Novels by Flaubert; a study of techniques* (Oxford: Clarendon Press, 1970).

Unwin, T., 'The Significance of the Encounter with the Dog in Flaubert's First *Éducation sentimentale*', *French Forum*, 4 (1979) 232–8.

Unwin, T., 'Flaubert and Pantheism', *French Studies*, 35 (1981) 394–406.

Wagner, B., *Innenbereich Ausserung. Flaubertsche Fromen indirekter Darstellung und Grundtypen des Erlebten Rede* (Munich: Wilhelm Fink, 1972).

Williams, D. A., 'Determinism in the first *Éducation sentimentale*', *Forum for Modern Language Studies*, 7 (1971) 101–8.

Williams, D. A., *Psychological Determinism in 'Madame Bovary'* (Hull: University of Hull Publications, 1973).

Williams, D. A., ' "Flaubert – le premier des non-figuratifs du roman moderne"?', *Orbis Litterarum*, 34 (1979) 66–86.

IV General Studies of The Novel and Critical Theory

Banfield, A., 'Narrative Style and the Grammar of Direct and Indirect Speech', *Foundations of Language*, 10 (1973) 1–39.

Banfield, A., 'The Formal Coherence of Represented Speech and Thought', *Poetics and Theory of Literature*, 3 (1978) 289–314.

Banfield, A., *Unspeakable Sentences: narration and representation in the language of fiction* (Boston and London: Routledge and Kegan Paul, 1982).

Barthes, R., 'Introduction à l'analyse des récits', *Communications*, 8 (1966) 1–27.

Barthes, R., *S/Z* (Seuil, 1970).

Barthes, R., *Le Plaisir du texte* (Seuil, 1973).

Bellemin-Noël, J., *Vers l'Inconscient du texte* (Presses universitaires de France, 1979).

Chatman, S., *Story and Discourse: narrative structure in fiction and film* (Ithaca, New York: Cornell University Press, 1978).

Cohn, D., *Transparent Minds: narrative modes for presenting consciousness in fiction* (Princeton: Princeton University Press, 1978).

Culler, J., *Structuralist Poetics: structuralism, linguistics and the study of literature* (London: Routledge and Kegan Paul, 1975).

Culler, J., *The Pursuit of Signs: semiotics, literature, deconstruction* (London: Routledge and Kegan Paul, 1981).

Dillon, G. L. and Kirchoff, F., 'On the Form and Function of Free Indirect Style', *Poetics and Theory of Literature*, 1 (1976) 431–40.

Felman, 'Turning the Screw of Interpretation', *Yale French Studies*, 55/6 (1977) 94–207.

Forster, E. M., *Aspects of the Novel* (Harmondsworth: Penguin, 1963).

Friedrich, H., *Die Klassiker des französichen Romans* (Frankfurt: Klostermann, 1966).

Garvey, J., 'Characterization in Narrative', *Poetics*, 7 (1978) 63–78.

Genette, G., *Figures III* (Seuil, 1972).

Genette, G., *Nouveau Discours du récit* (Seuil, 1983).

Hamburger, K., *The Logic of Literature* (Bloomington: Indiana University Press, 1973)

Hamon, P., 'Pour un Statut sémiologique du personnage', *Littérature*, 6 (1972) 86–110.

Hamon, P., *Le Personnel du roman* (Geneva: Droz, 1983).

Holland, N. N., *5 Readers Reading* (New Haven and London: Yale University Press, 1975).

Iser, W., *The Implied Reader: patterns of communication in prose fiction from Bunyan to Beckett* (Baltimore: John Hopkins University Press, 1974).

James, H., *Selected Literary Criticism*, ed. M. Shapira (Harmondsworth: Penguin, 1963).

Kaplan, M. and Kloss, R., *The Unspoken Motive: a guide to psychoanalytic literary criticism* (New York: The Free Press, 1973).

Kermode, F., *The Genesis of Secrecy* (Cambridge, Mass.: Harvard University Press, 1979).

Knight, E., *A Theory of the Classical Novel* (London: Routledge and Kegan Paul, 1969).

Le Galliot, J., *Psychanalyse et langages littéraires* (Nathan, 1977).

Lotman, I., *The Structure of the Artistic Text* (Ann Arbor: University of Michigan Press, 1977).

Maupassant, G. de, 'Le Roman', Preface to *Pierre et Jean*, ed. G. Hainsworth (London: Harrap, 1966) 35–47.

McHale, B., 'Free Indirect Discourse: a survey of recent accounts', *Poetics and Theory of Literature*, 3 (1978) 249–87.

Paris, B. J., *A Psychological Approach to Fiction* (Bloomington and London: Indiana University Press, 1974).

Pascal, R., *The Dual Voice: free indirect style and its functioning in the nineteenth-century novel* (Manchester: Manchester University Press, 1977).

Prendergast, C., *The Order of Mimesis: Balzac, Stendhal, Nerval, Flaubert* (Cambridge: Cambridge University Press, 1985).

Reinhart, R., 'Reported Consciousness and Point of View', *Poetics and Theory of Literature*, 4 (1979) 86–92.

Rimmon-Kenan, S., *Narrative Fiction: contemporary poetics* (London and New York: Methuen, 1983).

Sternberg, M., *Expositional Modes and Temporal Ordering in Fiction* (Baltimore and London: John Hopkins University Press, 1978).

Todorov, T., 'Les Catégories du récit littéraire', *Communications*, 8 (1966) 125–51.

Todorov, T., *Poétique. Qu'est-ce que le structuralisme?* (Seuil, 1968).
Torgovnik, M., *Closure in the Novel* (Princeton: Princeton University Press, 1981).
Ullman, S., *Style in the French Novel* (Cambridge: Cambridge University Press, 1957).
Vitoux, P., 'Le Jeu de la focalisation', *Poétique*, 13 (1982) 359–68.
Weinsheimer, J., 'Theory of Character: *Emma*', *Poetics Today*, 1 (1979) 185–211.

V Other Works (Novels, Criticism, General Reference)

Balzac, H. de., *La Comédie humaine*, 10 vols (Pléiade, 1950).
Barthes, R., *Fragments d'un discours amoureux* (Seuil, 1977).
Beauvoir, S. de, *Le Deuxième sexe*, 2 vols (Gallimard, 1949).
Benveniste, E., *Problèmes de linguistique générale* (Gallimard, 1966).
Du Camp, M., *Les Lettres inédites à Gustave Flaubert*, ed. G. Bonaccorso and R. M. di Stefano (Messine: Edas, 1978).
Eliade, M., *The Sacred and the Profane* (New York: Harper and Row, 1961).
Freud, S., 'A Special Type of Choice of Object made by Men', in *On Sexuality*, vol. 7 (The Pelican Freud Library, Harmondsworth: Penguin, 1977) 227–42.
Freud, S., 'On the Universal Tendency to Debasement in the Sphere of Love', in *On Sexuality*, 243–60.
Freud, S., 'Three Essays on the Theory of Sexuality', in *On Sexuality*, 33–169.
Freud, S., *The Psychopathology of Everyday life* (Harmondsworth: Penguin, 1975).
Freud: a collection of critical essays, ed. P. Meisel (Englewood Cliffs: Prentice-Hall Inc., 1981).
Goncourt, E. and J. de, *Journal*, 22 vols (Monaco: Éditions de L'Imprimerie Nationale de Monaco, 1956–8).
Lachet, C., *Thématique et technique du 'Lys dans la vallée'* (Nouvelles Éditions Debresse, 1978).
Laplanche, J., and Leclaire, S., 'The Unconscious: a psychoanalytic study' in *Yale French Studies*, 48 (1972) 118–75.
Lethbridge, R., 'Maupassant, Scylla and Charybdis', *French Studies Bulletin* (1983/4) 6–9.
Lethbridge, R., *Maupassant: Pierre et Jean* (London: Grant and Cutler, 1984).
Maupassant, G. de, *Pierre et Jean*, ed. G. Hainsworth (London: Harrap, 1966).
Millet, K., *Sexual Politics* (London: Abacus, 1972).
Nerval, G. de, *Les Filles du feu. Œuvres*, vol. i (Pléiade, 1952).
Prendergast, C., *Balzac: fiction and melodrama* (London: Arnold, 1978).
Renan, E., *L'Avenir de la science, Œuvres complètes*, vol. iii (Calmann-Lévy, 1947–61).
Ricardou, J., *Problèmes du nouveau roman* (Seuil, 1967).
Robbe-Grillet, A., *Pour un nouveau roman* (Gallimard, 1963).
Sarraute, N., *L'Ere du soupçon* (Gallimard, 1965).

254   *'The Hidden Life at its Source'*

Stendhal, *Lucien Leuwen. Romans et nouvelles*, vol. i (Pléiade, 1952).
Trilling, L., 'Freud and Literature', in *Freud: a collection of critical essays*,
    95–111.
Woollen, ' "Roland furieux" and "le roman d'analyse pure" ', *French Studies
    Bulletin* (1983) 10–11.
Zola, E., *La Joie de vivre. Les Rougon-Macquart*, vol. iii (Pléiade, 1964).

Index

255